Self-Creations

for Jane and David Ginn.
Friends, roaming travel-mates
and countrymen —
This is my favorite "self-creation"
Thanks for giving it your home!
with love,
Thomas B Morgan

9-18-00

Holt, Rinehart and Winston
New York
Chicago   San Francisco

Self-Creations: 13 Imperson-alities

Thomas B. Morgan

Designer: Ernst Reichl
85830-0115
Printed in the United States of America

To Joan,
for surviving

Contents

Contents

The Impersonal "Eye": A Survivor's Introduction

Twelve of the thirteen Impersonalities in this book were first published in *Esquire* and one in *Harper's*. They have been selected from one hundred and fifteen pieces about all sorts of people that I wrote from 1954–1964 for these publications and for *Cosmopolitan, Good Housekeeping, Holiday, Look, Redbook,* and *TV Guide* as well. I want to explain how these pieces were written.

Blithe and blue-eyed as I am, I have not gone around intending to think satiric thoughts about human folly; but looking back now, I see that I have. Out of my typewriter have come desperately amusing pieces about venerable Gary Cooper, lovable Roy Cohn, gorgeous Teddy Kennedy, et cetera, et cetera. I have brooded about this. Why desperate? Why amusing? Am I trying to tell myself something about my own workaday reality?

When I finish one piece, I go right on to the next. This makes me a professional, according to Scott Fitzgerald's definition, but there is more to it than that. A professional is one who takes all the time he needs to get his work done as truthfully as he can without starving to death. So, my *Esquire* sketch, "The Late Spring of Alf Landon"—a happy exception to my blues, by the way—required only a week of research and writing. Following that, I spent eleven weeks on "Elia Kazan's Great Expectations" for *Harper's*. Altogether, I write enough to live and enough more so that I can agree with Edmund Wilson about income tax.

I am, for better or worse, a pro, one wave in a sea of troubled writers. My distinction, if I may call it that, is not so much in what I have to say (writers have had the pip for some time now) as it is in surviving the particular journalistic process that determines what I research, write, and publish.

Survival has meant total dependence on direct encounters with my subjects. The essence of what I do is involvement. I write mostly about what a man does and how he seems in the days or weeks I am with him. It follows that I cannot write without special consideration from the people I am writing about. And this raises a substantive question about the Eternal Search for Truth: Why should anyone expose himself to the surveillance and criticism of a total stranger, namely me?

People I idolize, like J. Robert Oppenheimer, Lawrence Durrell, and Norman O. Brown, author of *Life Against Death?* Strays, like Tinker Bell and Blaze Starr, who strip in barrooms and burlesque houses? Unsung heroes, like A.P. Crary, the Antarctic explorer, and Frank Gerbode, the San Francisco heart surgeon? Just plain folks, like J.D. Davis, a North Carolina cabbage farmer, and José Rivera who, when I met him, was eleven years old, growing up in Manhattan on West 84th Street between Columbus and Amsterdam Avenues in the slum block known as Little Korea? The half-forgotten, like Alf Landon who, in case you've half-forgotten him, was the Republican candidate for President in 1936? And those well-known people in politics, the arts, and show business who, perforce (it's a buyer's market), are my basic raw material, like Brigitte Bardot, Ingrid Bergman, Pablo Casals, Bennett Cerf, Bobby Darin, Sammy Davis, Jr., Fabian, Barry Goldwater, Dick Gregory, Huntington Hartford, Krishna Menon, Jean Monnet, Pandit Nehru, Aristotle Onassis, Suzy Parker, Sidney Poitier, Prince Rainier, Nelson Rockefeller, Helena Rubenstein, Carl Sandburg, Arthur Schlesinger, Jr., Adlai Stevenson, Lawrence Spivak, David Susskind, and John Wayne?

Let the reader beware! The answer is that most people see me, talk to me, and let me live with them if necessary, because I represent a national magazine. Whether I like it or not, I come bearing the gift of potential publicity. They want to be better known and, for example, *Look* has twenty-eight million readers.

They want to be beautiful—I might be out of work if they didn't. But beauty is not all I need to know.

Under the circumstances, their motivation places an absolute limitation on the availability of truth. From the moment we meet, a kind of warfare begins in which the best that I can hope for is a moral victory.

I have made an assessment of my survival equipment especially in regard to those well-known people I write about most often, whose stories begin at the end of this interminable introduction. I have height and weight on most of them. I am six feet four and weigh two-twenty. My experience has been that interviews are more lucid when I am standing. I speak a disarming Corn Belt dialect. This has seemed to put some people at ease, but never completely. I think Sidney Poitier is the only subject who ever trusted me without reservation. Most importantly, my name is unknown to millions.

I am not Tom Morgan, the former Yankee pitcher, Tom Morgan, the Congressman from Fredericktown, Pennsylvania, or Tom Morgan, the chairman of the board of Sperry-Rand. I am not even Tom Morgan, the newsman who used to cover the Vatican for United Press. I have used my middle initial, B. for Bruce, in my bylines, but only librarians notice it—or my byline, for that matter. At parties, the questions most people have asked me include:

"How's the old arm?"

"What's in the hopper?"

"Should we sell at the market?"

Dryly as possible, I point out that I am the one who writes. But then I get, "Don't kid me—*he* interviewed Pope Benedict in 1921."

As one might expect, the lack of a bell-ringing name has made it difficult for me to open certain doors, especially those of people I'd like to interview for background material. As it happens, since there is nothing much to gain, most people would rather not get involved. But, despite protests from my ego, I am convinced that my subjects themselves are most likely to give me an honest interview if my name holds little or no meaning for them. I would rather not give examples here for obvious reasons.

But the fact is that those who associate my name with my pieces invariably have dissimulated more than those whose knowledge of Morgans stops with J.P. The small "I've-heard-of-you" group has seemed to think (a) that I'm a scold, (b) that I'm out to "get" them, and (c) that I am a sucker for high-mindedness. They have tended to volunteer thoughts on Art, Science, Foreign Affairs, and the Meaning of Life instead of answering questions.

As advantages, these are hardly impressive. But there remains the possibility of maximizing the truth (or minimizing falsehood) by relating observable or available facts to that which makes a subject co-operative in the first place: his desire to have a "beautiful" image.

Most better-known people tend toward an elegant solution of what they, or their advisers, call "the image problem." Over time, deliberately, they create a public self for the likes of me to interview, observe, and double-check. This self is a tested consumer item of proven value, a sophisticated invention refined, polished, distilled, and certified o.k. in scores, perhaps hundreds, of engagements with journalists, audiences, friends, family, and lovers. It is not really them, but curiously it is not *not* them either. It is the commingling of an image and a personality, or what I've decided to call an Impersonality.

There are gradations, from novice to consummate, among creators of Impersonalities. The latter are all but consumed by their creations. In the flesh, they suggest pictures come to life. They are Teddy Kennedy as *Teddy*, Bennett Cerf as *fun-loving Bennett Cerf*, Nelson Rockefeller as *Rocky*, and David Susskind as *the latest tycoon*. They do us a disservice by inflating the currency of necessary heroism. And, as for themselves, *personally*, they tend away from human complexity toward a single sterile meaning, a label, a handle, something that communicators (that's me!) can communicate and the hungering public mind can grasp, admire, love, and support.

Beyond a single meaning, some move on toward zero.

Consider the archetype, Brigitte Bardot. Some years ago, on an assignment for *Look*, I spent ten days in her orbit. On my last evening in Paris, she had invited me to dinner at the restaurant Androuet, whose specialty is cheese. Our dinner included seven courses, ranging from the weakest cheese to the strongest.

Toward the end of the meal, the *patron* brought his guest book to the table and asked Brigitte to autograph it. She wrote her name in her definite script, plus the comment, "Life is a slice of cheese." I think she meant the inscription to be a joke, but unconsciously she had also described the essence of a phenomenon: herself.

For me, the most telling thing about the real B.B. was how little she differed from the celluloid Brigitte. She had created herself in her own image. I could not distinguish substance from shadow-playing. I doubt that she could either. Egged on by Roger Vadim, the director, she had become a movie queen in the role of a sex kitten and had become a sex kitten in her life as a movie queen. It was impossible to *know* her, except as a self-creation. She was lovely architecture, a gorgeous house that she herself had designed, moved into, and never came out of.

Predictably, her movie roles were not merely imaginary constructions. Rather, they were adaptations from a character suggested by Brigitte Bardot, who was, in turn, suggested by an earlier move starring Brigitte Bardot. Only a decent regard for the nature of fiction kept her films from becoming documentaries. And only the physical limitations of her mind and body kept her from documenting the films in real life. She was her own work of art, a perfect self-created Impersonality. I won't say I wasn't impressed.

The existential focus of her self-creation was the exercise of power over men, to be unattractively unmanageable and unimaginably attractive. In her films, she played the girl-woman who loved men and betrayed them, alternately and endlessly— a latter-day Manon. And, day by day, her real life was a series of late arrivals (usually in high humor) and early departures (often in high dudgeon) to and from the company of men— directors, producers, scenarists, lawyers, promoters, and publicists—whom she baffled, amused, angered, or bewitched at every turn. She was a beach sparrow, a hummingbird, a pouter pigeon, a jackdaw, a duck. Speaking for all men who had to deal with her, her husband at the time, Jacques Charrier, said, philosophically, "With my wife, one has to be a philosopher."

Brigitte did not make me an exception. She was in St. Tropez one day and I thought we had made an appointment to meet at noon. I waited four and a half hours in the town square on the edge of the Mediterranean Sea. Then she drove up with Jacques Charrier in their two-cylinder Citroën. The car stopped a few feet from me. I waved good afternoon, but she made no move to get out. Jacques came around the car to shake hands and apologize for being late. But she remained in her seat and glared at me through the windshield. Ten minutes went by, then another five, like hours. At last, she stepped out, stroking Guapa, a dog she had found six months earlier in a garbage can in Madrid. Her first words, in very plain English, were: "Why are you here?"

"To see you," I answered.

I thought this was a reasonable reply. Through her husband, she had invited me to come over from New York to do the *Look* piece. In Paris, I managed to see her twice in five days. Once, along with fifty French journalists and movie-types, I was invited to her duplex penthouse to hear her announce that her son had been christened. At that time, she told me she had changed her mind about being "described" in an American magazine. "I am not Jayne Mansfield," she said. And besides, she and Jacques were going to St. Tropez in a few days; she was much too busy. "Sorry," she said, smiling, and walked away.

Henri-Georges Clouzot, the director of a film Brigitte was making, was standing next to me. "Don't worry," he said. "You must be patient. I'll take care of everything."

Of course, Clouzot failed, and the most Charrier could do was allow me to wait for Brigitte in his den in their apartment, hoping she would drop in. At the end of a three-day vigil, I saw her for the second time—as she passed an open doorway. She walked by rather quickly, and her hair was hanging over her face, but I recognized her.

Persevering, I followed Brigitte and Jacques to St. Tropez on the outside chance that the husband would change her mind en route. He didn't. She had met me in the plaza only so she could tell me to go away.

As we stood staring at each other in the sun beside the Citroën, she seemed to be looking through me to the boats in the harbor. She clung to the dog and leaned back against the car door. She wore a blue sweater, jeans, and sneakers.

"You should not have come here. I won't talk to anyone," she said.

I reminded her that her husband had sent for me.

"My husband is not my manager," she said. "This is final. I am having no more stories about me."

I do not remember exactly what I said next, but Brigitte suddenly started to walk—not really away, but around the car. She circled it gracefully from back to front, while I continued talking to her. The flight from New York had been very costly, I said. When she came by me, she put her face close to mine, puckered her lips and said, "No, no, no," in both our languages. Her eyes were very hot, wide, and well-shaped. Her nose was a little too flat. The mouth was moist, but too heavy to be perfect. The effect, though, dried my throat—even with Guapa thrown across her shoulder like a sack of salt.

Then Brigitte swung around the car again, and again. She walked briskly with a completely unself-conscious liquid motion of the hips. She came by, snapping French negatives. Then she passed on in increasingly wider circles that finally took her fifteen yards away from the car. I began to get the rhythm of her march and stopped talking when she was out of earshot.

On the eighth (so help me) circumnavigation of the car— as suddenly as she had started—she stopped, smiled and said, "Get into the car. We go to my home."

She had changed her mind about the story. The fact that she had changed it may have been simply female; her manner, however, was impersonality at work.

My experience, of course, was comparatively mild. Over the next few weeks, the papers were full of B.B., the self-creation, at some kind of peak in her life. She walked off the set of Clouzot's film in the middle of her suicide scene; the director's wife, Mme. Clouzot, went to a hospital suffering wrist wounds; Charrier entered another hospital with a nervous breakdown; the great director himself checked into yet another hospital for a little rest. And then Brigitte actually slashed her wrists (as in Clouzot's film) and nearly bled to death.

I had a hard time writing about Brigitte. Totally lost in herself, she brought the logic of impersonality to its ultimate conclusion—absurdity. In a world in danger of boring itself to death with the subject of sex, she had preserved her commercial viability by being incredible on screen and off. She was a sex symbol, and she was also a loud laugh at sex symbols. She represented an ideal of freedom from bourgeois morality, and, at the same time, she was passionately bourgeois. Her escapades were so thick that she even made freedom seem ridiculous. At last she had to dispense with meaning in her "real" life. She said she wanted to retire from films and become an interior decorator. Then she said she didn't want to change in any way. She complained that she was old and washed up at twenty-five. Then she laughed and said she would never grow old. She became angry when I asked her whether she had reached a turning point in her career. "I like my career," she said, "and I want to go on and on playing the lazy beauty with lots of men chasing after me." Then, in the next breath, she said she wanted to be known for her "character" and to be taken "more seriously as a comedienne." With B.B., all things were possible and, if you wished, impossible because her profession was absurdity. If, as a symbol, she stood for anything, she stood for this, for a profound, sad, dizzy, gay, self-created meaninglessness. Ironically, as she herself said at Androuet, the cheese restaurant: "If life is not a slice of cheese, then what is it?"

Well, I survived. I wrote about Brigitte substantially what you have just read. Now I would only add that she also symbolizes the loss of true identity, perhaps momentary but potentially devastating, that threatens all the hounds of publicity.

Vanity is the most deadly sin. Since we all possess it (suppose this book *sells*?), what we are considering is a matter of degree. Everyone wants to be better known, or at least, everyone I have met. We want to be loved publicly, perhaps to compensate for hating ourselves privately. The difference is only that some people strive to be better known than others. To the degree that some do, then to that degree are they in the process of becoming Impersonalities.

I do not always feel cheery about getting paid to exploit this. Self-creations sadden me, even those who do a great deal of good in the world.

But sometimes, when I am especially melancholy and wishing I were someone else, I allow myself one blast on a trumpet: the experience of writing one hundred and fifteen pieces seems to teach that at the end of wisdom we may understand human folly. If it is the hope of understanding that spins the earth, why not keep working? Obviously, there are better ways to search for the truth, but few as close to the action. So, I hang in. In another world, I might have liked being a Talmudist.

For a long time I had thought being a journalist was my worst folly. I did not expect such an ordinary life. As far back as I could remember, I wanted to be a real writer, that is to say, a writer of fiction.

I was born in 1926. My father was a lovable, inefficient merchant and a stiff at poker. My mother is a handsome, devoted, puritan lady. Our town was Springfield, Illinois, the sometime home of Abraham Lincoln. My older sister and brother and I grew up assuming that heroes were born, not made, and that if a man's fate was to become President of the United States, it would not matter that he learned to write with a hunk of coal on the back of a shovel. So much the better. It would make him humble. (That it might also be good for the old image never occurred to me. Apropos, in between writing the third and fourth draft of this introduction, I happened on Norman Mailer's *The Presidential Papers*. In *his* introduction, he used a word I have used and said something provocative: ". . . the hero is the one kind of man who *never* develops by accident . . . a hero is a consecutive set of brave and witty self-creations.")

My mother often assured me that there was a silver lining in every cloud, that no failure was a permanent bar to success, and that everything always came out right in the end. Late in the Depression, my father lost the store, our house, and our car. I believed this was only the dark before dawn. (He died broke.) And I decided I had been born an Artist.

I have lost the orange fountain pen my father gave me for my *bar mitzvah*. But I remember that he said, "You want to be a writer, write with Eversharp." A roly-poly, button-nosed spinster named Elizabeth Graham taught me high-school English. "Writers write," she used to say, paraphrasing Epictetus, and meaning fiction. Ten years later, after I had settled in New York, I returned to Springfield for a visit and called on Miss Graham. "Don't tell me about New York, son," she said, "tell me, how's the writing?" She meant the novel. At Carleton College in North-field, Minnesota, there was a lean, hawk-nosed English pro-fessor and critic *manqué* named Arthur Mizener, who always wore a tweed jacket, gray flannels, and white buck shoes. He was thin-skinned and Fitzgeraldy, but he settled any doubt I might have had that the novel was a church and that its practi-tioners were clergy. I can hear myself promising him I would start one immediately after graduation. Instead, I went to New York, got married, and divided the next nine years between the editorial departments of *Esquire* and *Look*.

As I saw it then, I had won the wrong race, but I would still be running that way were it not for two experiences in late 1957. First, I endured three weeks on an expedition in the Ant-arctic thinking about my life and its end, which seemed im-minent. Then, second, my father died. Nothing could have impressed me more, except perhaps the coming of the Messiah. Forthwith, I quit *Look* and wrote two novels. Both have yet to be published; but as mother used to say, nothing succeeds like failure. I began free-lancing for the magazines in order to live (I had become a father, twice) and discovered that a good thing had happened. The professional and the unacclaimed nov-elist in me had resolved certain psychological differences. Why, I don't know, but I had somehow assimilated attitudes related to fiction writing and these surfaced in my nonfiction pieces. My very first post-novel effort, a chronicle of an encounter with Sammy Davis, Jr., for *Esquire,* came out virtually as a short story, using dialogue, atmosphere, and character development to explore Sammy's personality and self-created image of color-lessness. Since then, I have written most of my pieces in this way. I plan more novels, but I no longer tell myself that jour-nalism is a preliminary before the main event. A writer, I have learned, writes many things. His media, at best, are means to his end. Among mine are magazines.

Many of my pieces have been suggested by such editors as Arnold Gingrich, Harold Hayes, and—until he resigned—Clay Felker at *Esquire,* Daniel Mich and William Arthur at *Look,* and John Fischer at *Harper's.* Clay Felker, for example, had watched Sammy Davis perform on the Ed Sullivan show one Sunday night in March, 1959. A few days later, I met Felker for lunch to celebrate the completion of my first novel. As is our custom, we were criticizing the magazine industry, this time for its indifference toward Negroes: "Sammy Davis, for example," Felker said. And he went on from there to assign "What Makes Sammy, Jr., Run?"

Most of my pieces, however, have been based on ideas that occurred to me for one reason or another. When I am enthusiastic about an idea, I usually have no difficulty finding an outlet for it. Often, a name in the news sets me off. Or a barroom anecdote. Or a press agent. It is a very random thing. Typically, I wrote "How Hieronymus Bosch (XVth Century) and Norman O. Brown (XXth) Would Change the World" because a friend gave me a copy of Brown's *Life Against Death* along with a feverish recommendation. At the time, March, 1961, Brown's book had just begun to move in the college underground. In *Mid-Century* Lionel Trilling had called it "the best interpretation of Freud I know," and critics in London and Paris had raved about it. But it had yet to be reviewed here in any major newspaper or magazine. *Life Against Death* was a hair-raising adventure for me. The moment I read the last line, I called Felker, who agreed that I should write about Brown for *Esquire*. He had not read the book, had never heard of Brown, in fact. He simply went along with my manic excitement.

Whatever the source, my pieces fall into one or the other of two idea categories, the timely and the timeless. Both Davis and Brown were timely. Blaze Starr was not. When I told Harold Hayes that I liked burlesque, he said, "So?" and I said, "How's Blaze Starr?" The result was "Blaze Starr in Nighttown," which *Esquire* published last July, but might well have held for another year.

Theoretically, people like Nelson Rockefeller and Teddy Kennedy are good story ideas any time. But usually, there is a moment when a man's name suggests a certain irony and, for me, that is the best time. It was ironic that Alf Landon had become a supporter of liberal causes. It was ironic that Roy Cohn had become a razzle-dazzle businessman and fight promoter. It was ironic that politically acute Teddy Kennedy would run for the Senate at the low point of his brother's administration. It was ironic that golden Nelson Rockefeller had become a brassy caricature of his own image. Each of these ironies was a signal that an idea's time had come. The unexpected had happened and I wanted to begin. Irony, it seems, is my subject.

Ideas, as everyone knows, are constantly pushed by press agents, who sometimes take me to lunch. Most of them now know that a phone call will do. I'm interested in their suggestions, but most press agents miss the point about irony. An exception was the late William Blowitz, my friend, who was the best in his field. He was killed last year in New York by a hit-and-run driver. Blowitz never called me unless the Ironic Moment had come. One of his clients, Gary Cooper, had suddenly grown old. Going on sixty, he was still playing Peter Pan in a Stetson. We agreed that there was irony in that. Another, Elia Kazan, was leaving Broadway to organize the Lincoln Center repertory theater. At the same time, he was making a mawkish film called *Splendor in the Grass,* which Blowitz hoped to publicize. That a director of such uncertain tastes should be appointed to develop New York's most ambitious art-for-art's-sake theater was, to put it gently, a story idea.

Some ideas have the proper ingredient, but still do not end as stories. *Esquire* assigned me four pieces in 1964 that I could not deliver. There was John Glenn, hospitalized with an ear ailment before I could get to him. Elizabeth Gurley Flynn died in the Soviet Union. Harry S. Truman never answered my letter. And when Lyndon Johnson prematurely ruled out Adlai Stevenson as a candidate for the vice presidency, the idea for a convention story called "Goodbye, Adlai" or "Adlai Returns" lost its meaning.

Often I turn down assignments because an idea that might be interesting to readers does not touch me. One I remember was an idea for a piece about Eddie Fisher in Las Vegas while Elizabeth Taylor was making headlines with Richard Burton in London.

Sometimes, I just don't like a suggested subject. I have learned that I am unable to hate in public. I may be amazed, offended, disgusted, antagonized, or saddened, but getting to know a subject always rules out hate. I may attack—too hard at times, I think—but never without feeling that I might do what the subject has done if I were in his shoes. I am sentimental. I prefer to write about evil in terms of its victims. I hope to change, but I don't know how. Not long ago, *Holiday* magazine asked me to get in touch with Ayn Rand, the novelist whose half-baked dog-eat-dog philosophy has attracted a substantial number of cannibalistic dogs. Routinely, I assembled her bibliography, talked to a few people who knew her, and read *Atlas Shrugged*, which weighs six pounds in the hard-cover edition. I hated what I read. I knew that I might ridicule her, but I also knew that my worst would fall far short of the mark. Besides, I would have to spell her name right. The project seemed futile, so I said the hell with it and turned down the assignment.

In any case, when an idea has been approved, I begin getting involved with my subject by letter or phone. He is occasionally too modest to admit, even to himself, that he cannot resist publicity. But then he has strong views on freedom of the press and that suffices. How can a good citizen deny a journalist his God-given right to interview him? Besides Harry S. Truman, only two potential subjects ever denied me at least an exploratory chat—De Gaulle and Fulgencio Batista, in exile.

The most eager subject I have yet encountered is David Susskind. Early in 1960, I sent him a short note saying I had been assigned to write a story about him for *Esquire*. I waited a few days, then phoned his office in the *Newsweek* building on Madison Avenue. His secretary invited me to come to the office right away, that very afternoon. When I arrived, Susskind seized my hand. His phone was ringing. "I want you to see everything," he said, "know everything, hear everything!" He picked up the phone. After listening for a moment, he covered the mouth-piece with his hand. "It's long distance—Hollywood—go pick up the other phone." He waved me toward his secretary's desk where, still wearing my overcoat, I listened in on his half-hour conversation with another TV producer. In the next three weeks, Susskind never allowed himself a moment of circumspection. He insisted that I attend meetings, luncheons, rehearsals, and screenings with sponsors, network executives, various talent, and his wife, and when necessary, he even introduced me as one Thomas Bruce, a member of his staff.

Another readily accessible subject was Teddy Kennedy. In 1962, before he had declared himself a candidate for the Senate, I called him in Boston. Teddy himself answered the phone, sounding like the man in the Northeast Airlines commercial. "Come on up!" he said. "Whatever you want . . ." As a member of the Kennedy family, he grasped the meaning of publicity. It was power and it would make no sense to be shy about it.

Some subjects are accessible, but not exactly eager. Brigitte Bardot has been mentioned. Roy Cohn wanted to be sure I had never written for *The Nation* or *The New Republic*. Presumably, if I hadn't, he would have a chance. And since I hadn't, he agreed to co-operate. Jean Paul Sartre, who recently turned down the Nobel Prize, said he thought he ought to be paid for answering questions. We never got around to discussing the amount. Frank Sinatra, through his press agent, said he was available only if he could censor what was written. I gave up on him, too.

Alf Landon, Robert Oppenheimer, Jean Monnet, Prince Rainier, and Norman O. Brown said they wouldn't mind having me around if they or their representative could *check* what I wrote. I acquiesced, but reserved the right to reject any suggestions. Writing pieces about Monnet, Brown, and Oppenheimer involved some precise, technical definitions, so I had no real objection to the conditions they had set. But I was unhappy about Rainier and Landon. The sense that someone was looking over my shoulder would make it that much more difficult for me to write as I felt. Besides, I was certain that they expected not only to check my work, but also to censor it. As it turned out, I was right. Rainier's American press agent complained that my piece was "too negative" and demanded a rewrite. "I let you see it," I said, "I didn't say you could change it." The press agent retreated. But he had more luck at the magazine, which had an interest in subsequent stories about the ever-popular Rainiers. The magazine shall be nameless, but I have since stopped writing for it. Similarly, Alf Landon, who had no press agent, took strong exception to the closing paragraph of "The Late Spring of Alf Landon." Here, I had quoted a long, funny story that he had told his son and me about the fiery mistress of an Oklahoma politician. After reading my manuscript, he wrote me from Topeka insisting that I delete the quotation on grounds of taste. In the short time I had spent with Landon (my visit to Topeka was cut short by another death in my family), he had captivated me. I cherished our relationship. But I wanted to use the quotation. At *Esquire,* Harold Hayes said the decision was up to me. The magazine would publish the piece either Landon's way or mine. So, the article ran as I had written it. Landon wasn't pleased, but he wasn't as angry as I had expected, either. Today, we still correspond.

Arthur Schlesinger, Jr., dreamed up the most restrictive precondition I have ever accepted. He said he would only go along with me if I promised not to quote him at all. At the time, Schlesinger had gone to work in the White House. His office was in the East Wing, far from President Kennedy in the West Wing, but he liked his job, liked the Washington whirl, and apparently feared that he might say something that would compromise his position. Foolishly, I promised not to quote him and didn't realize my mistake until I tried to organize my material. I wanted to say that Schlesinger symbolized the status of liberalism in the first two years of the Kennedy Administration. He, as an example, had steadily lost influence in JFK's inner circle. But this could hardly be demonstrated using paraphrases and lifeless anecdotes. In fact, nothing I could write on his terms would do him justice; he is a lively man. The cramp in my style produced a melancholy piece, but Harold Hayes kindly scheduled it for an early 1964 issue. Its press date was November 23, 1963, the day after President Kennedy's assassination. A few days later, there were reports that Schlesinger would resign to write a book about the Kennedy years. He had told me he would never write such a book because JFK would surely do it himself. Hayes decided to withdraw my piece. And it lies buried now in my files. No one will ever read it. Which is all right with me.

Finally, there are subjects about whom I will write for one magazine, but not another. The issue here is not the validity of a story idea, but the problem of expenses. *Look* can afford to send me anywhere, at any time, to write about anybody—to New Delhi for Nehru, Paris for Brigitte Bardot, and the Ross Ice Shelf for A.P. Crary. But *Esquire* could not send me to the Ganges to interview Allen Ginsberg unless somebody, not *Esquire,* paid my way. Indeed, nothing is more hopeless than an expensive idea submitted either to *Esquire* or that other excellent publication, *Harper's*. The problem vexes me. Two of my pieces might not have been written if editors hadn't approved air transportation paid for by the subjects themselves or their agents. Bill Blowitz, for example, paid my way to London to interview Gary Cooper. "Don't think you're buying me, Bill," I said. "Who'd want to!" he answered. Obviously, the practice is unhealthy. In recent years, I have not agreed to it. But neither have I returned to London. Once I tried to organize my assignments so that I could pool the limited expense allowances of two magazines. I paid my own air fare to Europe, interviewing Ingrid Bergman for *Redbook*, Lawrence Durrell for *Esquire*, and Aristotle Onassis for no one in particular. The pieces were sold, but my gain was merely personal, not financial. My accountant said it had been a dumb thing to do. Ever since, there have been people I wanted to write about whom *Look* did not want and all the others could not afford. So I have mourned for missed adventures.

The adventures I have had are, I hope, revealed in my pieces. Here I would only add a personal word. My conscience troubles me. In each encounter with a subject, whether it lasts a day, a week, or a month, I have been shameless. If one pretends that he is telling me the truth, I pretend that I think he is beautiful. I tell him truths about myself so that he will tell me truths about himself. In a short time, he may know more about me than my wife knows. Meanwhile, of course, he is telling me I'm swell, hoping that I will say the same about him. The relationship is gay on the surface, violent below. We are sophisticated apes. But, secretly, I admit to myself that I relish our struggle. If, as often happens, we become friendly, I do not expect our friendship to last past publication day. We may meet again, but I have never let that possibility affect what I write. I prefer remorse to regret.

Now I must qualify what I have just said. Some relationships have lasted, or so I believe. I feel that I am not only Alf Landon's friend, but also Sammy Davis'. Before "What Makes Sammy, Jr., Run?" appeared, Sammy had had few magazine stories to clip for his scrapbook. I suspect that he did not enjoy my observations, only the publicity. But soon after the story appeared, he called to thank me and I appreciated that. I think we discovered then that our feelings of friendliness extended into reality and, for several years at least, we maintained a warm relationship. I feel I am Sidney Poitier's friend, too. About halfway through my sojourn with him, he predicted that we would surely know each other for a long time. I doubted it. I was fairly certain by then that my piece would not flatter him. It happened that I was right about the piece, but not about Sidney's reaction. His prediction is coming true.

Another friend is Irving Gitlin, an executive producer of documentaries for NBC–TV. *Esquire* published my piece about him more than six years ago. He was not pleased by the title, "The Happier Time on TV," or the contents. Nearly three years went by before I saw him again. But then we met, more or less accidentally, and buried the hatchet. Last year, as he began to move into feature films, he commissioned a screen play from me and we have since been working together on the details of production.

My favorite subject was Suzy Parker, the model and actress. I liked her the moment I set eyes on her. In a mood for understatement, I titled her story, "The Most Beautiful Woman in the World." Was it love? Was it mutual? She did call to say she *liked* the piece. Need I say I was devastated when I read she had been married—and, of all people, to an actor?

A time comes on each story when I see that nothing more is to be gained by stalking a subject. By then, I have filled half-a-dozen notebooks with quotations, names, dates, and random details. I have interviewed the subject's friends, enemies, past and present wives, children, and other authorities. I have also collected pertinent books, reviews, and additional printed matter. And sometimes I have received the results of legwork by free-lance researchers who have spent some days digging up special material for me. By far, the best of these has been Miss Susan Black, who is now a brisk and resourceful writer for *The New Yorker*. Besides an ability to dig up useful information from unexpected sources, she had a faultless memory for obscure news events, esoteric history, and shop talk. She is pretty, too. I miss her.

Reading about how writers write bores me. If it bores you, too, you may want to skip ahead a few pages to the denouement of this open-and-shut essay, because I am now going to tell How I Do It.

When I sit down to write, I already know that I will try to avoid my subject's *private* private life, his more intimate family relations, sexual tastes, and medical record. He may have placed numerous juicy items on the record, but I believe there is a proper limit to the public's right to know, even if he doesn't. Avoidance, however, does not mean suppression. I tell whatever seems *necessary* even if it exceeds the proper limit: There was no way, for example, to explain David Susskind's passions and "flexible art" without revealing Mrs. Susskind, so I did it. Had I omitted mention of Blaze Starr's love life, I might as well have omitted Blaze Starr. And it seemed to me that one mention of Lawrence Durrell's mistress was required to help validate his attempted resignation from "the English Death." On the other hand, I would not reveal that Sidney Poitier no longer lived at home with his family. It was a secret then; today, he and his wife are legally and publicly separated. Nor would I report the psychiatric ailments of one subject or the sexual activities of another who, after I had been around for a few days, gave up trying to hide the girls.

I write to find out what I am going to say. Studying my notes, I am certain that I do not know any truth except that the need for publicity is probably a symptom of something I ought to have found out about and didn't. I am also reasonably certain that I've been had, a little or a lot. I sometimes feel I have been asked to restore a Rembrandt overpainted by an Eisenhower. At best, I'm an art critic. Here is a unique subject, unlike any other, particular in every sense. The subject has form and style, color and line, rhythm and tone. Above all, he must mean something or nothing. He is a singularly chaotic arrangement of molecules readily identifiable as an individual. He defies generalization and will certainly fool the judge. And here am I: The deadline is nigh. I need the money. I want to understand. Usually, I begin by reminding myself that, honestly, I don't know anything either about art or personality. I only know what I like. I will not discount the causal significance of heredity or environment. But because the coin I flip always stands on end,

I will hold this truth to be self-evident, that each man is responsible.

I write. And I lose. The subject always wins. He wins because, good or evil, rich or poor, it's nice to have publicity. I lose because what I write isn't him. He also wins moral responsibility for the self he has created. I just lose my pretensions.

As I write, I try to beat the devil with style. I have always liked J. Robert Oppenheimer for saying, "The problem of doing justice to the implicit, the imponderable, and the unknown is of course not unique to politics. It is always with us in science, it is with us in the most trivial affairs, and it is one of the great problems of writing and of all forms of art. The means by which it is solved is sometimes called style. It is style which complements affirmation with limitation and humility; it is style which makes it possible to act effectively, but not absolutely; it is style which, in the domain of foreign policy, enables us to find a harmony between the pursuit of ends essential to us, and the regard for the views, the sensibilities, the aspirations of those to whom the problem may appear in another light; it is style which is the deference that action pays to uncertainty; it is above all style through which power defers to reason." That, from *The Open Mind,* is what I mean by style.

How maximize the truth? How limit limitless failure? How survive?

Of the two classical schools, the biographical, third person, anecdotal stylist is more likely to fail for lack of genius than the narrative, first person, "this-happened" stylist. The anecdote is almost always apocryphal, commercially inspired, or precisely misinterpreted. The alternative is safer because the writer is reasonably certain about his own half of the truth. "I was there," he says, "and the subject said this to me." Furthermore, "I" is reassuring to readers who assume that "I" was a truth-telling eyewitness. I admire the masters of personal reporting. I also admire a whole slew of my contemporaries who have the *chutzpah* to write essays, reviews, and even footnotes in the first person perpendicular. But I have never been able to do it, except for this tumbleweed preface. I fall in between.

The occasional "I" in my pieces is as impersonal as I can make it. It is not "me." It is only a means of confining and defining another's Impersonality. Were I able to do the right thing by my readers and tell the Whole Truth, the Real Truth, and All of the Truth, I might risk the personal "I." But I can't. The best I can do is try to keep the subject in line so that when the truth does come out, I will at least know I tried.

When I am finished with a piece, I feel wonderful. I send it in and rest until I hear from the editor. Rewriting offends me, but I do it. "Elia Kazan's Great Expectations" required the most extensive rewriting of all my pieces. I completely rewrote it twice. At last, I pleased the editor, John Fischer, but then I was no longer pleased myself. I was simply fed up. The third version was published. I'm not unhappy with it now, but the original was livelier.

I like editors who acknowledge their own fallibility. Clay Felker, for example, asked for a new lead page on "Teen Age Heroes: Mirrors of Muddled Youth." I sat down in an empty office at *Esquire* and did the deed. About six P.M., I threw away the original and presented the new approach. Felker read it and exclaimed, "God, I've ruined it! Give me back the original!" I told him it had been my only copy, but that I could easily retrieve it from the wastebasket. When I returned to the empty office, the wastebasket was also empty. Desperately, Felker hunted down the cleaning woman and plunged into her enormous burlap bag full of wastepaper. After an hour spent uncrumpling wads of typing paper, he found my page. Since then, I have always made carbons.

Publication of my pieces is out of my hands. Magazines own "first serial" rights and editors do as they please, or as their publishers please. I once wrote an Aesopian jibe about Barry Goldwater for *Good Housekeeping*. Permission to publish it came from the chairman of the Hearst Corp., Richard Berlin, himself. I was surprised when he approved it, but then I was less surprised two years later when the Hearst press endorsed Lyndon Johnson. A delayed decision on the publication of another one of my pieces aggravated me more than any single experience I've had as a writer. The Norman O. Brown piece languished at *Esquire* for eighteen months before it saw print. Felker had resigned and neither Harold Hayes nor anyone else was *with* it.

It was scheduled only after I had asked to have it back to publish elsewhere.

I don't know what I would have done if *Esquire* had called my bluff.

Nowadays, I spend most of my time engaged in some phase of the journalistic process. On the average, I work a twelve- to fourteen-hour day. I do not need much rest. Looking back, I see how like my father I am. He played poker with his friends until three or four A.M., three or four nights a week. Father, the devotee, the addict, the pro, foolishly never stopped trying to fill inside straights and three-card flushes. He lost, but he always played the last hand. Then he would go home, sleep a few hours and be off for his busy day at the store. Today, I see more of my children, Katherine and Nicholas, than my father saw of me. I spend more time with my Mrs. than he did with his. But, by day, I am busy, as he was, with business—interviews, appointments, the library, lunch. I, too, am a devotee, an addict, a pro, who works through the night. Of course, I am alone, but my friends are no farther away than the telephone and I keep in touch. Finally, I, too, lose.

Perhaps it cannot be otherwise. Or perhaps it can. It is, I think, too early for irony. Let the winners laugh and joke. As my father used to say, I want to say, too:

Deal the cards.

                                                  —T.B.M.

Gary Cooper
The
American Hero
Grows Older

Aged fifty-nine going on sixty, Gary Cooper, whose image is one of the two most enduring ever created in Hollywood, was in London a while ago making a movie called *The Naked Edge*. (You probably can't imagine a more unlikely vehicle for Cooper: the story concerns an American businessman with a British wife —Deborah Kerr—who thinks Gary Cooper, of all people, is a murderer. Only a firm belief that movie people can lick any story ever written should sustain your faith that the picture will come out all right in the end, with Cooper's image intact and the whole thing adding up, willy-nilly, to a Thataway-on-the-Thames.) Cooper stayed at the Savoy for the nine weeks required to shoot the picture. His wife and daughter—Rocky and Maria—were with him. The family went to the theater (Cooper enjoyed *Ross*, starring Alec Guinness), hiked in Richmond Park, and visited friends in the estate country. But most of the time, Cooper conserved himself for the task at hand. Five days a week from about eight-fifteen in the morning to after six in the evening, he was getting himself ready to act, waiting to act, or acting on location or at the Elstree studios of the Associated British Picture Corporation, Ltd. Most nights, he studied his lines for the next day and got his rest. Although he had made a hundred movies in the past thirty-six years, acting still wasn't easy for him; he had to concentrate. He said, however, that he wouldn't mind if I hung around with him for a week or so, watching the work and making conversation from time to time

in an effort to find out how Gary Cooper was affected by being
Gary Cooper.

It is a nice coincidence that Cooper is the same age as *The
Virginian,* the novel which Owen Wister started writing in 1901
(Cooper was born on May 7 that year), published in 1902, and
lived to see made into Cooper's first talking picture in 1929.
Cooper says that movie made *him:* "That was the big one—you
had to survive the transition to talking pictures—*The Virginian*
put me over the hump and made millions." On rereading the
novel, one finds it difficult now to conceive of anyone but Gary
Cooper in the title role.

Take the scene in Chapter Two: "The poker game at the
Medicine Bow saloon; the villain, Trampas, is impatient with
the young Virginian, who inevitably takes his time about deciding whether to call, raise, or fold his hand. . . .

"Therefore, Trampas spoke: 'Your bet, you-son-of-a-b—.'

"The Virginian's pistol came out, and his hand lay on the
table, holding it unaimed. And with a voice as gentle as ever,
the voice that sounded almost like a caress, but drawling a very
little more than usual, so that there was almost a space between
each word, he issued his orders to the man Trampas:

"'When you call me that, *smile!*' And he looked at Trampas
across the table.

"Yes, the voice was gentle. But in my ears it seemed as if
somewhere the bell of death was ringing; and silence, like a
stroke, fell on the large room. . . ."

Who else but Gary Cooper? To this day, Cooper projects an
image from the screen that is the quintessence of Wisterism.
Wister's book contains the pure essence of the cowboy as an
American Hero. Before Wister, there was no literary category
called "Western." Out of Wister, whose novel sold over 1,600,000
copies, sprang a genre, a myth, and the basic plot for America's
horse-opera industry. Wister literally redefined the West, not
only for the folks back East, but for Westerners themselves who
probably didn't understand how romantic they were just running ornery cattle, eating salt pork, and getting themselves killed
by desperadoes. Wister created a West that was remarkably
akin to Never-Never Land. For his hero, he devised a slim,

roughhewn, self-effacing Peter Pan who never grew old, never found out, and could ride and shoot onetwothree justlikethat. "Daring, laughter, endurance—these were what I saw upon the countenances of the cowboys," Wister wrote. And, "What has become of the horseman, the cowpuncher, the last romantic figure upon our soil? . . . Well, he will be here among us always, invisible, waiting his chance to live and play as he would like. His wild kind has been among us always, since the beginning: a young man with his temptations, a hero without wings. . . ."

A review of Gary Cooper's film titles now suggests episodes in a long-running serial about such a hero: *Lives of a Bengal Lancer, A Farewell to Arms, The Plainsman, Mr. Deeds Goes to Town, Alice in Wonderland* (Cooper played the White Knight), *For Whom the Bell Tolls, Unconquered, They Came to Cordura,* and even the sophisticated *Love in the Afternoon,* at the end of which the hero leans down from a moving train and sweeps his little old gal off a station platform. Of course, a complete transference occurred long ago. Gary Cooper, the apparition on the screen, himself became the essence of the cowboy as an American Hero. It is always Gary Cooper as *Gary Cooper* who gives these films their meaning and provides the attraction for audiences that have paid in nearly 300 million dollars to see them.

Gary Cooper's *Gary Cooper* is second only to Charlie Chaplin's tramp among all the enduring symbols created by U.S. movies. "When the critic of the American cinema looks around for the film that can give him his clue to American thought," the *Times* of London said unhappily recently, "he can point to nothing but the Western." If one points to the Western, one must point at last to the archetype Gary Cooper. While Chaplin's tramp expresses our common humanity and inevitable tragicomedy, Cooper sums up the shifting American dream in terms of our national reluctance to grow older and our pioneer belief in the inevitable triumph of good over evil. On the screen, he is the essentially simple man who resolves complexities, finally, by taking matters into his own hands and simplifying them. The "critic of American cinema" could do worse, in fact, than look for his clues in Cooper rather than the Western itself. Cooper's films have often mirrored our democratic mood if not our nature. He was the hero of *A Farewell to Arms* when we were preoccupied with pacifism; he was the liberal-minded Mr. Deeds in the New Deal era, and both Sergeant York (pacifist turned warrior) and Robert Jordan (civilian turned guerrilla) in a world at war. He was the lonely hero of *High Noon* at the beginning of the Eisenhower era. If, in recent years, he has seemed to fumble about, unable to define a mood and break box-office records, perhaps that is a reflection of the end of the Eisenhower era. Outside of America, the impact of Cooper-as-*Cooper* is no less enduring, as Leslie Fiedler, the resident culture critic of Montana, observed during a recent sojourn in Europe. The American dream of innocence and achievement, he said, was a kind of religious belief, a post-Christian faith in which even movies were scriptures: "This faith has already built up in Western Europe a sizable underground sect which worships in the catacombs of the movie theaters. . . . A hundred years after the *Manifesto,* the specter that is haunting Europe is— Gary Cooper! Vulgar, gross, sentimental, impoverished in style —our popular sub-art presents a dream of human possibilities to starved imaginations everywhere. It is a wry joke that what for us are our most embarrassing by-products of a democratic culture, are in some countries the only democracy there is."

One day at Elstree studios, the creator-beneficiary (and victim) of democratic cultural by-products, Gary Cooper, was seen between scenes in his star-dressing room close by the set of *The Naked Edge.* As was his custom, he had retired to the tiny room where he might nap, study his script, or talk, but in any case get off his dogs. He had left the door ajar through which one could see the set—an upper-middle-class model home with some of its walls and the ceiling missing—and had turned on the electric heater. When I had entered, he had not, of course, gotten up from the day bed. He explained that he didn't mind being interrupted as long as he could converse from the prone position. He had the laconic air of a man who never stands when he can sit and never sits when he can get flat.

"Here I am, all the time talking about how hard actors work," he said, "and you find me lying on my ass."

Life-size, Cooper's face retained something of an atmosphere of make-believe. It was as though reality and the movies had combined long ago to make a face for a man with a unique role to play in his lifetime: himself as *Gary Cooper*. The face was seamed and worn in the Western way, but it wasn't stern the way some Western faces are. The sophisticated, sunny life of southern California was there, rather than the country life up where the winters last so long. The eyes were blue, often abstracted, but expressive and good-humored, too. The nose was straight and not small. When Cooper cracked a smile, not just the wide mouth but the whole face seemed to open up and he looked then most like Gary Cooper, the one you see on the screen who was simply born with the cowboy-man personality. A few years ago, Cooper had checked into a New York hospital for an operation requiring plastic surgery. The press had reported a "face-lifting," but both Cooper and the surgeon had insisted it was not that at all. A nose bone fixed, scar tissue and a cyst removed was all, Cooper had said. Whatever the results of that surgery may have been, Cooper close-up now looked his age—no more and no less.

His condition seemed all the more remarkable when you considered the real (as opposed to make-believe) beating his body had taken over the years. As a boy in Montana he had broken a hip in an automobile accident. The hip had healed imperfectly and had contributed to the Gary Cooper walk, a slightly bow-legged, slow-rolling gait that makes him seem like a cowboy even in a Savile Row business suit. In the mid-Twenties, breaking into the movies as a stunt rider, he had suffered innumerable sprains and bruises and had damaged his right shoulder so badly that he couldn't lift his arm over his head. When he had played Lou Gehrig in *Pride of the Yankees,* he had had to learn how to throw a ball again. (He was right-handed, but Gehrig was left-handed, so the throwing sequences in that movie were all printed from the reverse side of the negative film.) In the early Thirties, following much hard work and a romance with Lupe Velez, he had been put out of commission for nearly a year with jaundice and exhaustion. (He went on a safari to Tanganyika to recover his strength.) He had developed an ulcer after he had made *High Noon,* and last year he had been in surgery twice within six weeks for internal troubles. In addition, he'd had four hernias besides all the minor accidents connected with movie-making: pinned underwater and almost drowned; cut by falling debris after a bridge explosion; hearing impaired in the left ear by a dynamite blast; wrist-sprain, cut lip, and black eye suffered when a brother actor had become too realistic in a fight scene; left shoulder wounded by a blank pistol fired at close range by Burt Lancaster; and hands burned putting out a fire in his dressing room on the set of *The Naked Edge*.

"I feel real good," Cooper said. "Keep my weight to one hundred and ninety by backing away from the groceries every now and then." He fished in his pocket, pulled out a toothpick and began to gnaw it.

"Now I like the idea of this picture we're making. It's a whodunit—a good one, I think. Different sort of thing for me. I got to play this role on the ragged edge. Problem is to play it on the innocent side and still bring out to the audience the circumstances that seem to make me guilty. Well, there's a bigger problem. I don't know whether people will believe that Gary Cooper could commit a crime. For the picture to work, there has to be some believability that I did kill this other fella. Going to be interesting to see how it comes out."

Somebody knocked and called out, "Ready, Mr. Cooper!"

He sat up on the edge of the day bed and took another look at Scene 323 in the script. Then he tossed it on the bed and stood up.

"All a matter of script," he said. "Good script makes a good movie. Made *Ten North Frederick* and never read the novel. Liked the script and made the movie. This is a good script and I like it. Well."

Cooper ducked his head going through the door. He met Deborah Kerr, blonde and aristocratic, coming out of her dressing room. He asked her how she was, and she said she was fine. Cooper's make-up man put down his copy of *Model Railroading*, took up his comb and powder puff, and went to work. He paid most attention to Cooper's corn-yellow wig. When he was ready for the camera, Cooper joined the director, Michael Anderson, who was young, bushy-haired, and deferential. He had directed, among other films, *Around the World in 80 Days* and Cooper's *The Wreck of the Mary Deare*. They went over the scene together.

. . . Miss Kerr is sitting on the edge of a bathtub telling Mr. Cooper that she's been thinking of committing suicide because she is afraid of what he's done and might do. She has hysterics. Then Mr. Cooper moves toward her and says, "Stop it, Martha! You think I'm a real murderer, don't you. . . ." And so on for about thirty-five seconds of film. . . .

Cooper took his place on the chalk mark in the bathroom as Miss Kerr seated herself on the tub. The distance from his face to the lens was measured by an assistant cameraman. A bell rang and the outside stage door was automatically locked. Cooper began snapping his fingers and rocking back and forth on the balls of his feet. He tried his lines once for the technician operating the sound boom. He did not speak loudly, bearing out the legend of his understated acting style. (As one story goes, he and George Raft made a scene with a wooden cigar store Indian and the Indian was accused of overacting. And the moral of many others is that Cooper never seems to *act*, yet he dominates any scene in which he appears on the screen.) The man on the boom was satisfied although he would have to work the microphone closer to Cooper than to Miss Kerr. The cameraman and the director were ready. One man called for silence while another clacked the slapstick and announced for sound Scene 323. Take One. The audience—artisans, technicians, and workmen—froze.

"Action!" Anderson said.

Eyes filling with tears, Miss Kerr had hysterics and Cooper recited his lines.

"Let's try it again," Anderson said. "The 'Stop it, Martha!' ought to be a bit bigger, Mr. Cooper."

"Stop it, Martha! Goddamn it!" Cooper said.

"That's it. Bang it in there, Mr. Cooper."

"Stop it, Martha! You—"

"You're stopping my hysterics," Miss Kerr said.

Cooper forgot his lines on takes two, three, and four. He walked around in a circle, whistled, and pounded his palm with his fist. Then he forgot them again on take five.

"It's difficult," he said.

"It needs quiet strength, Mr. Cooper. Take a little more time."

"I'm sorry," Cooper said to Miss Kerr.

"Don't be silly," she said. "It's all right."

"It's difficult."

The sixth take wasn't bad, Anderson said, but still not right. On seven, Miss Kerr forgot her lines. Cooper botched eight and nine.

"This feels awful, Mickey," Cooper said. "Just standing here saying, 'Stop it, Martha!' for chrissakes!"

"No, it's all right, Gary," Anderson said.

A pause for make-up repair. Then takes ten and eleven both interrupted by a knock in the plumbing. Cooper more edgy now. Take twelve was flawless. "Simply marvelous!" Anderson said.

Cooper walked back to his dressing room. He chomped on the toothpick. The number of takes had been below his record of twenty-two set in an earlier film, but well over his average of four or five. The thirty-five seconds of film had required an hour of shooting.

"Goddamn it!" he said, stretching out on the day bed. "I hate this whodunit stuff. It's so contrived! Now what this character would really do in real life is not any 'Stop it, Martha!' bull. He'd slap her one on the behind and take her off to bed or on a trip. But for the sake of the goddamn plot you got to keep on doing things a man wouldn't do! Christ!"

Thus seen, Gary Cooper, the actor, was curiously indistinguishable from his own screen image of the slim, roughhewn cowboy-man. If he was not self-effacing, too, at least he was self-conscious, which comes close. And though he turned out to be normally talkative (he never once said "Yup"), whatever one heard from Cooper often seemed to be more an attempt to fortify the image than to justify the man.

When one asks Cooper why he has survived in the movies for so long, he is likely to say something Cooperesque like this:

"Everybody asks me how come you're around so long. Well, I always say I attribute it to playing the part of Mr. Average Joe American. Just an average guy from the middle of the U.S.A. And then, I guess I got to believe it."

Or: "Gary Cooper. An Average Charlie who became a movie actor."

Or: "My taste in art and literature is real ordinary. I don't pretend I know anything. I'm the average guy in taste and intelligence and if there's any reason for my success, that's it!"

Cooper doesn't seem to want it to get around that he is a highly skilled, high-priced actor who can act. His profession has earned him at least $10,000,000. He drives a Bentley, has three homes and an art collection (Picasso, Renoir, Walt Kuhn), and is tailor-made down to his shoes. Born in Montana, he spent more time in his youth attending public school in England (three years) than he did running cattle on his father's ranch (two years). He majored in art at Grinnell College in Iowa, leaving at the end of his junior year to earn enough money to continue his studies at a Chicago art school. He joined his mother and father (Charles Cooper, one-time Justice of the Montana Supreme Court) in Los Angeles in 1924 and found work eventually as a movie stunt rider and extra. His real name, Frank Cooper, was changed to Gary Cooper by his agent, who hailed from Gary, Indiana. In 1926, Samuel Goldwyn featured him in *The Winning of Barbara Worth* with Vilma Banky and Ronald Colman. He starred opposite Clara Bow in 1927 and, for a while, he was known as the It boy. In 1928 he made a picture with Fay Wray and early in 1929 he co-starred with Lupe Velez in *Wolf Song*. Then came *The Virginian*, followed by his emergence as a box-office phenomenon and world symbol.

Cooper would have you believe that he has been helpless before his fate. He declines most of the credit for being *Gary Cooper* and lays off the responsibility, too. When he talks, for example, about the theory and practice of choosing scripts, he either gives credit to someone else for telling him what to do or else refers to himself in the third person.

"I'm always looking for stories to do," he says. "And people tell me I should do certain things. Cecil B. De Mille told me— he said—'You look like the typical average American fella. There are roles like that to be had and you should stick to them. Heroic —adventure. The American people would like to think of a hero as a hero wherever he is around the world.' Well, I made a picture called *Along Came Jones*. About a cowboy who couldn't

shoot. De Mille said to me, 'You're letting your fans down.'
It's always been a question whether to let the public see what
they expect or whether you should give them something new.
It always comes up. There are things Gary Cooper shouldn't
do, things that offer great opportunities actingwise. My friends
tell me he could make an artistic flop, so why do it?"

Cooper, however, does make the final decision on roles he will
portray and on the way they are written. He has had this power
since 1933 when he signed a contract with Paramount giving
him "pretty much control" over his scripts. Since 1944, when he
became a free agent, Cooper has had absolute control. Today,
he makes movies with his own company, Baroda Productions,
alone or in association with other independents. The Naked
Edge, for example, is a joint production of Baroda and Pennybaker Productions, in which Marlon Brando has an interest, and
is financed by United Artists. One of Pennybaker's producers,
Walter Seltzer, has described the crucial points at which Cooper
makes decisions: first, a simple yes or no to the story; second,
yes or no to the screenplay with suggested modifications.

"We had this idea for Cooper to make a switch," Seltzer says.
"To play in a suspense picture and make him, Gary Cooper, the
suspect. So I called Cooper. He was in the West Indies and he
got a copy of the book, read it, and signed the contract without
ever seeing the screenplay. But, of course, he knew we had
Joe Stefano who wrote the Psycho screenplay for Hitchcock.
The financial arrangements were simple. Coop is the easiest deal
in the world. He never figures in it. His agent or his lawyer
handles the fiscal policy. Baroda Productions just gets so much
money and half of one-hundred per cent of the profits. Then
Coop had one meeting with Stefano and us before we started
shooting. That's all he needs. We had this meeting with Coop
in Paris about the story, the team, the plans. He was on his way
to go skin-diving in the south of France with Rocky and Maria.
He has a definite concept of himself as a hero. Definite. He
wasn't sure the audience would accept him as a possible murderer. So we convinced him they would. He wanted certain lines
changed in the script and certain things added to make his
character softer. Like, in the first version, Stefano wanted to
build up the fact that there was a warm, personal relationship

at the outset between the hero and his wife, so he wrote in some cute little sexy lines. Coop said he couldn't deliver those lines. He said we'd get laughed out of the theater. He said he can't deliver coy, sexy lines. So now, instead of those lines, we have different devices. For instance, we have a moment in an early scene where he's in court and she massages his shoulder. That shows the relationship Coop's way. There was another kind of scene which Stefano had in there where Coop was supposed to squeeze a tube of toothpaste into the lens of the camera. Coop said he couldn't do that either. Too phallic. And then, finally, Coop wanted bits here and there in the script that softened him, his character. So, for example, after his testimony sends another man to jail, he mumbles to the man's wife: 'I'm sorry.' Just that, but it does a great deal. Well, it was that sort of thing. Coop knows what he wants. After the meeting, he gave us the name of his London tailor, said he'd see us two days before the shooting, and took off."

Cooper's control of his screenplays actually goes much deeper —to the essence: the screenwriter knows as he writes or rewrites that the script is for Cooper and almost certainly he must be guided by a conception of his image. In approving or disapproving such efforts since the early Thirties, Cooper has assumed final responsibility for himself as *Gary Cooper*.

For a time after his first big successes, Cooper admits he went "the Hollywood route." He bought a snappy wardrobe, a Duesenberg, and whatever else caught his fancy. He participated in some highly charged and well-publicized romances with Clara Bow, Evelyn Brent, Tallulah Bankhead, and Countess Dorothy di Frasso. He almost married Lupe Velez. But the same year Cooper signed the Paramount contract, he met and married Veronica "Rocky" Balfe, a listee in the New York Social Register whose grandfather was Harry Balfe, one-time president and board chairman of Austin Nichols. (Their daughter, Maria, was born in 1937.) Cooper gave up the playboy life and got down to the serious business of managing his career. He has been an assiduous manager ever since.

Cooper's ambition seems to center on preserving his image even at the cost of repetitiveness and some bad films in among his better achievements. He has maintained himself as the cowboy hero by making a Western in between every two or three films with contemporary settings. Until recently he made three pictures every two years; his new arrangement calls for as many pictures as he can find good scripts. He has great will power when it comes to turning down juicy but unsuitable parts. He had a crack at the Rhett Butler role in *Gone With the Wind,* but rejected it. He did not, he says, see himself playing the part of a dashing ladies' man: "I wanted to do stories that were credible, that fitted my personality, and didn't clash with people's beliefs about me."

Seemingly ageless, Cooper has continued through the post-war boom what he started in '29 and nourished through Depression and war. Television may close movie theaters. Disc jockeys and crooners may replace Hollywood stars as teen-age heroes. Private eyes may vie with cowboys for popular attention. Yet Cooper persists. He allows that he hasn't been satisfied with some of the films he has made since *High Noon,* but his audiences remain loyal. Because of them, he was able to earn 311,000 dollars in the Depression year of 1935, become the highest-paid wage earner in the United States in 1939 with a salary of 482,819 dollars, and earn more than 500,000 dollars a year in most of the years since 1946.

Cooper is looking forward to a "three-picture deal" with United Artists, possibly including a dramatization of *The View from the Fortieth Floor,* Theodore White's book about the magazine business, Madison Avenue, and the executive life. "Possibly," Cooper says because "the one problem with the White book is that the hero is defeated in the end. I don't know if I should play a role like that."

Which, if nothing else, is a tip on how *The Naked Edge* ends.

At the end of a day's shooting at Elstree studios outside London, Gary Cooper bowed his head so that the make-up man could remove his corn-yellow wig. Underneath was a respectable head of brown-to-blond hair. He went to the room in which he had left his city clothes, peeled to the waist and washed off his make-up. He wore a St. Christopher's medal on a chain around his neck. (He had converted to Catholicism in 1959.) He scrubbed his face with a towel and then hung the towel neatly on a rack. Then he dressed himself in alligator shoes, gray flannel trousers, blue shirt, dark tie, yellow sweater, tweed sports coat with sky-blue hanky flaring from the chest pocket, and a Tyrolean hat. He put on his raincoat and led the way to the entrance of the building where an oversized Rolls-Royce was waiting for him. He stepped back and waved me in.

"After you, your Majesty—and sit on the side with my good ear."

Cooper directed the driver to the Savoy and settled back.

"How do you like these seats?" he asked. "You sink right in! They hired this car for me. One of the very few straight-eight Rollses in the world. Built for the Duke of Gloucester. Take a feel of that glass. Bulletproof and half an inch thick. No wild hare with a .22 will ever shoot you through that."

Cooper looked out at the sky. It was raining again.

"Going to stop soon," he said, "because it's slanting thataway." He pointed to the west. The rain stopped about halfway to London.

"TV? They may call that stuff on TV *Westerns*," he said, "but they're really Easterns. They're gangster stories with big hats and they're all crap. And the *hats* they wear! There's only one real cowboy hat and it's not the one those kids wear on television. Cowboy hat has to be made out of beaver. Would cost over two hundred dollars today, but hatmakers don't give a damn any more. Now they make hats for drug-store cowboys. A real cowboy lived out there where the mesquite thorns were three inches long and the weather always changing and he needed himself a *hat,* and not just crap!"

Cooper rubbed his knees, sighed, and slid down in the seat until his feet were comfortably resting on the jump seat.

"Well, wouldn't I like to get in a bit of shooting before I leave! Now what I really like is hunting bobcats with a .22 pistol. You have to have real good dogs. They tree the cat, and then you shoot him in the head. If you miss, you're liable to lose some dogs. Every fall, I meet Hemingway out in Sun Valley. We both have places there. Well, Papa and I go hunting. You know, it does you good to get out and get your butt wet every once in a while."

Cooper sighed again. "Well," he said, "I guess we've got a new president. I've known Jack Kennedy a long time. We happened to be together the day FDR died. I've known him that long." During the 1960 campaign, he had been torn between his friendship for Senator Kennedy and his own Republican heritage. Cooper's father had been active in Montana GOP politics and Cooper himself used to draw cartoons for Helena's *Independent,* a Republican newspaper. During World War II, along with John Wayne, Walt Disney, and others, Cooper belonged to the Motion Picture Alliance for the Preservation of American Ideals to "correct the gnawing impression that this industry is made up of and dominated by Communists, crackpots, and radicals." In 1944, he even risked the Cooper image supporting Thomas E. Dewey for president in an advertisement entitled, "I've been for Roosevelt before . . . but not this time." The advertisement, signed by Cooper, said, ". . . I disagree with the New Deal belief that the America all of us love is old and worn out and finished—and has to borrow foreign notions that don't even seem to work any too well where they come from . . ."

"The people have got to pay attention," Cooper said to me. "Can't let this moral decline go on. We say democracy is best because it's fairest to the average man, but if you get more socialism, more government control, more decadence, well, then you get more like the Marxists."

Cooper fell silent after that and seemed to doze. We arrived at the Savoy about twenty minutes later. Cooper instructed the driver to drop me at my hotel and pick us both up at the Savoy at eight P.M.

"If you get here before that," he said to me, "give us a holler on the lobby phone."

Cooper and I had dinner together that evening at a restaurant called *Quo Vadis.* We ate fettuccine and drank a good red wine. Cooper talked mostly about food and restaurants, especially in Paris. He signed a few autographs and, about eleven, we prepared to leave. As he made his way toward the door, people seemed politely happy to see him. At one table, however, a young man with two comrades looked up, recognized Cooper, and said nastily: "Look chaps, a movie star!" Cooper had already gone a step beyond the table. He stopped, turned, and towered over the three young men. A muscle twitched in his jaw and his lips became a hard, thin line.

And with a voice as gentle as ever, the voice that sounded almost like a caress, but drawling a very little more than usual, so that there was almost a space between each word, he issued his orders to the trio: "Stand up when you say that!" he said.

For a moment, the young men were motionless. Then one smiled. Gary Cooper turned away, walking out of the restaurant to the Duke of Gloucester's Rolls-Royce, at fifty-nine going on sixty, still playing *Gary Cooper*.

Personal

There is a reference to Gary Cooper's politics in the closing paragraphs above that did not appear in "The American Hero Grows Older" as published in *Esquire*. A copy editor cut the piece to fit the magazine's format literally minutes before a production deadline. No harm was intended, but I think the piece makes more sense with the cut restored. In the last analysis, it suggests Cooper-worship had a political connotation and Cooper himself observed it. Like many Impersonalities, he bought what he was selling. In his private philosophy as in his public imagery, he reflected nostalgia for a past that never was and hankered for a future that can never be. Someday, he may become a patron saint of the radical right (John Wayne is sure to make it). To my mind, nothing could have made this more understandable than to hear him talk about it, coupled with his views on the decline of the cowboy hat, in the back seat of the Duke of Gloucester's bulletproof Rolls-Royce. I am sorry that *Esquire's* readers missed it.

I console myself that the piece was destined to be misunderstood anyway. I had written a wry comment about an Impersonality. My point was satiric. The subtitle, which had been my original title, was "Yes, Santa, there is a Virginian." But, as it happened, Cooper died while the magazine was still on the newsstands—with his picture on the cover. Now, people who might have been amused or dismayed were curiously moved. In London six months earlier, I hadn't known he was ill. I wrote what I wrote assuming Gary Cooper would go on forever. It was his death that removed the sting.

Some who knew him best felt I had set out to write the definitive appreciation of their hero. I received several letters thanking me for saying so many nice things about "the Coop." I was told *he* had enjoyed reading the piece on his deathbed. Most astonishing of all was the macabre word I received from an actor named Robert Wagner, who was an old friend of the Cooper family.

One afternoon in Normandy, where he was on location with Darryl Zanuck's *The Longest Day* company, I met Wagner between takes. Unrecognizable in a G.I. combat costume, he had spent most of that long day running in and out of foxholes while the cameras turned and Darryl Zanuck sucked on a cold cigar. Wagner told me all about himself and about how this, here and now, was the most important role of his career, career, career. He was just warming to his subject, when a passing press agent happened to mention that I had "done" the Cooper piece. Then Wagner forgot about his own interview. Pressing my hand gravely, he told me that only the length of *The American Hero Grows Older* had prevented him from reading it aloud at Gary Cooper's funeral. "It would have been the perfect eulogy," he said.

My hunch is that there is nothing much a writer can do about this sort of thing, except write for the ages instead of for *Esquire.*

Roy Cohn
The
Pleasures
of
Roy Cohn

In the early Winter of 1952-53, when the defeated Democrats were in the process of moving out of Washington, Roy M. Cohn, the Attorney General's special assistant on matters of subversion, received a letter from Senator Joe McCarthy, who would be chairman of the Committee on Government Operations in the next Congress. McCarthy wanted him to stay on in Washington at 11,700 dollars a year as Chief Counsel to his Permanent Subcommittee on Investigations. They had never met (as Cohn says, "The letter came out of nowhere"), but McCarthy had been attracted to Cohn by his reputation as an investigator and prosecutor of subversion cases. Cohn talked to McCarthy and took the job. He was twenty-five years old. For the next eighteen months, McCarthy and Cohn seemed determined either to take the government apart or commit political suicide trying. They slammed into the Voice of America, the Foreign Service, and the Army. Cohn, who had been a moderate Democrat back in New York and had performed prodigies in the courtroom during the Rosenberg trial, wielded his new power as though trying single-handedly to prove all the old axioms about the dangers of too much power. On one occasion, in March, 1953, Cohn sat next to McCarthy, listening as the Senator interrogated a witness named Reed Harris. McCarthy offered as evidence against Harris the fact that he had been defended in court by the American Civil Liberties Union. His point made, McCarthy moved on to the next question. Cohn had not spoken up, although he himself had delivered an address to the ACLU three weeks before in New

York. Later that same year, Cohn flew off to Europe with his friend, David Schine, who had been made a consultant to the subcommittee, to carry on investigations of a sort in ten cities, in seven countries, all in seventeen days. They were roasted in the press of Europe, responded with some clownish antics, and probably started then the decline of McCarthyism, which could least endure laughter. As everyone who owned a TV set in those days knows, Schine was subsequently drafted, Cohn sought first his deferment and then favored treatment, and somewhat reluctantly McCarthy was drawn into his fateful struggle with the Army. In the wake of the hearings, Cohn was asked to resign as chief counsel by a four to three vote of the subcommittee members. Cohn had no choice but to quit, his career as an investigator terminated at age twenty-seven.

Roy Cohn is thirty-three now. Six years after leaving Washington, he has power again, albeit a different kind. Cohn today is a partner in the New York law firm of Saxe, Bacon, and O'Shea, from which he earns 250,000 dollars a year. He is the major stockholder of The Lionel Corporation, maker of toy trains, fuses, and electronic equipment; a subsidiary manufactures sporting goods and another is a leading producer of missile components. He is one-third owner of Feature Sports, Inc., which promoted, among other fights this past year, both of the Johansson-Patterson heavyweight championship bouts. He is a successful investor in the stock market, owns two middle-sized restaurants of no particular distinction in Manhattan, and holds oil leases in Texas, New Mexico, and Kentucky. He estimates his net worth (assets over liabilities) at about one million dollars, *not* counting the income from his law practice. And like many another triumphant entrepreneur, he has set up a foundation named after himself to distribute his philanthropies.

Since the McCarthy days, only one serious attempt has been made to suggest what Cohn's motives might have been in 1953-54. In *Senator Joe McCarthy*, Richard Rovere wrote: "In all probability, Cohn's anti-communism was somewhat less of a caprice and an improvisation than McCarthy's, for Cohn was Jewish and from New York, and at about the time he came to man's estate and participated in the Rosenberg prosecution, it seemed terribly important to many Jews not only to disassociate themselves from Jewish Communists, but to demonstrate a zealous and fiery anti-communism. . . ." Rovere's analysis no doubt has merit, but somehow it does not sound like Cohn. Rovere himself later suggests that Cohn enjoyed the hunt "for the hunt's sake," which probably comes closer, and in any case excludes any motive on Cohn's part springing from a desire to prove something.

Not long ago, seeking some further insight into the old Cohn, I arranged to meet him for lunch in a restaurant on the east side of Manhattan. Now that he had emerged, so to speak, as a millionaire lawyer-businessman-sportsman, it occurred to me that the new Cohn might produce some clues to the past. He could not, I felt, have changed so much in six years. When Cohn arrived, he created a minor stir and head-turning in the restaurant. He looked about the same as he had on TV. He had the same drowsy eyes and scar on his nose, slick hair, expressive hands, and boy-in-a-man's-job manner. His clothes had those earmarks of a good tailor and a fastidious owner. He could have been twenty-seven instead of thirty-three. I had, in fact, a curious sense of going back in time; he seemed to have brought the past with him. We talked for more than an hour. He was an amiable, often amusing luncheon partner. He seemed, on the other hand, not particularly vital, as though he had no commitment to anything in particular. He was not averse to being observed at work for a few days and answering questions as long as he was sure that I had not written anything at any time for such magazines as *The New Republic* and *The Nation*. I said I hadn't, but I might sometime. Cohn said: "All I am asking for is objectivity," which was disarming, given his record with McCarthy. I said I would try to be objective. Cohn said all right. He left then, taking the past with him. The week of the Johansson-Patterson rematch at the Polo Grounds, we got together again.

During that week, Cohn's days and nights, from early morning until the sleeping pill at night, were totally occupied with moves. His concern was the management of his three major enterprises—the law practice, The Lionel Corporation, and the championship fight. He was a bachelor, and therefore had maximum maneuverability. He told me he was not against marriage, but that he could not afford the time to "get involved." Cohn did the standard New York eighteen-hour business day, but not with the usually frenetic quality of the man on the make. Cohn seemed to work because the work was there to be done, not for any end that he desperately wanted to achieve. Each day was hypnotically similar, although the scene constantly changed from home to law office to Stork Club to the Lionel plant in New Jersey, in and out of the air-conditioned, black Fleetwood Cadillac, with a telephone in the front seat as well as the back. (Jokingly, Cohn once said he had the two phones so that his chauffeur, Jimmy, could pick up one and tell unwanted callers he was not in.) Cohn had telephonitis. He did much of his business on the telephone. The cost to him over a year was 10,000 dollars in phone charges. Virtually every call was a move, a play in a game. Besides the two radiophones in the car, he also had three in his apartment on Park Avenue and two phones plus a switchboard full of overworked phone lines in his law office in the financial district. Sometimes he carried small change for pay phones, sometimes not; the assistants who flocked around him *always* carried some for him. It was a matter of survival for all of them. If Roy didn't make his moves, they were all dead. "Roy," they said, flatly, "is lost without a telephone." They also pointed out that, prophetically, Cohn had even invested the first money he had ever made in his life in American Telephone and Telegraph securities (the amount was 10,000 dollars earned at age seventeen as a brokerage fee for helping a friend buy a radio station). In short, the telephone was more than a means of communication for Cohn; it was his unconscious symbol, and a rather complete one at that. Roy was running a race all by himself, I thought. As long as he had the phone in his hand and someone to call, he wouldn't really feel that he was all alone.

When we were together, Cohn's big day—probably his biggest in years—was the day of the fight. For Cohn, it was a little like old times, and yet it was not an untypical whirl for him. He was very much accustomed to parties, celebrities and the big time. He managed to touch all the bases besides going to the fight. He also managed to be a little bored from time to time. As much as any day could, this day helped define Roy Cohn, past and present.

Cohn awoke before eight in the morning. In the bedroom, between shaving, dressing, and eating chopped egg on a cracker, he made a dozen calls. The room was moderately large, with one wall full of books, two TV sets, and two framed, banal nudes. The other bizarre touch, besides the nudes, was the imitation leopard-skin comforter on the lounge chair. Cohn talked to someone connected with all of his enterprises, plus a politician, a broker, and a client. Phone in hand, he put on his shoes without untying the laces. It was going to be a warm day (the word had come directly from SAC in Omaha that there would be good weather for the fight), so he selected a monogrammed batiste shirt and a light silk suit. He dressed with care—matching tie, gold cuff links, gold watch. As he was about to leave, his mother came for the breakfast tray. She was a small, gray woman, a widow since 1959 when Judge Albert Cohn died at age seventy-four. She told me: "I run my house for the comfort of my son."

In front of the apartment, Cohn's chauffeur, Jimmy, was reading the New York *Daily News*. He opened the back door and Cohn climbed in, reaching for the telephone. Precisely at ten, Cohn arrived at a midtown office building. Waiting for him in the lobby was a client and his new wife; they were scheduled for a pre-trial hearing concerning charges of default on alimony brought by his ex-wife. In a paneled conference room, Cohn sat beside the client's wife and faced the opposing lawyer across the table. Cohn's technique seemed to be feigned disinterest, but if he was play-acting it was a very good show. Absently, he rubbed the back of his head, lightly tapped his pencil, or stared at his fingernails. The only thing he didn't do was whistle. When the lawyer challenged the husband's veracity, Cohn seemed not to care.

"Mr. Cohn, my recollection is that there is a conflict of testimony here," the lawyer said.

"Okay," said Cohn, "you've got a conflict. Do what you want about it."

"I shall, Mr. Cohn."

"Go ahead."

"Well, I certainly will."

"Oh, come on—" said Cohn.

The lawyer wilted. Cohn had defeated him with condescension and even the stenographer seemed to sense it. Shortly, the hearing ended and the lawyer departed, without the usual courtesies.

"I would do anything Roy Cohn told me to do," said the client, "because he is the most wonderful lawyer in the world."

After the couple had said their good-bys, Cohn drove on to the offices of Saxe, Bacon, and O'Shea at 20 Exchange Place, near Wall Street. Cohn's office was medium to large, overlooking the Narrows. It was pleasantly furnished with desk, chairs, and hi-fi console. Over the desk was a six-foot sailfish which Cohn had caught near his vacation home at Duck Key, Florida, in 1959. The walls were hung with mementos of Cohn's past, most of them dated 1954 or earlier. There was a plaque from the Catholic War Veterans, Christopher Post No. 841, Baltimore, Maryland, recognizing Cohn's "gallant fight against communism in defense of our glorious Republic, America"; similar plaques from the Baltimore American Legion, Patrick Henry Post 244; American Jewish League Against Communism; Joint Committee Against Communism; American Legion, Wall Street Post No. 1217; American Council for Community Education; and the New York County Council of Veterans of Foreign Wars. Cohn had hung up a photo of Judge Irving Kaufman, inscribed in 1951 after the Rosenberg case, when Cohn was twenty-four, to "a lawyer's lawyer"; a photo of Styles Bridges who called Cohn a "great American"; a photo of Senator McCarthy and his chief counsel; a photo of David Schine with Walter Winchell; a letter from J. Edgar Hoover, signed "Edgar," commending Cohn on his work in the 1952 Communist Party trials; a color photo of Francis Cardinal Spellman; a letter from J. Howard McGrath thanking Cohn for his help in the Rosenberg case; a scroll of honor from the lawyer's division of the Federation of Jewish Philanthropies; a photo inscribed to "my friend, Roy Cohn," from Carmine DeSapio, boss of Tammany Hall; another shot of McCarthy with Cohn whispering in his ear; a photo of George Sokolsky at the Stork Club; a letter from J. Edgar Hoover congratulating Cohn on his work in the Remington case; and a picture of the Duke and Duchess of Windsor with Cohn in Las Vegas, 1959. On the wall, Cohn also had his diplomas and a framed copy of a tribute to his father who had spent thirty-one years on the bench: the tribute described Judge Cohn as a friendly man with no pretense.

Cohn attacked the papers on his desk as his secretary, Miss Lawrence, and his young law associates moved in and out with their assignments. Often, he cradled the phone between ear and collarbone, talking and writing notes at the same time. He was sharp and fast with the younger men, sometimes sarcastic. One walked in with data on a potentially controversial stock transfer. Cohn listened, made his decision, and waited for the nod of agreement. The young lawyer hesitated.

"You know, Roy," he said, "this is subject, well, to interpretation."

"Everything is subject to interpretation," said Cohn.

"Well, the guy wants us to be cautious."

"He's not cautious," Cohn said harshly. "He's stupid. That's the opposite of being cautious. Let's go on it."

Sadder but wiser, the young lawyer departed.

Suddenly, Cohn leaped up, remembering a luncheon appointment. In the hall, he signed a document on the fly, then plunged into the elevator. The Cadillac waited for him. Jimmy tooled into the flow of traffic heading for the East River Drive and the Stork Club on East 53rd Street. Cohn discovered he had arrived before his luncheon companions. He sat at a table near the bar, ordered a telephone, and called people until it was time to eat.

The Cadillac dropped Cohn after lunch at the Lionel Building on East 26th Street. The building faces Madison Square Park, in the older, small-industry section of New York that is a little run-down at the heels; the building, too. The elevators were old and squeaky. Cohn rode up to the second floor to the main offices and showroom. In the foyer there is an almost life-size mock-up of the front half of a railroad steam engine coming out of the wall. Cohn was swallowed up by personnel: his sales manager, the production chief, the director of the sporting-goods subsidiary, and several other executives. They ushered him into the nearest empty office; he had no desk of his own at Lionel. Cohn grabbed a phone. He straightened a paper clip and began to chew it while waiting for his call. The business talk began. Cohn simply wanted more cuts in staff; names of employees were mentioned and their jobs described. Cohn suggested that Mr. A. would not be missed. The executives disagreed. "You all say he's doing a good job," Cohn said, "and I don't even know what he does." Cohn got his call through—the accountant on the other end announced that Lionel's profit was 170,000 dollars over budget thus far in the year. Cohn made the announcement and the executives relaxed, as though there would be no more talk now about cutting staff. "Now," said Cohn, "I want this company in fighting trim." The sporting-goods man protested against dismissing any more of his personnel. Cohn said: "Look, either you go along, or we'll drop your operation altogether. It's lousy anyway."

Cohn moved on with the day, uptown to see about the details of a possible merger, crosstown for a meeting with a client, then home to change into his tuxedo. He returned to the Stork Club at dinner time for the Feature Sports, Inc., pre-fight party. Cohn's mother was there and everyone from Lionel and the law office and a mixed bag of celebrities: George Sokolsky, Senator Barry Goldwater, Leonard Lyons, Elizabeth Taylor, Eddie Fisher, and Max Lerner. Sportswriters from all over were at the bar.

"Well," said one sportswriter, "I knew Cohn would never get rid of it once it got into his blood stream."

"Get rid of what?" said another.

"The limelight, old chap. Publicity! He loves it. Sports give a man a forum and it's not controversial. People quote you. You're a big shot. Be a promoter, old bean."

"Contrary. Trouble with you is you don't know what year it is."

"What year is it?"

"It's six years ago since Cohn did what he did."

"Well, you know what he can do—"

"Be my guest."

That sort of thing.

Cohn was at home at the Stork Club. As guests poured off the elevator into the second-floor room, he was hugged and shaken and pounded. One big fellow simply said, "I want you to know I love this guy." Someone said to Cohn: "Hey, Roy, I hear they're going to investigate payola among sportswriters." Cohn cracked back, "Good—that would save me a lot of money." A short man introduced himself as the reporter from the Bismarck (North Dakota) *Tribune*. "How's the gate, Roy?" he asked. "Fine," said Cohn, escaping. "Where's Bismarck?" Cohn asked me. A disgruntled ticket holder accosted Cohn. Between mouthfuls of curry and cold ham, which Cohn and Feature Sports had provided him, he complained about his seat at the Polo Grounds. Cohn, who wanted nothing more than peace this night, fumbled in his pocket for a pack of tickets. When the exchange was made, the man toddled off, and Cohn said: "Guess what? That guy had a complimentary ticket in the first place. I get no complaints from people who pay, only the freeloaders. Then, too, the foreign press is complaining. It's a foregone conclusion about my reputation in Europe, so why should I show preference to them when I still have half a chance in America?"

Cohn rode out to the Polo Grounds on one of the special buses chartered to take the Stork Club crowd to the fight. Among the passengers was Barry Goldwater, U.S. Senator from Arizona. The crunching mob at the gates proved (a) that the promotion was a financial success, and (b) that it was a terrible job of organization. Cohn had left most of the details to his partners. Now he had come to see the fight. He led the bus party through the crowd to ringside. The confusion was greatest here. Gate crashers were struggling with ticket holders for the hundred-dollar seats. The fellow trying to sing the Swedish national anthem in honor of Ingemar Johansson couldn't hear the organ in the uproar. The press complained of overcrowding in their section. Cohn was unperturbed. He gave up his seat for a friend and watched the fight kneeling on a piece of cardboard behind the press section. At the end of the third round, he said, "You have to admit that's a tough life, being a fighter. It's a matter of choice, though. They're doing what they want to do. And for three-quarters of a million dollars, I guess it's worth it." In the fifth, Patterson caught Johansson with a left, then a moment later with another left, and the fight was over. Cohn turned his palms up, helpless before the will of the gods. "I guess we'll have to have another fight after all," he said. "I'd say we'll make half a million dollars on it."

After visiting the dressing rooms, Cohn and some of his friends piled into the Cadillac which had followed him to the Polo Grounds. Cohn picked up the phone and called back to the box office.

"Are you watching them count the dough, Al?" he asked. "Like a hawk, Al. . . . My God, you got 120,000 dollars at the window tonight! We're going over 800,000 dollars. Al, you really watching them every minute?"

Cohn hung up. In the traffic the Cadillac had not moved far from the curb. Cohn suddenly called Jimmy to stop. "Somebody's got to be up there watching those guys count," he said. Jimmy parked and Cohn walked back to the box office. He rapped on the door. A guard let him into the room in which a dozen men in white shirts were counting the money and making tabulations. Several of Cohn's young lawyers were watching the proceedings. No one spoke. Cohn's Al stepped over to shake hands. Cohn whispered: "I just want to make sure we get all of it, Al."

When the money was counted and taken away by the armed guards, Cohn rejoined his friends in the Cadillac. Automatically, he reached for the phone and held it on his shoulder. He seemed to have no one in particular to call. He was gay. Then someone reminded him that Max Lerner, the liberal columnist, had come to the party at the Stork Club.

"Imagine him coming in with Elizabeth Taylor," said Cohn. "A lot of nerve."

"He did have a lot of nerve, Roy," said one of the riders. "Coming to a party with you as the host."

"I'll send him a bill," said Cohn.

"You *should* send him a bill, Roy."

"What I should have done," Cohn said, "is throw him out. But tonight, I was feeling kind to everybody."

From all this, it appears that the difference between the Roy Cohn of today and yesterday may not be so much in the man, but in his situation.

In 1953, it was this way: postwar America had been frightened by Soviet and Chinese Communist aggressions, angered by the war in Korea, and shocked to find Red spies and subversives at work in the U.S.A. Cohn pitched in *after* most of our sensitive government agencies had been combed out by the security investigations of his own ex-employer, the Justice Department. The atmosphere of fear, anger, and shock had been exploited by McCarthy; it was ripe for more of the same. Cohn did not pass judgment on his surroundings; he merely functioned within them, in this case using methods for manipulating public opinion that would get more of the kind of results McCarthy seemed to want. For Cohn, it was a matter of process and, in the course of doing what came naturally, he made himself one of the most formidable men in America—and all this without either financial position or political office as a base. It was a stunning feat, performed with headlines and TV shows, and abetted by a segment of the mass media which had, one supposes, motives of its own. Take one example: He darkly suggested that radio transmitters had been mislocated overseas by subversives working for the Voice of America. This gambit, following weeks of confusion and doubt created by the McCarthy-Cohn VOA inquiry, blew up such a public storm that many top Voice executives quit cold or were forced to resign. The bejesus was scared out of lower-echelon Voice employees—and many prospective employees, certainly at a considerable cost to our propaganda effort, simply withdrew their applications. It turned out, of course, that the transmitters had not been mislocated at all—but by this time, Cohn had moved his operation to Europe for an assault on the International Information Administration. And so on.

In 1960, the situation (for Cohn) changes. He's in business. A different methodology is required and Cohn is nothing if not an expert on methodology. There seems to be little doubt among his peers that his success will grow.

But whether the year is 1953 or 1960, the essential Cohn persists: he is the archetype of the Adjustable Man.

Once I asked Cohn his philosophy of living. He responded with a potpourri of ideas that mixed nihilism with Beat, and determinism with free will, yet it somehow fits.

"I have a basic sense of the unimportance of everything," Cohn says. "You live seventy years. Civilization goes on after you're gone, so what difference does it make?" He thinks about this for a moment; then he asks himself: "So why do anything? It's all a matter of opportunities and desires, conscious and subconscious. You are propelled into certain things and you do them. I must like what I do or I wouldn't do it. I have a choice of what I want to do." This may be very contradictory, but it is Cohn. It sets him free to go on about his business and to take his opportunities as they come.

Cohn's philosophy is, of course, a lonely one. It has neither ideology nor self-limiting purpose; it seems to exclude the idea of love. It could take a man in any direction—destructive or constructive—depending upon the circumstances. Its goal isn't ultimately power or money, but the "doing" of things, of being on the telephone interminably. Cohn is a means man rather than an ends man. His real talent is for techniques and tactics and gambits; these are really his greatest pleasures. And to a degree, it is a reflex. Cohn has lived in an era that has placed a premium on technique, which is a function of conformity; the goal in his time has often been to play the game by whatever rules happen to be in effect. For the old Cohn, McCarthyism was the rules maker; for the new Cohn, the business-social world he inhabits. Prior to both, he seems to have been getting ready for any eventuality.

Cohn was born in the Bronx, February 20, 1927. When Roosevelt was elected Governor in 1928, Cohn's father, Albert, was FDR's first judicial appointee; in time he reached the Appellate Division of the New York Supreme Court. In the early Thirties, the family moved across the river to Park Avenue. The mother and father doted on the only child. Roy was a very good boy, never in trouble, never spanked. His major childhood misfortune was the scar on his nose left after a cyst was removed by surgery. He preferred the company of his parents. He liked to please them. He was a diligent student of the piano, practicing regularly in the living room on the blue-and-ivory piano, which was decorated with cherubs. (Cohn still plays once in a while on the same piano. In fact, little has changed over the years in the living room. It still reflects the taste for eclectic elegance which was popular on Park Avenue in the Thirties: Oriental rugs, eighteenth-century French-style chairs, satin drapes, and a rack on the wall for plaster statues, jade, and trinkets.) Roy was thought to be a prodigy. He was an honor student in school and, in his early teens, his parents often took him to adult dinner parties at which he participated in the political talk far into the night. Everyone seemed to forget that most boys of his age were home in bed.

During his adolescence, Cohn was short, graceless, and unathletic. He was a fast reader, a quick study, and loved school politics. He was never the candidate, but always the king-maker. The 1944 yearbook of Horace Mann High School noted that Roy made good use of his political bent, "becoming Horace Mann's man behind-the-scenes." He applied for West Point, was turned down for physical reasons, and applied again. (The Selective Service law allowed deferments for West Point applicants until a final decision had been made. Cohn was rejected by the Academy for the last time in 1946, but in the meantime he had missed the tail end of World War II. Since 1950, he has been in the New York National Guard.) He entered Columbia College in 1944, accelerated, and graduated early in 1946. He was a loner, lived at home, and kept his nose in his books. Without pause, he plunged into Columbia Law School. He spent most of his campus time in the library and won his degree in 1947 at age twenty.

Still too young to take the bar examination, Cohn looked around for a clerking job. Through his father, he had met most of the judges and attorneys in New York City and was on a first-name basis with all whom he knew. He was well-liked and few doubted that he was going places. He had his pick of the openings at the bottom in either government or private law. Cohn chose the former, a photostat assistant's job at 1,765 dollars a year in the office of the U.S. Attorney for the Southern District of New York. He was admitted to the bar in the Spring of 1948 and sworn in as an assistant U.S. attorney, which increased his salary to 3,397 dollars. He cut his teeth as a prosecutor on seventy-five counterfeiting cases, bringing more pressure to bear in that quiet area of crime than anyone had in years. He was rewarded, at about the time the Hiss case was breaking, with a minor assignment in the prosecution of the first-string Communist leaders. Cohn was tireless, determined, and immensely talented, especially in cross-examination. He worked on many of the major subversion cases of the period—the Remington Case, the second-string Communists, and ultimately the Rosenberg Case.

Cohn did trial work every day from nine until one and from two-thirty to five. On his lunch hour, he sometimes guided a grand jury as it worked up fresh indictments. Besides, he joined the law firm of Curran and Stim, which soon after became Mahoney, Curran, Cohn and Stim, and launched his private practice. Curran and Mahoney were respectively state leaders of the Republican and Democratic parties. Cohn had little time for relaxation, but when he played, he chose the Broadway-night-club circuit. Both Winchell and Leonard Lyons were his friends. He dated a string of handsome women, from time to time got his name into the gossip columns, and was getting to be known as an influential personage.

After working with the grand jury that produced the presentment charging the U.S. State Department with "sheltering" Communists at the United Nations, Cohn and his friend, G. David Schine, sailed for a pleasure trip on the maiden voyage of the *United States*. On board, he again met Judge Irving Kaufman who had been on the bench during the Rosenberg trial. At sea, Cohn received an offer by phone to go to Washington as Attorney General James McGranery's special assistant in charge of subversive matters. He discussed the offer with Judge Kaufman who advised him, as a friend, to stay away from Washington. In the fall, however, Cohn went. He prepared the seven-count perjury indictment of Owen Lattimore (all of which was later dismissed or withdrawn) and got acquainted, at last, with Senator McCarthy.

McCarthy was then at the peak of his powers. He is said to have first heard of Cohn through Walter Winchell and to have been most impressed with Cohn's investigation of the United Nations. Cohn himself had called it "the most important investigation ever conducted in the history of the United States." There has been some speculation on what was in Cohn's mind at the moment when he made the decision to go with McCarthy. One theory suggests that Cohn was simply attracted by McCarthy's nihilism and by the opportunity to share the limelight with him.

Another suggests that Cohn, who was still too young to become either a U.S. District Attorney or a judge, didn't want to go back to mundane affairs in New York. G. David Schine, president of Schine Enterprises, Inc. (hotels, movie theaters, real-estate developments, etc.) and still Cohn's good friend, says, "Communism is a threat to our way of life. We wanted to give whatever effort at whatever risk, to render whatever service we could." But Cohn himself is not given to idealistic interpretations. He says, "It seemed to me like the thing to do. That's all. I didn't know that I was going to get in the middle of a war between McCarthy and the Administration." But he did, and as the first casualty of the hearings, he returned to New York in August, 1954, a hero to the supporters of McCarthy, otherwise a loser. "I wouldn't say he was bitter," says Schine. "Roy is very realistic." For six months, Cohn traveled on the testimonial-dinner circuit, which provided rehabilitation of a sort. Then he dug into the business of being a lawyer. His practice had been worth 20,000 dollars a year to him even while he was in Washington. He quickly built it up from there. Cohn thinks he was helped by the reputation he had gained with McCarthy, because it "brought me people who wanted a lawyer who wasn't scared of anybody." His clients ranged from corporations seeking to merge to society couples seeking a divorce. He represented the Stork Club, National Airlines, the San Francisco Giants, a distillery, two newspaper chains, and Albert French Restaurant of Greenwich Village in New York. The latter client came to Cohn after receiving sixteen summonses in an hour from a policeman who objected to a publicity stunt involving an automobile decorated by Salvador Dali. Crying foul, the *patron* told the police he would get Joseph Welch (who had opposed Cohn in the TV hearings) to fight the case. Failing that, he called Cohn, who was able to get fifteen of the sixteen summonses dismissed. Cohn especially enjoyed working in trial courts and never lost a case before a jury. In 1958, he moved over to Saxe, Bacon, and O'Shea. By 1959, besides his 250,000-dollar income, he had made substantial profits in the stock market. He was in a position to expand.

Cohn's great uncle, Joshua Lionel Cowen, had been the founder of The Lionel Corporation, and through this family relationship Cohn was known to several of the major stockholders. Dissatisfied with the management of the company and the depressed price of their holdings, they came to Cohn in the summer of 1959 for legal advice. Cohn saw an opportunity. Lionel was the nation's leading manufacturer of toy trains. It was losing money and the value of its stock was less than half the book value of its plant and equipment. Cohn felt that proper management plus a public-relations campaign designed to generate interest in Lionel's stock could cure what ailed the corporation. He decided to form a group that would buy "control blocks" of stock from a few stockholders with large interest in the corporation. His objective was ownership of about 200,000 shares of stock, then selling around $10.00 per share. To avoid a proxy fight, Cohn was prepared to pay $15.00 a share to get the stock plus options on additional stock at $10.50, which meant raising three million dollars. American banks are prohibited from lending money to finance stock transactions, so Cohn got in touch with friends he'd made on a trip around the world. "I met this banker," he recalls. "He said he'd get me financing any time I needed it. Just yell, he said, so I yelled." Cohn's razzle-dazzle performance in raising the money astonished even the most hardened pros on Wall Street. His technique was to borrow money from new sources as soon as he had control of Lionel, and pay off the first loans before the interest payments overwhelmed him. In October, 1959, he borrowed 532,000 dollars in Hong Kong and another 339,000 dollars from a money lender in New York. The interest rate was one-and-a-half per cent a month. With these funds, plus money put up by Cohn and his group, Cohn took control of Lionel. After a month had been spent studying the corporation's financial structure, Cohn lopped off one hundred twenty-five supervisory personnel and saved 600,000 dollars in salaries. ("If you don't clean out a place right away," Cohn says, "you're dead.") He instituted a new production schedule which was certain to save money by cutting pre-Christmas overtime. And he hired a public-relations firm, Tex McCrary, Inc., to get the message to the people. With things looking up, Cohn skipped around borrowing 400,000 dollars in Panama to pay off the New York loan, and then 365,000 dollars from another New York lender to pay off a third of the

Hong Kong debt and buy more Lionel stock. Last April, he borrowed enough to close out his indebtedness in Hong Kong, and Lionel was in the black for the first time in two years. It had been a bold, seemingly brilliant job and Cohn was pleased. ("Usually I'm ninety per cent wrong," he says. "But when I'm ten per cent right, we can do something.")

In the meantime, Cohn also became a fight promoter—again through his law practice. He was approached for legal advice by a friend named William Fugazy, a travel-bureau operator, on a possible purchase of the rights to promote the Johansson-Patterson rematch. The rights were owned by the promoters of the first fight, Vincent Valella and Bill Rosensohn. They were in difficulties and willing to sell. All that stood in the way was the New York Boxing Commission regulation which prevents anyone from assigning a fighter's contract without the fighter's permission. Cohn proposed a move that was simple, if roundabout: let Valella and Rosensohn form a corporation which would own the rights to the rematch. Then Cohn, Fugazy, and a group of investors would buy the corporation outright and no assignment of contracts would be involved. Thus Feature Sports, Inc., was born and sold to Cohn and friends for 243,000 dollars. Once again, Cohn had demonstrated his mastery of technique. The fight was promptly scheduled for June at the Polo Grounds in New York. Although Cohn didn't know who Ingemar Johansson was before Fugazy came to visit him, he himself flew to Sweden to discuss arrangements for the fight.

When he returned, he continued looking for ways to expand. He had become, he said, "acquisition-minded" for The Lionel Corporation. Last spring, he looked at financial data on fifty companies before he found one that looked good: a company called Anton-Imco which manufactured components for the Nike missile and various space rockets. Cohn was fascinated. The company was sound. It had 8,000 stockholders who, if merged with Lionel's 3,000, would broaden Lionel's public participation and increase market activity in its stock. Finally, Cohn felt that Lionel would have reached its peak by 1964 or 1965, while a company in the missile field had potential far into the future. "Look at the international situation," Cohn said. "It's going to continue as it is or blow up. One thing, it's not going to get better." Cohn discussed the merger with Harry Roth, chief executive of U.S. Hoffman, the electronics company which had spun off Anton-Imco earlier in the year. Roth said he was prepared to sell for one million dollars cash, plus Lionel stock. Cohn sought advice from several accountants and financial experts. He sent investigators to look at Anton-Imco plants. In less than a month, the deal was closed. "If you're going to do a thing, do it fast," Cohn says. And, "It was a sweet deal." As soon as the merger news got around, Lionel's stock jumped. Then it jumped again (selling for more than double Cohn's purchase price and triple his option price) when Cohn announced that the corporation's new chief executive would be the Army's former missile chief, Major General (ret.) John B. Medaris. In hiring an Army man, Cohn was only following the recent example of many private industries. But the irony was too obvious not to go unnoticed, even by Medaris. "Let us forgive the mistakes of youth," he said.

Sweet deals, expansion, techniques, the telephone, and obvious ironies—these are at the heart of Roy Cohn's adjustment to life today. For now, at least, Cohn is not crusading, not advocating, not bitter, and not true-believing. Some of his friends are still in there swinging, but Cohn is mostly smiling. He likes to call his friend, George Sokolsky, "Our Great White Father" or "The Grand Lama." He calls Russian salad dressing "MacArthur dressing." And he likes such jokes as: "You know what C.I.A. stands for after the U-2 incident? Caught In the Act." This is not the humor of a man passionately dedicated to his cause. The fact is that Cohn still supports the Joint Committee Against Communism and others, but he is not at all busy in them. "This is off-season on communism," he says. And, "I'd like to do more, but I haven't got time."

Still, the old Cohn is an inseparable element in the new Cohn. Like Mary's lamb, everywhere that Cohn goes, the past goes with him. He is recognized everywhere by almost everyone who was not unconscious during his heyday. On the street, in restaurants, and in most public places, strangers stop and stare. As a celebrity, he seems to have the staying power usually associated with only unique movie stars—like, say, Garbo. Some strangers look kindly toward him and some look as though they have just sucked a lemon. It is about fifty-fifty. Once I asked Cohn if he had any regrets about the McCarthy era. "Some," he said. "For one thing. I can't go any place and have some fun without people knowing who I am." He said this lightly, though, and it seems that he really has no regrets. "I know how some people feel about me," he says. "In certain circles, I'm a hero, and in others, I'm a Hitler." Faced with the inevitable, Cohn relaxes. He does not seem to be hurt easily.

Cohn does not want to forget the past, but even if he did both enemies and friends regularly remind him of the passions he once roused. At a session of the directors of a charitable organization, one member protested naming Cohn (who was not present) to the board and refused to sit on it with him. A counter-protest arose and the objection was withdrawn, but such incidents keep cropping up, six years after the fact. Cohn's friends keep the memory alive another way; they are defensive about him, a bit wary of strangers who are as yet undeclared for or against, and ready to describe their own feelings for the man whenever an opportune moment arises. They tend to protect him even before he is fairly acquainted with a newcomer and often with Cohn himself right there listening.

"I didn't like Roy when I met him," one of Cohn's latter-day friends volunteers. "I didn't like him for all the usual reasons. I was against McCarthyism, so I was ready to hate Cohn. But you get to know Roy and you like him. He's like your brother. Roy is a great guy. A great guy!" This last is accompanied by an arm flung about Cohn's shoulder and Cohn says: "I could tell you didn't like me. I've got a sixth sense now about how people are going to react to me." Then the friend laughs, but Cohn doesn't. Roy doesn't mind a little adulation, but demonstrations of affection leave him a little cold.

Personal

Roy Cohn is one of the most absorbed people I have ever met. As I knew him, he was either purposefully aimless or aimlessly purposeful, I couldn't tell which. He was constantly in motion, moving in circles, straight lines, zig-zags, up and down, in and out, through a tangle of business, legal, and political confusion leading, as time has shown, almost nowhere. He never seemed to enjoy himself. I rarely saw him laugh. His smile was like the midnight sun. A girl he has dated once said, "You feel a certain type of man will take you to the races, another to the theater, another to a night club. When Roy calls, you feel he'll take you to a funeral."

Roy had little time for ordinary pleasures. He moved in a tight little world of tension, reaching for the telephone the way I reach for a cigarette. He played a little golf, but the telephone was his real hobby, his stamp collection, fishing rod, mystery thriller, flower garden, deck of cards, and, for all I know, his mistress. Looking back, it seems that he relaxed only when his hand found that smooth black receiver.

I expected a reaction to "The Pleasures of Roy Cohn," but I did not hear from Cohn until four years later and then only indirectly. He did tell a mutual friend that he thought the piece was fair enough. But a few months later, he threatened to sue *Esquire* for a humorous, pictorial feature that identified him as one of the worst-dressed men in America. If there was a connection, he didn't mention it. Then, as the years passed, Cohn seemed to run out of luck. He was overthrown at Lionel in 1962, a year in which the corporation lost about four million dollars. Lionel's stock plunged and has yet to recover; today, it sells for about $5.00 a share, thirty-three points below the high of Cohn's heyday. Under pressure in 1963, he resigned as director and chairman of the finance committee of the Fifth Avenue Coach Lines Corporation; this is the company that runs the Fifth Avenue buses in New York, acquired by Cohn and sundry associates after a raucous struggle involving the Mayor of the City, the head of the Transport Workers' Union, and a purple cast of characters. And last year, Cohn stood trial on charges of bribery, conspiracy, and perjury growing out of his weird relationship to certain principals in the case of the five-million-dollar United Dye and Chemical Corporation stock fraud. Cohn was acquitted (despite a particularly yellow effort by *Life* to convict him in the court of public opinion), but once again his affinity for scoundrels was exposed.

As often happens when a man's image has been badly tarnished, Cohn decided to write his autobiography—and not long ago, his agent asked my agent if I wouldn't like to work on it with him. Since I declined, I have been thinking about that offer. It was Roy's idea. He is still the Adjustable Man.

I wouldn't be surprised to hear that he's asked Max Lerner.

Edward Kennedy
Teddy

The face is familial: the detached expression in the eyes, the slightly aquiline tip to the nose, the big white teeth, the flaring jaw, the good ears. From one end of Massachusetts to the other, Edward M. (Teddy) Kennedy, the Boston brother of the President and of the Attorney General of the United States, is available almost any day of the week for two speeches before ten A.M. and three or four between four P.M. and midnight. The hours in between are reserved for his duties as one of the twenty-six assistant district attorneys for Suffolk (Boston and environs) County. But after work, just give him time to go home to change his shirt ("This is what makes it all possible," he says, meaning he would have a minute with wife, daughter, and son), and he is ready to talk, giving essentially the same brief, modest, middle-of-the-road-liberal lecture about Latin America, slightly edited to appeal to the dominent interest—religious, racial, national, commercial, or merely human—of each audience. He tells Catholics about the missions in Latin America, Jews about Israel's example for Latin America, and businessmen about the future of business in Latin America. Not only are his listeners untroubled by his conceptions, they are enormously happy to see him, Ted Kennedy, on his own. He is the fraternity, sorority, school assembly, communion breakfast, B'nai B'rith, Parent Teacher Association, alumni, and benevolent society program chairman's *coup* for the year. At the same time, at age thirty (on Washington's birthday in this election year), he has something more in mind. As has been said, no man talks so much unless he is getting paid for it or unless he is campaigning for public office. Kennedy accepts no fees, although he would not turn down the gift of a football or a brace of linen hankies. He is, then, doing what he does as engagingly as any American who comes to mind—*campaigning*.

It cannot be said that he is campaigning specifically for the U.S. Senate seat that his brother, John F. Kennedy, held from 1953 through 1960, that its current occupant, Senator Benjamin A. Smith, 2d, will (apparently) relinquish at the appropriate time, and that will, in any case, be contested again in another two years. That he might become a senatorial candidate was reported in the New York *Times* as long ago as January, 1961, but it is traditional to pretend doubt about a politician's intentions until he has made a formal announcement. In Massachusetts, of course, almost no one except reporters and party regulars are pretending. For example, two Bostonians looking at two-button suits in Filene's basement were overheard, one saying, "He's a fine lad, but too young to be a senator," and the other, "Bother! And what about William *Pitt?*" A Suffolk school principal said young Kennedy couldn't lose because he has "an ideal political personality." A director of a Boston lawyers' club said, "He's a whiz and a better speaker than Jack was at his age." A civil servant said, "The Kennedys say you make allies but not friends in their business, but Teddy's different. I *like* him." And, best of all, a Harvard fellow said, "Ted is the Bobby Fischer of Massachusetts polity." Conversely, there was the young ruffian prosecuted for armed robbery by Kennedy, the assistant D.A.: As he was led away to serve seven-to-ten years in the state penitentiary, he said, "I'll never vote for that son-of-a-bitch." (Dead pan, the guard replied, "You ain't never going to vote, laddie.") But when Kennedy's father, Joseph P. Kennedy, was asked what problems his youngest son might have if he ran for the Senate, the former Boston newsboy and Ambassador to the Court of St. James's put his fingertips together and didn't mind saying, "None." Kennedy himself even forgets sometimes that as of the moment no one is supposed to know what, if anything, he is campaigning for. Once as I was watching him go and go and go and trying to find out a little more about Political Man *genus Kennedy,* he said, "Listen, this thing is up for grabs and the guy who gets it is the one who scrambles for it and I think I can scramble a little harder than the next guy."

With the broad shoulders, the brown-carrot mop of hair, and the impeccable, monogrammed taste in clothes, Teddy looks so much like his older brother one can believe that an elderly lady did ask during the West Virginia primary campaign if it wasn't a bit early for him to be running for President. At six-two and two hundred ten pounds, however, he is taller and heavier and, in some ways, rather different. He is actively seeking the political career that, after all, came unexpectedly to his brother at roughly the same age. In this, he is more like Joseph P. Kennedy, Jr., the brother who died in World War II and who had every intention of becoming President of the United States. As opposed to the President's intellectuality and aloofness, young Kennedy has no overwhelming enthusiasm for ideas. He compensates with enormous life-of-the-party exuberance, gregariousness, and willingness. As the President told me, "It was easier for Teddy than it was for me." Finally, Teddy also has an extra dose of the much-publicized athletic *élan* of his family. He came to campaigning in 1961 with a history of highly personal and frequently dangerous exertions. At Harvard, after breaking his shoulder in a skiing accident, he had a leather brace made so that in two weeks he was back on the slopes, continuing the season. On another occasion, he bet a college chum that he could drive a golf ball across the Charles River with a seven-iron. Fifteen balls later, he succeeded with a five-iron. When he was in the Army in France, he went on pass to Switzerland where, with no previous experience, he entered the one-man bobsled races and scored the fastest time of the meet. During a summer between semesters at law school, he attempted to scale the Matterhorn with his roommate, Varick Tunney, a son of the former heavyweight champion. On Rimpfischhorn, he slipped, dangled over a three-thousand-foot chasm, and fell to a ledge. "Anybody else," Tunney recalls, "would have called it a day, but Teddy ate an orange and five minutes later we were climbing again and went on to the top." While campaigning for his brother in Wisconsin, he donned skis and went off a long ski jump because somebody had announced to the crowd that he would. And later, in Montana, after telling some locals about that first ski jump, he accepted a dare to ride a bucking bronco at the Miles City rodeo—which he did, for five-and-a-half seconds. So far, it seems that the only challenge Kennedy has failed to accept was that of an Indian who offered to shoot a cigarette out of his mouth with a .22 bullet. "He would have done that," a friend has said, "but Teddy doesn't smoke." Someday, all of this may help us understand his activities as a statesman, assuming the nation survives.

Watching Teddy campaign, the endless repetition of set speeches, family jokes, and the platitudes of good fellowship (a trial for many men) seem to be as satisfying to him as the sequence of plays in a football game is to the players. Each play is a challenge met and enjoyed for its own sake as well as for the hope of ultimate victory. In the phenomenology of U.S. public life, he could qualify as the quintessence of a well-educated athlete-as-politician, an archetype who is learning at an early age all the technical skills of the Old Pol and for whom campaigning is a sporting contest in which a man proves himself and is approved. So much for talking sense to the American people.

Not long ago, I found that Teddy had taken over the three-room office just back of the county court building on Bowdoin Street that had been the President's Boston office and legal residence until he moved to the White House. In two of the rooms, six secretaries and two part-time office assistants worked on various shifts maintaining mail contact with, and keeping up the files on, virtually every Massachusetts civic organization and nationality group (in Boston alone, twenty-six nationalities each with more than five thousand people are represented in the population), besides some three hundred forty-five "Kennedy Secretaries" spread out in towns and villages across the state. The "Secretaries" had been organized for John F. Kennedy's senatorial campaigns of 1952 and 1958, the list had been updated for the 1960 campaign, and Ted Kennedy had met with the new group in 1961. In Worcester, Massachusetts, for example, there were two "Secretaries" plus several hundred ward and precinct workers ready when necessary to do the doorbell ringing and leaflet passing that still counts for many votes. The office had a homey atmosphere, but it was essentially a place of business.

The President's old Navy uniform was hanging in one of the closets, but whatever might have suggested the identity of the previous tenant had been removed from the walls and, instead, there were the usual plaques and framed citations that indicated a new Kennedy was making his move—thanks to Edward M. Kennedy for being General Chairman of the Massachusetts 1961 Cancer Crusade, chairman of the United Fund Health and Fitness Fair, orator of the day at the Independence Day Exercise, Faneuil Hall, July 4, 1961, and so on. In the inner office, where Kennedy worked out his plays and called signals, there was a big map of the state with two hundred four red and black pins showing incorporated communities (including one on the island of Nantucket) that Kennedy had visited in less than a year.

And a notebook lay on the desk, a calendar page for each day, a neat listing of engagements (e.g., a random month—one hundred eight speeches), every day different, every day more or less the same, a record of discipline and determination which has led one admirer to say, "He's like one of those old Oklahoma football teams. He's just going to run the Republicans to death."

At seven-thirty one morning, Jack Crimmins from the D.A.'s office called for Kennedy at his home in Charles River Square at the foot of Beacon Hill and they drove in Kennedy's Dodge to Newton South High School in the suburbs. In the assistant principal's office, he was interviewed by three girls from the high school weekly. (Q: "Is Congress going to pass the aid-to-education bill?" A: "Well, they're doing everything they can.") Then he walked around to the stage entrance of the assembly hall where six hundred boys and girls waited to hear him. Before going on, he asked one of the monitors for the name of the principal. He received a standing ovation going on, another going off, and was caught up in a riptide of coeds squealing for his autograph. At ten, he was in court. ("The President calls and wants to know how he is doing," District Attorney Garrett Byrne told me. "And Bobby has called and I see his father at the Cape. I give them a regular report and it's always the same. Teddy's the hardest worker I've got.") And at four, Teddy was in the office on Bowdoin Street. For the evening, he had three speeches scheduled—a dinner at six-thirty, a PTA at nine, and a women's club at ten. "I keep my speeches short," he said. "I don't present myself as an expert. I just give my views. If you give them too much, it goes over their heads. I talk on Latin America, mostly, and Africa and physical fitness. Later, I'll move in on state problems. . . . You have to know your audience. You can't give women too much. They get confused. Besides, if they've seen you on TV, they can't think anything bad about you. . . . And after ten at night, you don't read your whole speech. You tell some jokes and get it over. The main thing is to move around and meet people." At five-thirty, he had gone home, changed, spent some time with the family, drank a glass of milk, and left again with Jack Crimmins. It had started to snow. At the dinner, the toastmaster arose and told a joke. "So Mayor Jim Curley died and soon after, we received the glad news that one of our own had been elevated to Cardinal, our own Richard Cardinal Cushing—and Mrs. O'Reiley said, 'Isn't it wonderful, and Jim Curley up in heaven only two weeks.'" Beginning with the potato blight in Ireland in 1846, the toastmaster next reviewed the history of the Kennedy and Fitzgerald families. Then he introduced "Ted Kennedy, whose brother incidentally is President of the United States." Beaming, Kennedy told the story of the two brothers who went fishing and one had a rod and reel and the other just had a pole, a line, a hook and a can of worms, and that brother caught all the fish, so the next morning, the first brother borrowed the pole, line, hook, and worms and went out alone and still didn't catch anything, but when he was going home, a fish jumped out of the water and said, "Where's your brother?" and so, "I hope none of you wonderful people is going to ask me where's my brother." Which reminded him of another story, "About these three boys who rescued Jack while he was out swimming." It seems that the President gave each one a wish and the first boy wanted an appointment to West Point, the second wanted an appointment to Annapolis and the third wanted to be buried in Arlington Cemetery because when he got home and told his father who he'd just saved, he'd be *shot,* but "I know that doesn't apply to any of you wonderful fathers sitting here tonight." Which reminded him of the time he was sitting on the platform and this fellow introduced the president of a brotherhood and he jumped up and started talking because he thought he'd said "brother of the President." Which led him, abruptly, into Latin America "where the problem is not only hunger, but ideas and minds." On schedule, he left, pausing only to shake hands with the chef and two waiters. In the car, driving through the snow to the next appointment, he asked Crimmins who the guests had been at the dinner just concluded. "A good bunch," Crimmins said. "There were some contractors. You can't tell about contractors. They play both ends against the middle. Otherwise, a good bunch. A is in real estate. B is in furniture. C is in textiles." And Kennedy nodded: "I don't think we pulled any of them before—it was a good meeting." And so on into the night, twice more being reminded of the pole, line, hook, and worms, the three boys who rescued Jack, and the president of the brotherhood, until at the end of the last meeting, Kennedy was stopped at the exit by an ancient lady who had known his grandfather, Honey Fitz, and who remembered when Honey Fitz used to come to the Irish dances and sing "Sweet Adeline." "You know, Mrs. Regan," Kennedy replied, "at the fights, my grandfather used to get into the ring between the fifth and sixth rounds and give a speech. They threw things at him, but he never lost an election." Honey Fitz had lost, of course, to Henry Cabot Lodge.

Thus played by Ted Kennedy, politics is a daily scrimmage, an unabashed, tightly organized, relentless competition against all comers. Going at it, he seems happy as a Boston clam. He is not unaware of certain shortcomings, wisdom yet to be gained, political experiences yet to be had. "What are my qualifications?" he asks. "What were Jack's when he started?" But neither happiness nor humility should obscure the unfunny seriousness of his desire to win public office. He has no sense of the ridiculous, of his own as well as others' essential folly. He seems to subscribe, without humor, to Mr. Dooley's hollow dictum: "Politics ain't bean bag." If he has doubts, he keeps them to himself, relying on his ability to play the game using the equipment that was born and bred into him. For better or worse, he didn't grow up absurd.

He was the ninth child of Joseph and Rose Kennedy, born in Brookline, Massachusetts, on February 22, 1932. As he was growing up, his father was in banking, movies, liquor and real estate; then for 431 days chairman of the SEC, effectively outlawing the

Wall Street shenanigans at which he himself had once excelled; then chief of the Maritime Commission assigned to reclamation of our merchant fleet; and subsequently Ambassador to Great Britain, with very little understanding of Nazi Germany. For the youngest Kennedy, there were houses to live in in Bronxville (New York), Washington, Palm Beach, and the thirty-six-room American Embassy in London, but "home" was the house in Hyannis Port on the Cape. The eight other children in the family were a constant source of both rivalry and affection. "Whenever Teddy poked his head out the door," a family friend has said, "Jack would hit him with a pillow." At age thirteen, for the memorial book, *As We Remember Joe*, privately printed in 1945, Teddy wrote, "I recall the day before the year we went to England. It was in summer and I asked Joe if I could race with him. He agreed to this so we started down the pier, about five minutes before the race. We had our sails up just as the gun went off for the start. This was the first race I had ever been in. We were going along very nicely when he suddenly told me to pull in the jib. I had no idea what he was talking about. . . . Suddenly he seized me by the pants and threw me in the cold water. . . . I was scared to death practully. I then heard a splash and I felt his hand grab my shirt and then he lifted me into the boat. We continued the race and came in second. . . . One fault Joe had was that he got very easily mad in a race as you have witnessed. But he always meant well and was a very good sailor and swimmer." Young Kennedy was, it seems, closest to his brother Bobby, who taught him how to play games. His father was strict. "I remember," he says, "that we always kept a tight ship. We had a clear idea of what we could do and what we could not do. You could ride your bike on the property, but not off. You had to be in the house when the lights went on. We had to pick up our clothes." With the rest of the children, he had to appear at the meal table five minutes early and often heard his father's reminder that Lord Nelson attributed *his* success to the fact that he was always fifteen minutes ahead of time.

Given both paternal discipline and competition from eight older children, Kennedy might have soured. Instead, he developed the sunniest disposition of all. "We used to sail together," the President recalls, "and Teddy was always willing to put up the boat." Not long ago, he went skiing in Switzerland with his sister, Jean; it turned out that the lodge had only one room available, which he gave to her, and—without complaint—he slept three nights in the communal bathtub. Today, he is the spark plug of the family get-togethers, the organizer of activity —an hour of touch football followed by an hour of water skiing followed by an hour of golf followed by an hour of parlor games. The only member of the family more vivacious than he, some of his friends say, is his mother. Rose Kennedy showed him no special favoritism. "My mother's great theory," says Jean Kennedy Smith, "was to concentrate on the older children and the younger ones would come along." But mother and son were close all the same. Rose Kennedy taught him to dance and encouraged him to read newspapers. She corrected him on what he read, always attended to his grammar, and helped him interpret the meaning of events. When he was grown, she still had advice for him ("My mother," Kennedy says, "is the pol of all pols"). She set an example of efficient organization for him. His illnesses were recorded in her card file and he had to wear one of the identically colored bathing caps that all the children wore so that she could keep track of them at the beach simply by counting caps. Finally, she devoted time and patience to his religious education. She drilled him in the catechism over the luncheon table. In England, according to her wishes, his nurse took him to church during afternoon walks to teach him that piety was a seven-day-a-week requirement. At age seven, Rose Kennedy let him come along to the coronation of Pope Pius XII. He sat on the Pope's lap and later granted an interview to the press. "I wasn't frightened at all," he told the reporters. "He patted my head and told me I was a smart little fellow. He gave me the first rosary beads from the table before he gave my sister any." One result of all this was that he became his Harvard roommates' religious policeman, determined to rouse the boys at seven to go to Mass every day during Lent. And, at law school, he wrote his mother for some books on Catholicism which he gave to Varick Tunney, who had been baptized a Catholic but had never become a member of a church. Having since joined, Tunney says, "The books had a very definite impact on me." But more importantly, from a political standpoint, Rose

Kennedy's ability to give attention even to her ninth child seems to have provided the cheery balance of his personality. It also seems to be a major source of the happy warrior spirit that urges him to take bigger steps quicker than any of his brothers —and, when seen, makes the professional pol weep and convinces the political reporter that Teddy will more than likely do it.

Until he entered prep school, Kennedy led an erratic boarding-school life. The family moved around so much that he attended at least ten different schools. The constant change, he feels (in a rare moment of self-analysis), accounts for his gregariousness. As an outsider, he wanted to be in, and usually was by the time he had to pick up and leave again. It also accounts for the fact that he had little interest in education itself until, at last, he settled into a stable academic community. He stayed four years at Milton (Massachusetts) Academy, discovered that he liked teachers and history books, *Ivanhoe* and the possibility of a career in public life, and the idea of going on to Harvard, where he went—a modest scholar with a passion for football.

The Harvard freshman football coach, Henry Lamar, remembers all the Kennedy boys: "They all played end. Jack had an injury and finally had to go in for swimming. But Jack hit hard for his size and he'd hit anything. Bobby was more a defense type. He didn't have the size that makes for a blocker, but boy, was he *mean*. All those kids were battlers. Teddy was good at everything. The outstanding thing about Ted was that he'd do everything you told him to do. If you gave him a job to do, he'd do it, exactly as you asked it to be done."

At the end of his freshman year at Harvard, Kennedy was involved in a cheating scandal and expelled. He volunteered for induction into the Army. He trained as an infantryman and later was attached to a Military Police honor guard at SHAPE headquarters in Paris. He declined officers' school, served twenty-two months, and was discharged as a private first class.

Readmitted to Harvard in 1953, Kennedy moved into Winthrop House, where his brothers had lived as undergraduates, and rejoined the battle of the books. In his senior year, he made honor grades, scored a touchdown against Yale, studied speech,

coached basketball at a Boston settlement house, read three
newspapers a day, and dropped everything when a member of
the family was in town to devote himself to his or her pleasure.
During summer vacations, he looked for demanding projects;
he was a forest ranger and a crewman on a transpacific yacht
race to Honolulu, and spent two months with the French Army
in Algeria on which he reported for International News Service
(in *their* day, both the President and the Attorney General had
worked for INS, too). After Africa, he followed the family
trail to the University of Virginia Law School where he "overwhelmed his studies" and won the moot court competition
teamed with Varick Tunney. He did a summer at the International Law School in The Hague and another working on
Senator Kennedy's re-election campaign. Meanwhile, on a visit
to Manhattanville College of the Sacred Heart for women, he
met Joan Bennett, a tall, pretty blonde from Bronxville whose
father was president of an advertising agency in Manhattan.
She had come out at the 1954 Debutante Cotillion, was an ac-
complished pianist, and intended to teach music. They were
married during Kennedy's last year in law school. "Ted's roommate moved out and I moved in," Mrs. Kennedy says.

After winning his law degree and passing the Massachusetts
bar exams, Teddy did not have to think twice about a career.
He was over twenty-one and therefore receiving about $100,000
a year after taxes from two irrevocable trust funds that his father
had set up for each member of the family. He was free to go
into politics full time and, indeed, had been in it since 1957,
when his brother had decided that 1960 was *the* year. Although
his mother and father had once wanted him to be a priest, as
he sees it he had no career alternatives. "It was impressed upon
us," he said, "that our opportunities carried with them certain
responsibilities. My sisters have been active in charity work and
the boys have all been interested in public life."

It was true, too, that the status of the politician was changing.
His occupation remained hazardous and expensive, but since
World War II it had steadily gained respectability. A new breed
of young men was going into politics less for idealistic reasons
and more for an open-faced desire to win respect through public power. It remained a question whether their pragmatism

would be, pragmatically speaking, a fair substitute for the amount of idealism lost, or whether it would be, as it had often been in the past, only a more efficient means of acquiring power. In any case, Ted Kennedy, whose athlete's nature was especially suited for this version of the game, was one of the new breed.

He was involved in his brother's planning from the start. In late 1959, Teddy began visiting the Western states, establishing alliances that would produce delegate votes at the Democratic National Convention come July, 1960. After a trip to Latin America in the Summer of 1959, he returned to the West Coast to take soundings for Jack, who told me, "He's the hardest political worker I've ever known." He was appointed Western manager of the preconvention campaign, responsible at age twenty-seven for working the delegations of eleven Western states plus Alaska and Hawaii. In addition, he would be counted on to campaign in the states holding presidential primary elections. Until January, 1960, he roamed the West from Nogales, Arizona, to Nome, Alaska, making speeches, representing his brother, getting movements started, finding leadership, and helping build an organization.

Between January and July, Ted Kennedy crisscrossed the country countless times. Besides canvassing the Western states, he spent the better part of seven weeks in Wisconsin helping make sure that Hubert Humphrey (who apparently never had a chance) didn't pull a Truman in the primary. And about seven weeks more in West Virginia (where Humphrey had even less chance) helping make sure that the victory was particularly crushing. He was an asset of extreme value. He not only looked like Senator Kennedy, he sounded like him. It was as though the candidate were able to be in two places at the same time. Once, in West Virginia, young Kennedy was even called in to share the Senator's platform and speak for him because his voice had failed after weeks of twenty-speech days. As the story goes, Ted Kennedy began, "Do you want a man who will give the country leadership? Do you want a man with vigor and vision?" Whereupon, Senator Kennedy took over the microphone and whispered to the audience: "I'd just like to tell my brother that you cannot be elected President until you are thirty-five years of age." On primary day in West Virginia, our man landed in Wyoming, listened to the returns in a phone booth in Thermopolis, and went off in a rented DC-3 on one of his seven preconvention tours of that one state. The results of his efforts, especially in Wyoming, were apparent at the convention. Not only did Lyndon Johnson arrive in Los Angeles with less strength in the Western states than had been estimated, but also Wyoming cast the necessary votes to give the nomination to Senator Kennedy.

Soon after the convention, the youngest Kennedy, now age twenty-eight, was appointed Campaign Coordinator for the Rocky Mountain and Western States, Alaska and Hawaii. He moved his wife to a rented home in San Francisco, but only managed to be there with her thirteen nights in the next three-and-a-half months. "Being the wife of a campaigner is exciting," she says. "But it has its drawbacks. I've had to get used to being alone." In August, Senator Warren G. Magnuson, a Johnson man, was named "chairman" of the Kennedy forces in the West. He was to "work closely with Ted," which meant that he had been assigned to repair whatever breaks and fissures still existed between Johnson loyalists and the Kennedy people. Teddy remained the effective head of the Western campaign against Vice-President Richard M. Nixon. "If we had carried California," Kennedy now says, "I could have done no wrong." As it turned out, Nixon won ten out of the thirteen states under Kennedy's campaign control, *including* California.

The difference in California was 35,623 votes. Although it has been said that President Eisenhower made the difference by going on TV while the polls were still open on the Pacific Coast, it seems more likely that mismanagement at all levels of the Democratic organization caused the narrow defeat. Perhaps Eisenhower did spur on GOP workers who had begun to sag as the returns came in from early-closing polls in Connecticut. But, more importantly, *absentee* voters gave *two-thirds* of their 200,000 votes to Nixon while the rest of the state was divided about 51-49 *for* Kennedy. Young Kennedy had many problems in California. Since that state is never organized for political combat except in the months just before an election, there was an inevitable scramble for position in the early weeks of the campaign. Lines of responsibility were blurred. Some districts were overrun with volunteers; others had none. Preconvention supporters of Stevenson and Johnson only gradually developed enthusiasm for Kennedy—some never did. Governor Brown was little help because he had so few political appointments available through which he could discipline party workers. ("The civil service is killing us," one California professional said.) Moreover, many of the Democratic clubs were happy to thwart Brown because their members felt he had betrayed the Stevenson movement. On the other hand, the Citizens-for-Kennedy state chairman complained to anyone who would listen that he wasn't being consulted on the candidate's speaking engagements. While sunk in this morass, Ted Kennedy might still have salvaged the victory if he and the local pols had not neglected to work on the absentee voters. In California, most absentee voters are not out-of-the-state at all—they are in hospitals and homes for shut-ins. A special Absentee Voters Committee had been organized by the Republicans to go after their ballots, county by county. Republican doctors, nurses, and attendants were contacted to get out the Nixon vote. Presumably, Democrats were similarly situated, but none were asked to help. Elsewhere the Democratic defeats and victories were more or less expected. The President lost Wyoming by about 14,000 votes, closer than the 25,000 by which Stevenson lost in 1956, but not enough because the game isn't horseshoes. Arizona and Utah were, it seems, hopeless to begin with. The Denver *Post* blamed Ted Kennedy for losing Colorado because of "inexperience." Others more accurately blamed the religious issue ("Their bigots beat our bigots.") and, as one leathery pol has said, "Nothing but the second coming of Christ could have changed the outcome in the Rockies." All perhaps true, but California should have been won. It was a rude shock to the Campaign Coordinator, who perhaps learned once and for all that *nothing* human and eligible to vote can safely be neglected in a political campaign. "Next time," he says, ruefully, "I think we'll do much better out there."

After the election, young Kennedy paid his way to Africa for a five-week, sixteen-nation fact-finding tour with members of

the Senate Foreign Relations Committee, while his wife looked
for a house in Boston. And the new President's old roommate,
Benjamin A. Smith, 2d, a Gloucester, Massachusetts, fish proces-
sor, was appointed by Governor Foster Furcolo (as he was
leaving the Governor's mansion, permanently) to warm the
Kennedy seat in the Senate until the next general election. Although the interrelation of these three events was not immediately apparent, the hindsight-eye can, of course, see the start of
Teddy's campaign.

"The maneuvers in a battle are like the maneuvers in politics," Harry S. Truman once said. "In the military they have
what they call a five-paragraph order. In the first paragraph,
you make an estimate of the enemy, his conditions and what he
can do. In the second paragraph, you make an estimate of your
conditions and what *you* can do. In the third paragraph, you
decide what you are *going* to do. In the fourth paragraph, you
set up your logistics and supply sources to *carry out* what you are
going to do. And in the fifth paragraph, you tell *where* you
are going to be so that everybody can reach you. That is all
there is to politics."

One way or another, more or less, Ted Kennedy has covered
or will soon cover all the paragraphs. His Republican enemy,
now an avowed candidate, is George Cabot Lodge, whose great-
grandfather, Henry Cabot Lodge, defeated Kennedy's grandfather, John "Honey Fitz" Fitzgerald, in the Massachusetts U.S.
Senate race of 1916, and whose father, also named Henry Cabot
Lodge, lost his Senate seat in 1952 to Teddy's brother, John F.
Kennedy. Lodge, age thirty-four, can hardly make an issue of
Kennedy's age. Lodge is on the faculty of the Harvard Business
School, but Kennedy was recently appointed to the Board of
Trustees of Boston University. Lodge has been an Assistant Secretary of Labor under James Mitchell and under Arthur Gold-
berg, serving both as chairman of the governing body of the
International Labor Organization. He talks well about places
he's been and leaders he has seen; but since Africa, Kennedy has
became a public servant ("He happened to be looking for a job
so I gave him one," says D.A. Byrne), has represented his home
state at Italy's Centennial celebration (during which trip he col-

lected enough footage of the countryside and himself to make a twenty-minute film that has gone over with a nostalgic bang among Boston Italo-Americans), and has toured Latin America (where he gathered material for five pretty good articles in the Boston *Globe* and for that adjustable twelve-minute speech mentioned above). While Lodge still holds the edge on the experience issue, Kennedy is second-to-none in (a) savvy and sensitivity gained in intense campaigning and (b) moxie.

Behind his own lines, Kennedy has had to endure some minor sniping. Edward McCormack, Attorney General of Massachusetts and nephew of Speaker John McCormack, has also hankered for Ben Smith's seat in the U.S. Senate. *His* friends, following the tradition of Massachusetts Democracy, have been saying worse things about *Kennedy* than the Republicans. Few Bostonians, however, can conjure a situation in which Ted Kennedy would not be able to run for the Senate this year if he wants to. The political power that could be ranged against young McCormack is too awful to contemplate. As one Boston political reporter has said, *sotto voce,* "Eddie McCormack will do what he's told or get killed." Still, the "dynasty" issue which has been raised against Kennedy behind his own lines has even worried Democratic pols who want very much to win with him. Only Teddy himself is serene. "The question of a dynasty," he says, "applies to a self-perpetuating order. The people of Massachusetts know this is unrealistic. A series of brothers are interested in public service. Any consideration of this issue would be treated in the proper perspective. I don't think people would expect me to sit on my hands for the rest of my life because my brother is President and my other brother is Attorney General. I wasn't brought up that way."

And as we have seen, Kennedy has logistics and supply well in hand. And everybody knows *where* he is: somewhere in Massachusetts, available almost any day of the week for two speeches before ten A.M. and three or four between four P.M. and midnight. The hours in between are reserved for his duties as one of the twenty-six assistant district attorneys for Suffolk (Boston and environs) County. But after work, just give him time to go home to change his shirt. . . .

Now if that ain't bean bag, what game is it?

Personal

One sunny, autumn Sunday afternoon while I was in Boston, Ted Kennedy and a chum proposed that I join them in street clothes and low shoes for a fast hour of horseback riding, after basketball and before touch football. Not being a horseman, but compulsively willing to experience anything, I agreed.

At a public stable on the edge of town, a polite groom presented each of us with a saddled jumping mare. Mine was a large, somewhat bloated, bobtailed nag. The moment I put one foot into the stirrup, the bloated look was explained. The saddle slipped under the horse's belly, she reared, and my left foot was squashed under her front hoof. As soon as the saddle was adjusted, I mounted again. I was unwilling to quit or to inspect my injury for fear I would have to quit.

Teddy led the way over a bright green meadow and into a deep woods. We rode in silence until we came to a pile of brush that had been arranged for jumping. First Teddy and then his friend leaped over it, mounted, of course. And then they turned and waited for me. As in steeplechase movies, I backed off, urged my horse into a gallop, and headed straight for the pile of brush. We flew, but at the last instant, my steed balked. I sailed over her head, somersaulted in the air, and landed flat on my back. A sharp branch opened four inches of flesh in my right hip. When Teddy saw that I could stand, he had a good laugh. Except for that, I might have quit. Instead, I saddled up once more, pressed a handkerchief to my wound, and walked around the jump. In the next hour, I walked around thirty of them.

Several weeks later, after I had talked to most of the members of Teddy's family, I went to Washington to see President Kennedy, whom I had never met. Pierre Salinger, his press secretary, scheduled an interview for me. But two days running, my appointment was broken, reset, and broken again. On the third day, as I cooled my heels in the White House lobby, Salinger sent for me. If I could leave Washington right away, Salinger said, I could fly to New York with the President and, hopefully, discuss Teddy in mid-air. Within the hour, I arrived at Washington National Airport. A Secret Service officer examined my press card, checked my name off a list, and waved me aboard the President's Constellation. A few minutes later, President Kennedy and his entourage arrived. He retired to the rear compartment while sundry aides filled most of the seats in the plane. Airborne, the President sent for me. We were to have lunch together.

I found him seated at a small table, a sandy-haired, warm-eyed man, who seemed to have no interest other than mine. As we shook hands, he repeated my name. "Morgan?" he said. "Oh, you're the one Teddy told me about. Knocked off that horse twice. Got back on both times. We like that in our family!" Such charm is very hard to resist.

And the youngest Kennedy had it, too. It is the only excuse I have for a major error of fact that appeared in *Teddy*.

Early on in my research, a Boston newspaperman suggested that I look into the circumstances of Teddy's decision to join the Army at the end of his freshman year at Harvard. Later, from another source, I heard that he had been expelled from Harvard, but my source didn't know why. Then, as I interviewed several of Teddy's Harvard classmates and his freshman football coach, I asked them the question, but each to the best of his knowledge said that there had been nothing unusual about Teddy's departure. Finally, I called the office of Harvard's registrar. Student records are confidential, I was told.

At an opportune moment, I then asked Teddy why he had left Harvard. He said that "the Korean War was on" and it had seemed to him "a good time to get my service over." He did not hesitate. Nor did he explain overmuch. Balanced against rumor, his forthright charm convinced me. It did not occur to me that he had not answered the question. So, I published his response in *Esquire*.

Within days after the magazine was on the stands, the Boston *Globe* exclusively reported that Teddy had been expelled from Harvard in the aftermath of a cheating scandal. Ironically, Teddy himself had furnished the story which was printed along with his contrite observation that the experience had taught him a lesson. The *Globe* story was a masterful example of news management. Teddy had owned up to an incident in his life that could have damaged his political career and, at the same time, he had destroyed its significance.

I won the booby prize. Instead of pursuing the matter, I had been charmed out of my shoes. Teddy had not exactly lied to me. He had merely answered another question. But like Teddy, I had learned a lesson, too. Nowadays, I respect a healthy rumor. And I discount charm.

Teddy, despite a broken back suffered in a plane crash in June, 1964, has been re-elected for a full term in the U.S. Senate. I will give odds that one day he, too, will run for President.

Sammy Davis, Jr.
What
Makes
Sammy, Jr.,
Run?

In a typical ten-day period recently, Sammy Davis, Jr., had this schedule: the final week of an eighteen-day engagement at the Copacabana (sixteen performances interspersed with general frolicking, a record date, television and radio interviews, and two visits with Cye Martin, his tailor); a one-night stand in Kansas City to receive an Americanism award from the American Legion; one night at home in Hollywood; and the opening night of a two-week date in Las Vegas at the Sands Hotel, the management of which has a contract with him for the next four years, eight weeks a year, at $25,000 per week. The schedule could have been extended. The day after closing in Vegas, Davis was due for three weeks in Hollywood at the Moulin Rouge, another night club with which he has a five-year million-dollar deal, followed by two weeks in Australia, followed by an Eastern tour. Photographer Burt Glinn and I, however, arbitrarily pursued Davis through that ten-day period. Since this short, skinny, one-eyed, broken-nosed, umber-colored singer-dancer-musician-actor-mimic may be, as Milton Berle has said, "the greatest entertainer in the world," and may even be, as Groucho Marx has decided, "better than Al Jolson, who could only sing," we wanted to find out what we could about what makes Sammy, Jr., run.

Like most men, Davis lives a life of quiet desperation. The only differences are that he has little privacy to live it in and that on the average of twice a night, thirty weeks a year, he must stand in a spotlight and be Sammy Davis, Jr.—comic, senti-

78

mental, bursting with energy, and immensely talented—no matter how he feels inside. If he were an average performer, the challenge might not be so great.

"But you see," says Davis, "what I do is different. Most Negro performers work in a cubicle. They walk on, entertain, and sing twelve songs before they say good evening. They never make any personal contact with the audience. Long time ago, I knew I could only make it if I broke through this wall. I was convinced that a Negro boy could do comedy—you know the kind I mean. Not the yassuh, nossuh thing. I decided I could make it as a person, like Jolson or Danny Kaye made it. Well, to do that, you have to be honest with an audience. You got to have antennae and feel what they want. And you have to try to keep your personal feelings from interfering with your communication."

The Davis act has a basic structure—songs, impersonations, dancing, laced together with comic patter or sentimental chit-chat. The structure never changes, yet every performance is different.

"The patter between songs," says Davis, "is something that can't be planned. You can't write it if you're going to be honest. I can vary the act at any minute with a signal to Morty Stevens, my conductor. I snap my fingers a certain way and he knows we are going to go into 'Let's Face the Music.' I tap my foot just so, and it's going to be 'Old Black Magic.' If you're honest, you can feel the right way to get to them every time. Otherwise, Dullsville, Ohio. I don't mean all good shows are alike, either. You've got three kinds of shows—a routine show, a fun show, and a performance show. The fun show is lots of tumult and laughs. The performance show is the one, like opening night, where you belt it all the way. What I do works because I am trying to be honest.

"You take most of the material in my act: aside from the songs, I don't do any bits that I didn't contribute to. I have a choreographer—Hal Loman—but we work out the dances together. Nothing fancy about my dancing. I like to make clear sounds with the taps. Bojangles—that's Bill Robinson, who taught me a lot—he used to say, 'Make it so the people can understand it.' That's what I try to do.

"Sometimes the impersonations get in the way. They blur your image with the people and you die as a performer without a distinction of your own. I used to do a song called 'Why Can't I Be Me?' That's the story of most of my life. Every guy wants to sound like himself. But I keep the impersonations in the act because the audience wants them. They're like a frame. The audience says, gee, that's his best stuff, what's he going to give us next?

"The big thing is understanding the songs and projecting them honestly. When I sing 'I Got Plenty o' Nuttin',' I think about a guy who is happy with his life. Doesn't make any difference how *I* feel. I think how *he* feels. When you have that, daddy, you don't need any tricks. All I want is they should like me—say this is a nice guy. Just let them give me one thing—applause—and I'm happy."

Night-club audiences do curious things when Davis is on stage. For one, they are prone to give him standing ovations. For another, they tend to gasp out telling comments—telling about themselves as well as the performer. Early in his act, Davis comes on wearing a gray porkpie hat, black suit, black shirt, white tie, with a trench coat flung over his shoulder, a cigarette in one hand and a glass of whiskey-colored water in the other. He blows smoke into the microphone, sips the drink, and says, "My name is Frank Sinatra, I sing songs, and we got a few we'd like to lay on ya." Davis puts the drink on the piano, throws the trench coat on the floor, and begins "The Lady is a Tramp." The audience always applauds wildly and somebody is certain to cry out: "My God, he even looks like Sinatra," or words to that effect. A broken-nosed Negro does not look much like Sinatra, even though the latter is no work of art himself, but the illusion of Davis's voice and visage and movements, plus the complete rapport which has been established between entertainer and entertainees, produces a kind of Sinatrian hallucination.

For the full sixty minutes of his act, Davis sustains this kind of communication. It could be defined as an atmosphere of colorlessness in which he not only makes the audience forget that he is a Negro, but also makes it forget that it is white. This is why one of his closing bits has a special irony that is all Davis.

He is sitting on a stool in a circle of light. He has, it seems, almost sung himself out in an effort to entertain. His coat and tie are off. He takes a few deep breaths and suddenly he brightens. "What do you say?" he asks. "Let's all get in a cab and go up to my place!" For one goofy moment, nobody laughs. Here is the source of his power and also the reason for his private desperation. In the spotlight, he and they are colorless. In the real world, he is a colored man who has made it and yet can never make it all the way. When the applause finally comes, it is deafening. The performance drives to a rocking, exploding, belting finish, and Davis is gone. As someone once said, "The only thing that could follow that act is World War Three."

Thus driving and thus driven, Sammy Davis made 1,200,000 dollars last year—over half from night clubs and the rest from records, TV, and movies. When you say it slowly, it sounds like a lot of money, but his net is considerably less. Besides taxes (he's in the ninety per cent bracket), he has eleven people on his payroll: valet, secretary, conductor-arranger, drummer, guitarist, office manager, typists (for answering fan mail), and various assistants; his overhead is 3,500 dollars a week. His agent takes ten per cent. And even though his father retired from the act in 1959, because of a heart attack, and his uncle, Will Mastin, moved over from dance manager to manager in 1958, he still splits what is left equally with them, and presents the act to the public as the Will Mastin Trio featuring Sammy Davis, Jr.

The three-way split of the profits is unique in show business. Davis believes he must spend on the "millionaire" level, yet the contract with father and uncle provides him with a mere thirty-three per cent, of which still another ten per cent goes to a group of Chicago "investors."

Davis has not saved much money nor has he put his earnings to work for him with any conspicuous success. He owns a piece of an unspectacular restaurant in Hollywood and has an interest in a line of sports shirts ("Creations by Sammy Davis, Jr.") and a hand grip for cameras. He put money into some TV and movie properties. But mostly the money goes for living well, if not too wisely. It would be surprising if it went any other way.

Davis was born in Harlem, December 8, 1925. His mother, father, and uncle were all in show business. He went on stage before he was three in a theater in Columbus, Ohio. He did a talking act with Uncle Will when he was three and a half. He appeared in a movie, *Rufus Jones for President*, made at Warner Brothers' Long Island studios, at age four. The next year, in the midst of singing "I'll Be Glad When You're Dead, You Rascal You" at the Republic Theater in Manhattan, he was pulled off the stage by a member of the Gerry Society, which enforced child-labor laws in those days. Until he was eleven, he trouped with his uncle's fifteen-person vaudeville act. When the authorities became suspicious, his father put cork on his face, stuck a cigar in his mouth, and passed him off as a dancing midget. In 1936, the vaudeville act was disbanded and the Will Mastin Trio, a straight dancing act, was born. They danced in beer gardens and theaters all over the East, making as little as 30 dollars a week (for the trio) and spending part of the time on relief. Davis's education consisted of less than two years in school and a few lessons from a now-and-then tutor.

In 1943, Davis was drafted into the Army. He passed the Air Corps cadet tests, but Negroes with less than two years of college training were not being accepted. He was transferred to the Infantry, in which he took basic training in one of the earliest integrated units. Three times he was rejected for overseas duty because of an athletic heart. Toward the end of the war, he was transferred again, to Special Services. In camp shows, he developed as a singer and mimic. "What was more important," says Davis, "I met a sergeant by the name of Bill Williams who gave me about fifty books to read. He's really the guy who educated me."

After the war, with Davis's songs and impersonations added to the act, the trio's luck improved. They traveled six months with Mickey Rooney, who encouraged Davis to develop all of his talents instead of concentrating on just one. Frank Sinatra, whom Davis had first met in 1940, got them three weeks on his bill at the Capitol on Broadway in 1947. In spite of favorable reviews, nothing happened. They toured the West Coast with Jack Benny, through whose help they were booked into Ciro's, Hollywood, in 1951. Herman Hover, the owner of Ciro's, offered them 300 dollars a week to open a show starring Janis Paige. The trio held out for 350 dollars. Finally, Arthur Silber, their agent, put up 50 dollars of his own for the first week, and the contract was signed. The act caught fire. By the second week, the Will Mastin Trio was co-starred with the headliner. They moved on to a date at the Chez Paree in Chicago at 1,250 dollars a week and were not headed again.

After twenty-three years, Davis had become an overnight sensation. In the eight years that followed, the trio went round and round on the night-club circuit—New York, Miami, Chicago, Las Vegas, and Hollywood. Davis made eleven record albums for Decca Records. He took intermittent turns as a guest performer on TV—notably the Comedy Hour and the Steve Allen show. He appeared in *Mr. Wonderful* on Broadway—a mediocre show that ran for a year because it was cheaper for Davis's growing audience to see him in a theater than in a night club. In Hollywood, he made *Anna Lucasta* and the spectacular *Porgy and Bess*. The money simply poured in.

"After that night in Ciro's," Davis recalls, "every day for three years I had a new chick—wine, women, and song. After the war, I'd been hungry and mad, baby. You couldn't work certain hotels because of the Negro bit. Certain headliners refused to go on with us because we stole the show. I was so hungry. I was trying to do everything. We used to do an hour-and-forty-minute show. I could do fifty impersonations. Play the drums. Play the trumpet. Play the bass fiddle. Play the piano. Dance. Sing. Tell jokes.

"Well, then we made it. It's the old story of the guy who doesn't have it and then gets it. He fluffs friends. He does a hundred things wrong. He *knows* he's doing wrong, see, but he can't stop.

"I bought twelve suits at a time—one hundred and seventy-five dollars a whack. I bought tailor-made shirts, cars—fast ones. Once I bought twenty-one pairs of shoes from Lefcourt in New York. All my life, I wanted to buy something in a store and not ask how much. I lost all sense of value. I had credit everywhere and just signed my name. Between 1951 and 1954, I must have blown one hundred and fifty thousand dollars. My head got *so big*. I wanted to pick up every check and pay every tip. The first time I was booked into the Copa in New York, I bought a pack of cigarettes and left the girl change from a twenty-dollar bill.

I wanted to do that because once I went in there as a nobody and they put me on the side. I bought a Cadillac El Dorado. I bought gold cigarette cases for everybody. I remembered when, for Christmas presents, my dad and uncle and I used to exchange a carton of cigarettes. Every day was like Christmas. I got snotty. Everybody I saw, it was, 'Hello, chickee. Love ya, baby. See you later.'

"It takes a terribly long time to learn how to be a success in show business. People flatter you all the time. You are *on* all the time. And if you're a Negro, you find yourself using your fame to make it socially. Let's face it. The biggest deals with the big moguls are made in a social way, around the pool, that sort of thing. If you're not there, well, you're not *there*. So I used to think the greatest thing in the world was to be invited to a movie star's house.

"Things got bad. One night in Vegas, I lost thirty-nine thousand dollars playing blackjack. That's how bad it was. There's nobody who's got that much money to lose.

"I feel I've been changing. If a man doesn't change, he isn't one to swing with. But his friends stick by him while he's changing.

"November 19, 1954, I'm driving along with a buddy at eight in the morning near San Bernardino on the way to Hollywood. It was a beautiful, typical, happy California morning. A car pulled out of a blind drive and I hit it going fifty-five or sixty. The steering wheel hit me in the face. I got the car stopped and ran over to see if the lady in the other car was all right. She was, until she looked at me. She turned green. Then I felt my left eye. They took me to the hospital and Dr. Owen O'Connor and Dr. Frederick Hull removed the eye. If they hadn't done that, I might have gone blind in a month. I spent three, four days in total darkness. I began thinking about my faults. I was sure God had saved my life. That's when I began to change.

"I met a rabbi at a Jewish benefit in Las Vegas and got interested in Judaism. I found the faith gave me something I'd been missing—peace of mind—so I converted. When I am home, in Hollywood, I try to attend services whenever I can. For a long time, I was reluctant to go into a synagogue. I was afraid people would think I was trying to pull something. While we were working on *Porgy and Bess*, Sam Goldwyn thought I was kidding when I said I wanted to be excused for the high holy days. Then he had to believe me when I said I would take off anyway.

"I admit the Jewish thing has been a bit of a problem. It couldn't have been more of a problem if I'd have had my eyes fixed and become Japanese. But I think everyone has to find God his own way. Sometimes it takes something like the loss of an eye to get you thinking about it. Life is very confused and you need something. I accept the Jewish idea of God. As I see it, the difference is that the Christian religion preaches love thy neighbor and the Jewish religion preaches justice. I think justice is the big thing we need."

Davis has not been without a sense of humor about his religious conversion. During his night-club act he is likely to say, "I could have starred in *The Defiant Ones*, but I lost the part when they found out I was Jewish," or "The Irish kept me out of the St. Patrick's Day Parade for *two* reasons." On the *Porgy and Bess* set he looked accusingly at German-speaking director Otto Preminger and said: "You made lamp shades out of my people." But the justice he seeks, of course, is the most elusive of human ideals. Instead, there is irony, which Sammy Davis runs from and into almost every day of his life.

During his stay in New York last spring, Davis's dressing room was a small, seedy, two-room suite on the third floor of the Hotel Fourteen, which adjoins the Copacabana. One night after his late show, the average crowd of thirty people was milling in the twelve-by-fifteen-foot living room. Among them were Sidney Poitier, the actor, and Archie Moore, the fighter; Fran Warren, the singer, and Althea Gibson, the tennis star; three plain-clothes cops ("just friends"), and a Mrs. Goldman and her daughter ("We're fans!") from Queens, Long Island, and twenty-or-so-other people who were helping themselves to the liquor, watching TV, and fooling around with the expensive portable stereo rig on the mantel—yakking and puffing as though none of the satires on show biz had ever been written.

Davis was in the bedroom, wearing a white terry-cloth robe with a torn pocket and drinking bourbon-and-Coke from a ster-

ling-silver goblet, which a friend had given him. With him were
his valet, Murphy Bennett; his secretary, Dave Landfield, who
looks a little like Rip Torn and is an aspiring actor; and a man
from Hollywood, one Abby Greshler, who seemed proudest of
the fact that he originally brought Dean Martin and Jerry Lewis
together as a team. Greshler was there to organize a movie
vehicle for Davis based on Joey Adam's novel, *The Curtain
Never Falls,* about a Broadway-Hollywood star and heel. As
usual, Davis was conducting his business in a fish bowl. He has
no secrets from his valet, his secretary, or from almost anyone
else. In exchange, his employees are deeply attached to him.
A guest once said to his valet: "Tell you what, Murphy, I'll kill
Sammy, and you come work for me." Bennett replied: "If
Sammy dies, I'll just have to go with him."

Davis was passionately convinced that *The Curtain Never
Falls* with himself in the lead would be an important step forward for all Negro actors and entertainers.

"So the hero in the book is Jewish," he said. "We make him
a Negro. It works, motivation and everything. Look, I want to
make it as a movie actor. I always wanted to act, but what
chance was there? I remember when the reviews came out for
Mr. Wonderful—everyone was crying about the beating we took
and I was walking on air because Brooks Atkinson said I was
a believable actor. Atkinson said that. Or you take *Porgy and
Bess.* Now I simply *had* to play Sportin' Life. I mean, he was
me. I worked to get that part. My friends—Frank and all the
rest—worked to get it for me. So one night after Sam Goldwyn
saw me perform, he called me into his office and pointed his
finger. 'You,' he said, 'you are Sportin' Life.' Let me tell you, I
mean, playing that part was the gasser of my life."

"Well, this'll be great, too," said Greshler.

"The way I see it, Abby, the movie positively can't preach. It's
got to show it. Here's this hero. He knows there are only three
ways a colored cat can make it: as a fighter, ballplayer, or entertainer. He's got to make it, see? I remember one time a guy
asked me, 'How far you going to make it, Sammy?' and I said,
'I've got an agent, some material, and talent.' So the guy says,
'Yes, but you're colored.' And I said, 'I can beat all this.' Now

this is what the hero in the movie wants. Only he's ready to re-
nounce everything he is to make it. He's a character who's
ashamed of his father, see? That's the way we'll do it. People
have to believe it's honest."

"They will, Sammy, they will," said Greshler.

Davis and Greshler shook hands, re-sealing their contract,
which will never be more formal than that until and unless the
money talk begins in Hollywood. Davis turned and walked into
the living room to join his guests. In the crowd, he looked
smaller than he seems on stage. He is about five foot six and
weighs only a hundred and twenty-five pounds. His hair,
combed flat, is neither brown nor black, but somewhere in between. It is next to impossible to determine which eye is the
blind one. He has a U-shaped scar across the bridge of his nose,
which was broken in the 1954 accident. His face is thin, the jaw
slightly underslung. As Bob Sylvester once said, he looks as
though he had been hit in the face with a shovel.

Davis spied Sidney Poitier, who is husky and tall and reminds
you of an unspoiled Belafonte who can also act.

"Sidney!" cried Davis. "I'm glad to see you, baby!"

Sidney Poitier embraced him, lifting him off his feet. The
room, which had been shaking with noise, became quiet, except
for some shooting on the TV and Tony Bennett, crooning on the
stereo.

"Everybody's got to see it, baby," said Davis, turning to a clot
of people on his blind side. "I mean, you have to see Sidney in
Raisin. Only the end—a definite gas!"

Now Davis embraced Poitier, then backed away, bending
over, shoulders hunched, hands dangling in a precise imitation
of Poitier in *A Raisin in the Sun,* crying: "I'm thirty-five and
what am I—I'm *nothing!*"

A girl laughed, "Oh, you're something, Sam, and you're only
thirty-three," and everyone laughed with her.

"She's got to die," said Davis, pinching her cheek. "If she
makes one more remark, death!"

The crowd began to thin out after a while. Poitier and Moore
and many of the people that no one knew departed. Davis
paused to say good-by as each one left. At the door, he did a

short bit with a girl who asked him how he was getting along with the head doctor. Davis has had some psychoanalysis, but he is rarely in Hollywood long enough to accomplish much.

"Well, I've had a little, baby," said Davis. "I'm still sick, but I understand it now, see what I mean? I told the doc I didn't want to understand myself, I just wanted to be better. So he says, what you got, a cold or something—what better?"

Then Davis kissed her cheek and sent her on her way. A hard core of a dozen cordial-to-very-close friends remained. Dave Landfield, the secretary, strapped on one of the two-gun belts which had been hanging in the closet and practiced his fast draw.

"Not that way, Dave! Dave—God, I could draw faster with a pencil and paper," Davis said. "Get the thumb on the hammer, man, and do it all in one motion."

Over his bathrobe, Davis buckled on a gun belt holstering a single-action Colt .45 six-shooter. He tied the holster thongs above his knee. He drew the gun, twirled it three times over his trigger finger, and brought it down smartly into the holster. He drew again, very fast, cocking and dry-firing in a split second. Then he twirled the gun vertically, horizontally, over and back into the holster. (In Hollywood, Davis has a collection of thirty Western guns and, next to Mel Tormé, he is the fastest nonprofessional draw in town. Once I saw him hold a bottle at waist level, *throw* the bottle to the floor, and draw, cock, and shoot before it hit the carpet. "I love things Western," he says. "Morty, Dave, Arthur Silber, and I go to Phoenix and dress up in the tailor-made jeans and the tailor-made shirts, the cowboy hats, .45's on our hips, and Winchesters in the saddle holsters. We ride out like cowboys and talk about the south forty, tip the hat back with the thumb, and chew on filter cigarettes.") Davis demonstrated the fast draw a few more times.

"You dig, baby?" asked Davis.

Landfield nodded and Davis retired to the bedroom to dress. As he hung up his gun belt, he said to me: "I'm crazy to make a Western. Can you imagine a colored Western—they'll never do it! But if they do, it'll be the first time they let the Indians win!"

From the Hotel Fourteen, Davis and the hard core of friends

rode three cabs to the Hotel New Yorker. Davis was living there in the penthouse. Going up in the elevator, I remembered a story I had once heard about Bert Williams, a great Negro song-and-dance-man of twenty-five years ago. When Williams played New York, he also rented a penthouse at a midtown hotel. The only difference was that his lease required him to enter and leave the hotel by the service elevator. One night, Eddie Cantor was riding up with Williams and asked him if it bothered him using the service elevator. "Mr. Cantor," Williams said, "the only thing that bothers me is applause." A good deal of progress has been made since then, I thought, but there was still a strong trace of Williams in Sammy Davis, Jr.

Parties of varying intensity were held every night at the penthouse during Davis's eighteen-day engagement at the Copacabana and this night was no exception. When Davis arrived, three Copa girls, a former owner of the Chez Paree in Chicago, Davis's lawyer, another one of Davis's assistants named John Hopkins, the columnist, Bert Boyar, and his wife, Jane, and the comedian, Jack Carter, and his date were waiting. Hopkins and Murphy Bennett tended bar. Landfield sent out for hamburgers and Davis turned up the stereo. The hamburgers arrived and talking stopped as the guests leaped to the feast. In a twinkling, the hamburgers were gone. Everyone got one, even the pretty girl reclining on the floor underneath an oak bench—everyone, that is, except Davis.

"It's a definite steal," he said, cheerfully, but for an instant he looked as though he would have liked a hamburger.

The party broke well after dawn. Only a few bitter-enders remained when Davis's father and stepmother came in from their room down the hall. They had flown to New York from Hollywood, where they live with Sammy, Jr., for a vacation and to see him at the Copacabana.

"How's my baby?" asked Sam, Sr., and kissed Sam, Jr.

"I'm fine, Dad."

Davis stepped back to examine his father. The older man is taller and heavier and the family resemblance is faint. He wore a new suit.

"You're getting fat, Dad," said Davis.

"I'm going to get fat as I want to."

"Well, then, get into your old clothes. Nothing looks worse than a fat man in a Continental suit."

"See what kind of a boy I have," said Sam, Sr., and the two men embraced, laughing.

To me, Sam, Sr. said: "We have a fine house out there. We all live in it together—the wife and me, Sam's two sisters, grandmother, and Sammy. A fine house, yes! Believe me, it's a kick for a man who was born on West 39th Street."

Sam, Jr. was proud of the house, too. It had been built by Judy Garland on the side of one of the Hollywood hills, just up the road from where Davis's friend, James Dean, used to live. Davis had bought the house a few years ago for 75,000 dollars. Built on three levels, it provided an apartment for Davis's grandmother and more-or-less private quarters for the family of Sam, Sr. The upper floor—living room, bedroom, terrace, and guest room—was Davis's domain, furnished with white rugs, mostly black furniture, and gigantic lamps. The terrace overlooked the inevitable swimming pool. The most unusual piece of furniture was Davis's bed, which was twice the size of the average double bed; otherwise, the house was ordinary-California-expensive without being lavish.

"It is a fine house," Davis said. "It means a lot to me. Someday, I'd like to arrange things so I can spend some time there."

Davis finally went to bed that morning at eight. He was up at noon in high spirits. After lunch at P.J. Clarke's with Dorothy Kilgallen, the columnist, he walked crosstown. Everywhere he went, people on the street spoke to him, a bus driver pulled over to the curb to shake his hand, and teen-agers chased him for his autograph. A few days earlier he had been taking such a stroll on Seventh Avenue and had obliged a middle-aged lady with his signature. A crowd had formed and had followed him to the door of a haberdashery. From inside, he had seen a hundred noses pressed to the window. The crowd had grown, tying up traffic on the street. At last, an irate police sergeant had forced his way into the shop.

"Mr. Davis," the policeman had said, "you got a crowd outside."

"I didn't bring them," Davis had said.

"I'll call some more cops for you."

"No, I'll get out all right."

"How can you stand it?"

"I worked twenty years for this, sergeant. I can wait."

Now as he walked, Davis enjoyed the waves and glances of passersby again. "This sort of thing started a couple of years ago," he said to me. "All of a sudden, it was there. People knew *me*. Then I was sure I'd made it." His high spirits lasted through a sloppy recording session at Decca studios late in the afternoon. He was not in good voice and, besides, the songs were not right for him. When Dave Landfield, the secretary, asked him, "What's next?" Davis said, "Well, Dave, baby, it's a definite leave from here in two-oh minutes, maybe even one-five, followed by a definite cab, which will speed me to Danny's Hide-a-Way for a little din-din. Then it will be another cab-ola to the Hotel Fourteen, that is, one-four. After that, chickee, it is a definite lay-down with closed eyes, and Morpheus dropping little things in them for about forty winks, until I awake again, as myself—like refreshed—ready to go on. I mean, baby, is that clear?"

Davis laughed. When he is very happy indeed, his talk often becomes a combination of Hip, show biz, jazz, and a little English. It is in-group lingo of the kind he shares with his Hollywood friends—Frank Sinatra, Dean Martin, Peter Lawford, Eddie Fisher, and Tony Curtis—who are members of a determinedly informal organization known as "the clan."

In about one-five, Davis said to me, "Let's split," which meant *leave*, and we rode a definite cab to Danny's Hide-a-Way, a midtown restaurant in which Davis frequently dined. He ate his one big meal of the day with gusto. At seven, I followed him to the hat-check counter where he retrieved his derby, cape, and umbrella. A teen-age girl asked for his autograph. Davis signed a postcard for her.

"Thank you, Sammy," she said.

"You're welcome," he said, walking toward the door.

A heavy-set blond man, waiting to get to the hat-check room, said: "That's very nice, but why don't you do that in the *street—*"

A car was waiting for Davis. He stood inconclusively on the

sidewalk. He looked through the window into Danny's, trying to spot the blond man. Then he got into the car. By the time he arrived at the Hotel Fourteen, he was deeply hurt and enraged.

"What a Jackson!" he said.

"What Jackson?" I asked.

"A Jackson is some guy who calls a Negro 'Jackson' or 'Bo,' " he explained. "I'd like ten seconds with that rat!"

What can happen to Davis at any time, no matter how high he is flying, had happened.

Davis's early show was, in many subtle ways, below par. His timing was off. He did not kid with the audience. The beat of his songs was slower. It was not a happy show. Afterward, he returned to the dressing room, changed into the terry-cloth robe, and lay on the couch. Mike Silver, the drummer who travels with him, sat in a chair with his sticks in his hands, watching TV. Murphy Bennett straightened the bedroom. Davis was almost as alone as he ever is.

"I've never, never tried to be anything but what I am," he said. "I am a Negro. I'm not ashamed. The Negro people can mark a cat lousy for that and they won't go to see him perform. Well, we have Negroes here every night. If you go hear a Negro and see some Negroes in the audience, then you know how they stand. They'll ignore a guy who's marked lousy, see? So, I've never been the kind of guy who was ashamed. See, it's a matter of dignity. That's what makes something like that Jackson so tough on you. One time I went on in San Francisco and a guy down in the front row says to another guy, 'I didn't know he was a nigger,' and walked out. It's tough to play against that. In the Army, the first time anybody called me a bad name, I cried— the tears! I had spent all my life with my dad and uncle. I was loved. I was Charlie-protected. But now, this is the thing that is always just around the corner. It's like you can't get into El Morocco because you're colored. See?"

Davis's second show that night was better than the first, but he still seemed chilled. About four A.M., accompanied by fifteen men and women, he went to a West Side night club. Legally, it was closing time, but the bartender gathered up bottles, mix, ice, and glasses and carried the makings into a large back room. Cecil Young and three-fourths of a Canadian jazz quartet were having a last drink before calling it a night. Like the patrons, the fourth member of the quartet—the bass fiddler—had already gone home. Seeing Davis, Cecil Young began telephoning around to find another fiddle player. When the man arrived, sleepy-eyed and still wearing bedroom slippers, the jam session began. Davis, Young, the Canadians, and the new man played wildly and wonderfully for ninety minutes. Davis sat in on drums, blew the trumpet, and sang scat with Cecil Young. When it was over, the hurt was out of his system.

During a break, Cecil Young had said to me: "Jazz isn't polite, son. Jazz is, pardon the expression, screw you. If you don't like it, well, that's all. But if you do like it, then I like you, dig? With jazz, you thumb your nose when they don't like you. You get the message out, daddy."

Davis picked up the check for his friends and the group moved over to his penthouse for the sunrise.

A few days later, Davis landed in Las Vegas after overnight stops in Kansas City and Hollywood. Murphy Bennett had arrived a day ahead of him and set up the suite at the Sands Hotel which would be Davis's home for the next two weeks. The stereo was rigged and 250 records (from Davis's collection of 20,000) were stacked neatly in the bedroom. There was fresh ice in the ice bucket and the silver goblet had been polished. After the rehearsal and a steam bath, Davis settled on a couch in the living room to relax until it was time to dress for the opening.

Jack Entratter, manager of the Sands, telephoned to report that five hundred reservations had been turned down for the dinner show. A friend called to tell Davis that his wife, Loray White Davis, was in Las Vegas divorcing him. Davis had been married in 1958 and had separated from his wife in less than three months. During the separation, a settlement had been made, but this was the first Davis had heard of the Nevada divorce proceedings. He shrugged. It was all over long ago. Another friend called to give him the latest on the romance of his friend Eddie Fisher who, with Elizabeth Taylor, was exciting Las Vegas at that time.

Davis sighed. "Vegas I like," he said. "I feel like I've come home. You know, I've performed in this town like twenty-nine times. We used to come in here before we were anything and when there were only a couple of hotels. The Sands I like. I was offered 37,500 dollars a week to go into another hotel, but I turned it down. Very low pressure here. Easy. You're not fighting the knives and forks. It builds, but the pace is slower. You're running all the time, and then it's nice to come down to the Vegas pace."

Davis called to Landfield, the secretary.

"Hey, baby, call up Keely [Smith] and Louis [Prima] and tell them we'll be over after our show tonight. And find out what the Count [Basie] is doing. We'll swing with him tonight. And chicks. Chicks, we need. Ah, it's like a vacation. You can tumult all night, sleep all day, get a little sun—sun, I need—play a little blackjack. Oh, fine!"

And he lay back on the couch, running.

Personal

After this piece was published, Sammy Davis and I were bosom pals for several years. Whenever he was in New York or I was in Hollywood, we would spend some evenings together. I must have seen his nightclub act a hundred times. Then, one day, we decided that I should write a screen story for him. It would be based on an incident I had witnessed while researching a *Look* story on juvenile delinquency. We agreed on a price and I produced an eighty-page treatment. Davis liked it and, moreover, Frank Sinatra liked it. But the months slipped by and nothing came of it. Sammy couldn't pay me and, as creditor and debtor, we could no longer be Sam and Big T.

Last fall, a few days before Sammy opened on Broadway in *Golden Boy,* I visited him backstage at the Majestic Theater. He has changed since 1959. He is not running so hard. The hangers-on are still hanging on, but he does not seem to need them as much as he once did. He appears happily married to May Britt, who sat quietly in his dressing room while Sammy and I reminisced. I had had more pure fun working on "What Makes Sammy, Jr., Run?" than any other story I have written. As I was leaving, Sammy said call, but we have not had many opportunities to get together again.

Sammy's friendship was and still is important to me. We have much in common. We are both Jewish. But the illusion of color-lessness—all swinging cats are golden—that we both cherished six years ago no longer obscures our differences. Too much has happened. The American paradox has become obvious for all to see. Our system must work as a congress of differences or it won't work at all. It must be equitable, regardless of differences, or it will destroy itself. Either we function on these paradoxical terms, or we crack up. Perhaps a miracle is required, but since colorlessness is inconceivable and inequality is intolerable, what else can save us?

It has become the fashion for white authors to write about *their* Negroes. The result is never without condescension. And when it comes from good-hearted authors, it is depressing. Here, again, is that question of style, the allowance that ration-ality makes for the possibility of miracles. Sammy could not be *my* Negro. I could not be Sammy's white man. Such as it was, our friendship was based on feelings more fundamental than race. And so was the dispute that cooled it. Love and money, I think, are at the bottom of the human crisis. And, until we take to heart the necessity of both, there can be no miracle.

Elia Kazan
Elia
Kazan's
Great
Expectations

Elia Kazan, as director of the repertory company of New York's Lincoln Center for the Performing Arts, has been given a chance to do something important in the American theater. As an actor and director, Kazan has survived thirty years in the jungle of show business. On Broadway since 1937, he has directed two plays by Arthur Miller (*All My Sons* and *Death of a Salesman*), four plays by Tennessee Williams (*A Streetcar Named Desire, Camino Real, Cat on a Hot Tin Roof*, and *Sweet Bird of Youth*), and fifteen other plays and musical comedies. In addition, since 1944, he has directed sixteen movies, including *On the Waterfront* and *Baby Doll*.

At the new Vivian Beaumont Theater in the Center, he will command physical resources for play production which are unmatched in America and equal to the best in Europe. He will have nearly four times as much working space—11,000 square feet of stage area—as there is in any playhouse on Broadway, plus uniquely automated technical facilities. He will be able to rehearse plays for as many as thirty weeks, ten times the average Broadway rehearsal period. (Kazan rehearsed the cast of *J.B.* a few years back "for exactly nineteen goddamn days.") At the end of his fiscal year he won't be required to balance his considerable budget, let alone earn a profit for angels. If he shows a loss on ticket sales, the deficit will be made up by patrons such as Mrs. Vivian Beaumont Allen who gave three million dollars toward construction of the theater. Most impor-

tant, Kazan will have a choice of plays, players, and methods
of production limited by his own aims and not much else. He
must make certain decisions with Robert Whitehead, his co-
director whose functions are largely administrative. He must
also satisfy Laurance Rockefeller, chief sponsor, and William
Schuman, president of the Center. But these men are inclined
now to defer to Kazan in artistic matters. "I'm going to work
for Lincoln Center," Kazan says, "as long as I can do what I
want to do. When I can't do that, I'll quit." So, for all practical
purposes, he is quite free to create the repertory company in
his own image.

Along corrupt, commercial old Broadway, something has always been going wrong with the American theater. Either audiences are becoming insensitive, critics more dastardly, unions
more intransigent, performers more repetitious, playwrights
soft on their earnings, or directors, producers, and property
owners hungrier for a hit. Where Broadway people have gathered, one has eternally heard fanciful talk of an ideal theater.
Every profession, of course, has its dream—in journalism it's
"let's start a magazine"—but in the theater the dream has had
singular intensity for the simple reason that so much *has* been
wrong.

The dream has had many shapes; but eventually it has always
been defined as a theater where a group of players could work
continuously, free from box-office pressures, to put on the great
plays of the past as well as the best new work being written.
Beyond this, the dream theater has always had some significant
collective attitude toward the contemporary world which it
would express through its art. The Provincetown Players, founded in 1915, and the Group Theatre of the 'thirties were attempts
in this direction, but eventually they floundered without suffi-
cient funds to support them.

In Europe, the dream has been realized to varying degrees in
state-subsidized theaters: France's Théâtre National Populaire,
Germany's Berliner Ensemble, and England's Old Vic (soon to
be part of a National Theater). And since 1958 in America, plans
for Lincoln Center's theater have evolved precisely with a view
to forming an ideal repertory company. Robert Whitehead con-

siders the appointment of Kazan as evidence of the group's vision: "We wanted a living theater aimed at a more civilized world, an institution with a recognizable stamp, and we felt Kazan would give us this."

Not long ago, Kazan spent some days and evenings with me talking about the Lincoln Center and other aspects of his career. He is a short, congenial, ambiguous man with unruly-to-wild black hair (now graying), eyes too close, nose too much, and a taste in wearing apparel that ranges from wrinkled tweeds to sweat shirts. He complains that strangers often mistake him for a taxi driver. He has a sinewy quality and an intense way of expressing himself that often make him seem to be one of nature's own forces. You suspect that he is aware of his own super-intensity but, at age of fifty-two, is still a little in awe of it.

His surface manner is informal, tending toward raffishness. The knot of his tie customarily hangs an inch or two below his collar button. Invariably, he is the first person in a room to remove his jacket, slip out of his shoes, and put his feet up. He wolfs food, smokes big cigars, calls males as well as females *baby*, and swears just about all the time, using all the words in any company. All this gives a strong impression of aged-in-the-wood nonconformity. On the other hand, privately, he is extremely neat and well organized. Ten minutes after Kazan moves into a hotel room, his suitcase is emptied, his clothes are put away, and his toilet articles are regimented in the medicine chest. Even when he is not actively engaged in a production, his days are carefully (and usually completely) scheduled; recently, it was 8:30 to 9:30 A.M. at the psychiatrist's, a full morning of appointments, a light lunch at his desk, and a four-hour stint on the script of his new film, *America, America*. Then, too, he meticulously collects the opening-night reviews, telegrams, letters, memos, souvenirs, and news clips that touch on his professional life and has them pasted into thick scrapbooks, now numbering eighteen volumes. He explains the scrapbooks by saying that some day he is going to write a book.

Kazan is aware that he is expected to create something new and significant in the theater at Lincoln Center. He, no less than other show people, has shared the dream. "I am ready," he says, "for work in something that is more the way I think the theater should be. The theater is a collective art and in the back of my heart I've always hoped to have this kind of theater. I believe people value good theater. They recognize it and flock to it when it happens."

Having said (in a public statement issued in 1961) that he would never again direct a play on Broadway, he obviously feels that an extension of the Broadway stage at Lincoln Center would hardly be worth the effort. He passionately predicts that he will do better things at Lincoln Center than he has ever done before. He says he has been frustrated by "disgusting" commercialism on Broadway (and in Hollywood, of course), by "the people with money who pressure you to make something popular." Now, he promises, he is going to get "the best actors, directors, and writers and make this a living art center for the theater. . . . We're going to have about forty actors and actresses and they'll have a chance to play many roles. . . . We're not going to ask them to work for nothing, but for a living wage—what a fine actor wants is to have pride in and respect for what he does and he'll have that in the repertory company."

Kazan is discussing plays with a number of playwrights. *After the Fall*, Arthur Miller's new play, Kazan says, will be the first offering. Simultaneously, a "classic" play (something Greek, a Shakespeare, or an Ibsen, perhaps) will be rehearsed and will open a few days after the Miller play. Six or seven weeks later, the company will present a new comedy by S.N. Behrman. The first year's repertory will be rounded out some ten weeks later by a Eugene O'Neill drama. During any given week, then, the company will be presenting two or three different plays. The first two will be Kazan productions—"to stamp the purpose of the theater," Whitehead says. Thereafter, Kazan will direct one or more a year as other directors are invited in to work with the company.

Meanwhile, in a supplementary 299-seat auditorium, a different type of theater will be presented at the Center. "Here our writers and directors will have an opportunity to try things that are far out," Kazan says of the smaller theater. "They will be given an opportunity to say what they must say about living here and now in America. It will be a place where they can have the right to fail!"

But surely saying what "must" be said and its corollary, the right to fail, must turn out to be part of the *larger* theater's essential purpose, too, or it cannot amount to anything. At least for the present, however, Kazan apparently draws a distinction between criteria for the work to be done in the big 1,100-seat Vivian Beaumont Theater, where his own directing efforts will be concentrated, and the little auditorium. One will offer "conventional," the other "unconventional" plays. It is as though he would combine Broadway and off-Broadway under a single, but segregated, roof without remedying the defects of either. He seems to have thought much more about creating a theater to which people "flock" than about what might or should be presented to them. For instance, long before he had read Arthur Miller's play or had any idea what it was about, he had made up his mind that he wanted it for the repertory company's opening show. Also, he has signed for the play by S.N. Behrman, who seems a strange choice, given the pioneering ambitions of the Center. While Kazan has taken himself out of Broadway, it appears that Broadway has not yet been taken out of Kazan— all this raising some doubt as to whether Kazan's "recognizable stamp" will actually realize the Center's full potential.

Among the assets Kazan will bring to Lincoln Center is his characteristic directorial technique. He describes it as an attempt "to catch the thoroughly saturated essence of a type." As a former actor, he has the actor's anxiety to connect with the audience at all times, to grip the viewer at every moment so that the people on the stage are never left hanging or ignored. His work, therefore, seems supercharged. "When Kazan directs," Arthur Miller explains, "he wants to dramatize the metaphor in every human action. There is always the overt action and something under the surface. You kill a man, but in what attitude? In anger? Or as though you were praying to him? A good deal of the time, Kazan finds the inner metaphor and that is why his best work has tremendous depth. Now, other directors also try for this, but with Kazan it is in the forefront of his mind. If he finds nothing below the surface, his work tends to get clouded or seems overloaded. He is always on a quest for metaphors. That is his art."

Beyond technique, Kazan comes equipped with a knack for human relations in the theater. The director of plays and films is expected to form a brotherhood with a writer, a fatherhood with a company of players and craftsmen, and an alliance with producers, bankers, lawyers, and bookkeepers. He must form a family that takes him away from his own family. He must be the leader of a safari, the foreman of a construction gang, chancellor of the exchequer, and a counselor on emotional problems. "You're expected to do this," Kazan says, "and still keep yourself soft inside to do the creative work." Kazan has been able to do these things, pull a production together, convince a writer he ought to tighten up his script, and somehow get the best—or very nearly the best—out of performers.

No writer working with Kazan gets his play on without revisions. And none to whom I have talked (Miller, Williams, Robert Anderson, and others) has admitted that they are sorry about any changes inspired by Kazan. (The rumor that Kazan rewrites plays to make them work appears to be exaggerated; at least, no writer has admitted that Kazan ever did any rewriting of *him*. Arthur Miller made substantial revisions in *Death of a Salesman*, adjusting his script to the staging conceived by Kazan and Jo Mielziner, the set designer. When Archibald MacLeish's *J.B.* opened in Washington, a friend called Kazan from New York and learned that the local critics were sure that the play would never reach Broadway. Kazan, however, was unperturbed. He said, the friend recalls, "MacLeish is working." Williams rewrote the third act of *Cat on a Hot Tin Roof* to suit Kazan, who was then belabored by the drama critic, Kenneth Tynan, because the play seemed to him to be "an edifice tilted, like a giant architectural folly."

Williams, however, takes Kazan's side. "Kazan's suggestions resulted in making the play more affirmative," Williams says. "He has a much more sanguine attitude toward life than I do. I'm more a pessimist. My taste is my taste, but I am fallible. Basically, the play was there with either third act and Kazan simply staged it more brilliantly than anyone else." Tynan, after seeing the same play in London, directed by Peter Hall and offering the last act as originally written by Williams, still insisted: "I prefer the author's third act to the modified version approved by Mr. Kazan," but even Tynan "missed, more than I would ever have thought possible, the galvanic inspiration of Mr. Kazan's direction."

Kazan could not guide his playwrights if he were not able to get along with them as well as he does. Kazan respects writers (and until he started writing the screenplay for his new film, he even seemed to envy them). Furthermore, he has had a considerable range of contemporary plays and scenarios from which to choose, and has turned down the offerings of many, including Lillian Hellman, Paddy Chayefsky, and Williams. He had first look at *Oklahoma!* and *The King and I* and rejected both. He by-passed *Luther*. Thus writers assume that when Kazan selects a script, he believes in it as much as they do. From here on, it seems, Kazan gets what he wants through a combination of chemistry, sympathy, and mutual regard. "Most directors are nervous," Williams says. "Whenever I feel I am making a director nervous, I slink away. But Kazan is different. He makes you feel he wants you around."

On balance then, writers at least seem to feel that Kazan is an able script editor. But one can't help wondering how a play can say "what must be said" if it is to be radically altered for the sake of theatrical effectiveness. What will happen to the content of significant plays after many long weeks of rehearsal at the Center?

Kazan's way with writers is matched by his influence with performers. Again, it is Kazan's ability to inspire the feeling that he believes in the other person's work that forms the basis of his relationships. Kazan was a founder of the Actors Studio, the drama school led by Lee Strasberg and dedicated to the Stanislavsky method by which an actor uses his imagination and sense of reality to "become" the character he must portray. Here, actors and actresses have been trained and exercised like Kentucky thoroughbreds and many have gone into Kazan productions. (Oddly enough, Marlon Brando and James Dean, two of Kazan's faster horses, were not Studio products; the former attended about a dozen times and the latter just twice.) Studio membership, however, has been no guarantee of a job with Kazan. He lets nothing, not even friendship or the performer's needs, influence his casting selections. "Besides being in the Studio," Eli Wallach recalls, "I had known Kazan for fifteen years before I worked with him. He's a toughie. He knows what he wants and that's all that counts."

Kazan also hates to use stars. He avoids them whenever possible, even those he himself has created. "You lose something with stars," he says. "It always helps to have an unknown. The unknown hasn't got an investment in himself, he isn't goods for himself, his value to himself isn't diminished when people see him in something that doesn't make him look like a hero, and he isn't protecting his face. He's not an actor, he's just a person. Marlon Brando has never been as good again as he was in *Streetcar*. It isn't the bloom that comes off the well-known star —it's the humanity." Such is Kazan's ruthlessness in casting, that his choices feel they couldn't be in Kazan's play unless he believed in them. They are then ready for rehearsals.

During the rehearsal period, as Kazan leads his people toward his goal, he invariably establishes a honeymoon relationship with them. Actors work hard for Kazan because few directors work harder for actors. He is willing to absorb more than his share of the routine pressures of show business—so much so that he usually develops a somatic disturbance, such as a brief illness or a sudden need for new eyeglasses, soon after the work begins. The ordered tumult that characterizes a typical Kazan rehearsal quickly wins the performers' respect. His industrious preparations for each day's work ("It's like he sleeps in the theater," one actor said to me) reassure them that the master is in control. Actors are most afraid of making fools of themselves and Kazan gives confidence that he won't let this happen.

In return, although Kazan is frankly devious and known to use any technique that will work, including mild torture, to get a performance, the actors let Kazan fool them. They may fear and resent him, but they also worship him, and so far they have willingly worked with him. "He sloshed me with attention and charm," Geraldine Page says, recalling the rehearsals for her role as the faded movie queen in *Sweet Bird of Youth*. "He wanted me to feel right in the role, so he dug up old screen magazines showing poses of old Hollywood beauties and left them around to inspire me. Meanwhile, he was using talk-therapy on Paul Newman, who was co-starring. Paul was nervous about acting on the Broadway stage. And Kazan kept telling him 'Don't be nervous.' And the more Kazan talked to him, the more anxious Paul became. He started worrying that maybe he really needed all the help he was getting from Kazan. The result was that Kazan made Paul so nervous that he gave Kazan the kind of nervous characterization he wanted for the play."

For Lincoln Center, Kazan's single-mindedness, his personal magnetism, and his professional know-how can be invaluable. These qualities, however, are largely procedural. The real questions about Kazan and Lincoln Center must concern his creative purposes. "I have a great belief," Kazan says, "that just below the surface there is a great gap between what we profess and what we do. It's a disease. You can die from it. I want to show it up." And one can gather some notion of what he means from his own life experience.

Kazan's is a familiar American success story—the ironic kind. Born in 1909 in Kadi-keu, a poverty-stricken suburb of Istanbul, he was one of eight Kazanjoglou children. The family belonged to a community of Greeks who had been victimized for generations by the Turks. At age five, Kazan was brought to Ellis Island wearing an identification tag. The memory of once having been unidentifiable except for a tag still aggravates him. In Manhattan, he went to public school and attended the Greek Orthodox church. Then, as his father's rug business began to prosper, he moved with the family to New Rochelle, a suburb of New York which even then could hardly have been more different from Kadi-keu. Being Greek and looking Jewish, however, Kazan did find that Turks and Americans could share the same prejudices. Growing up, he was an outsider who wanted in.

As there were few Greeks and no Greek churches in New Rochelle, Kazan was sent to a Roman Catholic church. He remembers his first confession: "I kept trying to think up some sin I'd committed, but I was lily white. I hadn't robbed anybody and I hadn't told any lies. So, I made up something—I said I'd disobeyed my *mother*." He found it impossible to fib about disobeying his father. In spite of psychoanalysis, Kazan has a grudging memory of the man. "He used to tell me, 'Go shine your shoes. Go get a haircut.' He was always concerned about how I looked," says Kazan, who has made it a rule in his adult life to dress carelessly. "And when I said I wanted to be an actor, he wouldn't believe it. He said, 'Go look in the mirror.'" Kazan recalls that he had one great teacher in high school and has not forgotten what made her seem great to him: "Her name was Anna B. Shanks. I just did not want to go into any kind of business for a career and Anna B. Shanks taught me that it was all right to be different from my father."

At Williams College, Kazan was too small for varsity football, so he played quarterback on the nonfraternity touch team. With pride, he remembers that "we were all the freaks, the Negroes, the Jews, Greeks, and outsiders . . . and one year we had a hell of a team and beat all the fraternity-house boys."

Kazan directed the rest of his considerable steam into studying English (he graduated with honors), waiting on tables, and joining as many extracurricular campus clubs as he could. He maintained a pace that was, according to a former roommate, "almost threatening." Because he was so busy, he was given the nickname, "Gadget," which has been shortened to "Gadge." Already, it seems, he felt an out-sized compulsion to get ahead. Yet, he had no particular career in mind while at Williams. He had been greatly impressed by *Potemkin* and other Russian films. He had worshiped Eisenstein. Coming of age in the Depression and with the vague idea that he might like to make it as a film director, he decided to go to Yale Drama School. Here he met Molly Thacher, a fellow student, who became his wife and the mother of his four children. But he did not accomplish much in the way of theatrical efforts and left before completing the full course of study.

In 1932, he joined the Group Theatre, a repertory company with strong political impulses, as an assistant stage manager. Three years later, he was "discovered" as an actor in their production of *Waiting for Lefty* by Clifford Odets. In subsequent performances, especially as Fuselli, the gangster, in Odets'

Golden Boy, he was highly praised. Brooks Atkinson of the New York *Times* declared that Kazan was "one of the most exciting actors in America." He appeared in two movies, type-cast as a gangster and touted as the successor to George Raft. He might well have gone on as an actor, but by 1941 he had directed several plays, including two for the Group Theatre, and he had made up his mind that his future lay in directing. The next year, he was hired to direct Thornton Wilder's *The Skin of Our Teeth.* Since, at age thirty-three, he had little to lose, he was willing to tackle the Wilder play, a highly dubious property before opening night, and the formidable, preselected cast, including Fredric March, Florence Eldridge, and Tallulah Bankhead. The play was a hit, running for 359 performances, and Kazan became one of the most sought-after directors in America.

For the next twenty years, he was a "success"—pursued by the powerful and highly paid. "Yes, we've got show business in America and not a theater or film art," Kazan says, reflecting on his career. "By luck, once in a while, something comes through this mess made by freaks, this floating crap game. But I have done my best all the time—my flops have simply been my failures. I think of Shakespeare. He wrote five good plays and five pretty good plays. . . . No man is a machine. You can say this about me, though: I've always done the scripts I wanted with the actors I wanted the way I wanted. That's the way I've played the game and I'm proud of it."

In the early days of glory as a director, Kazan tackled one play after another in rapid succession, and made a picture a year for Twentieth Century-Fox. He approached theater and films as an actor might approach them—he had work to do rather than a particular idea to express.

Out of his next four plays and two movies, Arthur Miller's *All My Sons* was the only one of any significance. The play was inferior to Eugene O'Neill's *The Iceman Cometh,* which was staged in the same season, but the Kazan-Miller combination carried off most of the major Broadway awards for the year. More importantly for Kazan and Miller, they became best friends. And, as it turned out, Tennessee Williams enjoyed the production of *All My Sons* so much that he decided to offer *A Streetcar Named Desire* to Kazan. In 1948, *Streetcar* opened and Kazan's press notices were as ecstatic as Williams'. Newspaper critics proclaimed the dawn of "the age of the director" in which the director of stage plays would receive the kind of billing that formerly had been reserved for playwrights. And many, when they referred to Kazan's *Streetcar*, really meant that it was his. Yet, Kazan remained essentially the actor who had become a director.

The year of *Streetcar*, for example, was the year in which Kazan won an Academy Award in Hollywood for directing *Gentlemen's Agreement*. The film was about as far from Williams' tragedy of frustration as one could imagine. Its apparent point was that anti-Semitic prejudice cannot survive exposure. But Moss Hart, who had written the screenplay from the novel by Laura Hobson, once defined the point more accurately. Wryly, he told of the lesson a stagehand had learned from it: "From now on, Mr. Hart, I'm going to be good to the Jewish people because you can never tell when they might turn out to be gentiles." Kazan himself now feels that the picture was glib. The same kind of variations in Kazan's work occurred the following year when he was represented on Broadway by Arthur Miller's *Death of a Salesman* and in the Fox theaters by *Pinky*, a superficial little film on miscegenation. But if, as Kazan claims, these were really the scripts he *wanted* to direct, what went wrong?

By concentrating on movies for several years after *Death of a Salesman*, Kazan improved his technique in that medium, but he himself was still not satisfied with the results. Then, after studio executives cut 25 minutes from *Viva, Zapata!* without asking his aproval, he thought he knew what the trouble was: "Once and for all, I learned that the guy who signs the checks in Hollywood is the guy with the big voice in making artistic decisions." So he set up his own production company, Newtown Productions, Inc., with offices in New York, and determined to make films for himself. He seemed to have every chance for success although he would still have to depend upon the banks involved in the motion-picture industry for financial support— and upon the established Hollywood distribution facilities to get his Newtown pictures before the public. Yet, even before he had launched his first film, he almost lost everything.

Kazan's career was nearly ended by the fact that, back in the Group Theatre days, he had been a Communist. For eighteen months in the early Thirties, he had been a member of a cell with several other friends in the troupe. He had joined for the usual 1930's reasons—the party was then an accepted organ of social protest—and resigned when the cell members plotted to control the artistic policies of the Group. Nothing came of the plotting, times changed, and by January, 1952, one member of the cell was dead and most of the others had long since quit the Communist Party.

In that month, Kazan was summoned to Washington to testify before an executive session of the subcommittee of the House Committee on Un-American Activities looking into Communist infiltration of the Hollywood motion-picture industry. The position of the movie industry had become so hardened that anyone who for any reason withheld any information from "The Committee" could have no future in Hollywood. The situation on Broadway was equally menacing. And, further, the committee's procedure had also hardened: the ex-Communist could only absolve himself by *publicly* naming everyone he had known in the Communist Party, whether or not the names were already on the public record. "The ritual," as Murray Kempton has said, "was more important than any revelation." At first, in the executive session, Kazan withheld some names and gave others. But this did not satisfy the committee or anyone else, no matter where they stood on the conflicting principles involved.

"Four months went by," Molly Kazan recalls, "and Gadge was in a pressure cooker. He had to take stock of himself and decide what he believed in. We could have lived. We could have gone to England and he could have worked there. But this was a kind of political psychoanalysis for him. It was the best thing that ever happened to him. He had always been such a fair-haired boy."

Kazan voluntarily reappeared before the subcommittee in April and gave the rest of the names. In his public testimony, he stated that after long and careful deliberation, he had decided that secrecy could serve only the Communists, and that the American people needed the facts to deal effectively with the Communists. "I hated a lot of the company I was testifying in," he now says, "but I also hated the Communists." His performance, however, disappointed many of his former friends. It lost him the friendship of Arthur Miller. "We disagreed," Kazan says, "on what was the right and just thing for me to do about the committee." Kazan and Miller had been together almost daily when Miller had written *Death of a Salesman.* They had been best buddies. Now, their plans for staging *The Crucible,* Miller's play attacking witch hunting, were abruptly canceled. They would hardly speak to one another in the next nine years. Perhaps the most poignant thing about Kazan's later films and plays is that none of them were written by Arthur Miller, a loss to both men. Recently, however, the friendship has been restored, as Kazan says, "on a new basis."

After the hearings, Kazan made his best, and perhaps his most deeply felt film, *On the Waterfront.* Since the movie makes the point that to inform is morally right, many critics see in it Kazan's personal justification for his Washington testimony.

Through the Fifties, Kazan divided his efforts between plays and movies. With Tennessee Williams he made a good film, *Baby Doll,* whose ambiguous story line seemed more Kazan than Williams. Kazan was on the verge of becoming something more than an interesting film-maker. Thereafter, however, he tended to overload and overcook his stories, passing through such notable non-successes as *A Face in the Crowd* and *Wild River,* and culminating in *Splendor in the Grass* in 1961. Written by William Inge under Kazan's close supervision, the latter film struck many critics as vulgar and foolish and grossed over five million dollars.

Kazan has never been able to make films with the imagination and insight of a Bergman, a Fellini, or a Truffaut. He has missed the new era in film-making, the flowering of intensely personal directors who write their own scenarios and say only what they have to say. He may make his voice heard yet, however, depending on the outcome of *America, America,* the first Kazan film to be made from a Kazan screenplay. "I have always given life to the feelings of other writers," Kazan says, "but now I am going to make people feel what I feel."

On Broadway during the past decade, Kazan has not ventured

far from nor gained on *A Streetcar Named Desire* and *Death of a Salesman*. Besides *Cat on a Hot Tin Roof*, he made hits out of a weak Williams play, *Sweet Bird of Youth*, and Robert Anderson's mawkish *Tea and Sympathy*. With the exception of *J.B.*, he did not test himself on any play with an unfamiliar theme. He shunned all but the contemporary Broadway theater. He did not direct any Ibsen, Shakespeare, or O'Neill plays, nor any by the Greeks. Indeed he has shown little interest in the classical repertory which should be a part of a purposeful theater; nor has he done more than acquaint himself with the disciplined styles of acting these plays require. He has in fact confined himself to the realistic dramas which have predominated in the commercial American theater since the Thirties. And these, of course, are only a part—and hardly the major part—of the dramatic tradition available to the Lincoln Center company.

Finally he was not tempted by the new wave of angry, mystical, or absurd playwrights. "It is unthinkable," Tennessee Williams says, "that Kazan would direct a *Waiting for Godot*." He found the command to succeed at the box office onerous but, for himself, unavoidable, and he lived with it rather than turn to off-Broadway, experimental, or even university theater. "I've been making my living doing the things I most want to do," Kazan says. "I'm what I am. I can think of no other way to be."

What hope is there, then, for the Lincoln Center project? In 1958 in the New York *Times Magazine*, Kazan selected ten plays for a theoretical repertory company. They were all plays by familiar twentieth-century American playwrights—Miller, Williams, Odets, O'Neill, Inge. One hopes that Kazan's actual selection will show more variety and daring. Kazan's "stamp," thus far, is a mixture of artistic and commercial values hardly calculated to rescue the living theater from the one on Broadway. Once Kazan even told a reporter that he equated "good plays with successful plays," to which Harold Clurman, the drama critic and director, replied, "If this is taken literally, we are preparing for the burial of the theater as an institution of significant expression." Yet, it would be unsportsmanlike to put down Kazan as he begins his new venture. Presidents of the

United States are not the only ones who grow and change in their jobs.

One just has to wait and see.

Personal

As I recall, before my piece appeared in *Harper's*, ten years had passed since the last time Kazan sat still for a magazine portrait, which was published in *Collier's*. He was testifying before the Committee that season. Thereafter, he shied away from this type of publicity partly, I believe, to avoid the pain of rehashing his anti-Communist recitation. I do not know why his press agent, Bill Blowitz, pressed for the *Harper's* piece, but I suspect he wanted to enhance the chances of *Splendor in the Grass*. After two unsuccessful films, Kazan's Newtown Productions company badly needed a winner. In any case, the Lincoln Center aspect of the story is what made it interesting to me.

The piece ends on a note of "wait and see," and I have done this. Kazan had been extraordinarily articulate and gave an enthusiastic impression of sincerity. Despite the evidence of the past, I felt that *Splendor in the Grass* might be a good film, that *America, America* might be a great film, and that Lincoln Center might be the crowning achievement in the theatrical career of an idealistic man. He made me hope that he would be right.

Unfortunately, *Splendor* was a stinker, although it scored for Kazan at the box office. *America, America* had its moments, but suffered from Kazan's excessive theatricality and finally became tiresome. Above all, in its first year, Lincoln Center was a disaster. The repertory company produced a banal Behrman, an irrelevant O'Neill, and an incredible Miller called *After the Fall*. The latter was notoriously autobiographical, and even included a Kazan-like character, played by Ralph Meeker, who spent most of his time with his hands in his pockets and his back to the audience. It wasn't even good Broadway.

In 1961 and 1962, while I researched the piece, Kazan and I got along famously. We fought our war with kindness. Yet, after publication, there was no comment on my conclusions from him or Blowitz, except that Bill once said, "All I do is make the arrangements, you do the writing." I did not see or hear from

Kazan for nearly two years. Then last summer, he invited me to dinner at the Pantheon, a Greek restaurant on Eighth Avenue. We ate Kabob and spinach and drank Greek red wine. Afterwards, Kazan lit a cigar and told me that he was writing a new screen play. He wanted to know my thoughts on an aspect of the plot. Suppose, he said, a magazine writer was assigned to a subject, and suppose his magazine editor demanded that he change his conclusions, what would the writer do?

Of course, nothing of the sort had happened in the writing of "Elia Kazan's Great Expectations," but I couldn't help but feel that perhaps Kazan thought it had, given the cordiality of our subject-writer relationship and the chilly nature of the piece itself. My answer was that most writers I know would not change the conclusions of a piece, nor would they be asked to.

I wasn't denying the limitations of American journalism. These are serious and severe. The editing at *Harper's,* in fact, is an exception to the editing at most magazines where, for example, attacks on advertisers and their products, the practices of fellow journalists, and the financial interests of publishers are prohibited or softened. It follows that the worst journalistic sins are sins of *omission*—stories that are *not* written about fatal flaws in auto design, misinterpretation of events, or loopholes in the upper-income tax laws. What has been done is often well done, with maniacal attention to factual and technical detail. What has not been done is simply ignored—and the longer a story is ignored, the more likely it is to be thought of as "not for us." This is the curse, but not subornation. The story of the bushy-browed editor who buys the soul of the self-pitying writer doesn't wash. The wretch doesn't have to sell; he can always quit.

After Kazan had thought about my answer, he said he'd work it out. Since he seemed as enthusiastic as ever, I can't help hoping that he will.

Nelson Rockefeller
The Pitfalls of
Personality Politics

"I'm not one who has made a chart of his life. My course
has been zig-zaggy. I've believed in moving when the
opportunity came. Where my course goes next, I have no
idea. Time and events will tell as far as I'm concerned."
—Governor Nelson A. Rockefeller,
June 13, 1961.

The aerie of Nelson A. Rockefeller is a five-story double brownstone office building on West 55th Street in Manhattan. Out of
habit, preference and convenience, the charismatic governor of
New York more often works here in an atmosphere of super-
efficiency than at the clumsy old state capitol on the crest of
State Street in Albany. His office is on the second floor, a large,
cool, green room dominated by a big desk, flanked by the flags
of the United States and the State of New York. On the wall
closest to the desk are two photos of President Eisenhower and
Rockefeller posing self-consciously at the White House. The
respective photos seem to have been snapped when Rockefeller
joined the Eisenhower administration as Undersecretary of
Health, Education, and Welfare, where he was known as "a guy
who gets things done," and when he was promoted to Special
Assistant to the President, in which job he was frustrated, and
quit. You can't be absolutely sure of the origin of the pictures
because neither is inscribed (as one might expect) by the President. This makes you feel that the two men were never pals.
Propped up on a ledge below the photos is a plaque certifying

Rockefeller's lifetime membership in the National Association for the Advancement of Colored People and, next to the plaque, a stack of books: *The War Called Peace* by the Overstreets, *Executive Public Speaking Techniques* by Harry Simmons, and *Putting Faith to Work* by Robert J. McCracken. On the far wall, three prints from Brazil recall Rockefeller's early service as coordinator of Latin American affairs in the Roosevelt administration, while the silver lid on a cigarette box in the center of the conference table commemorates the 1960 G.O.P. Convention— *International Amphitheatre: presented to Nelson A. Rockefeller* —without sentiment. Legal pads are strewn about the table, too. Rockefeller likes to doodle while he talks: long firm lines, crosshatches, and arrows piercing circles.

Outside, the brownstone façade is painted blue which, for the neighborhood, acts as a camouflage: you could walk right by thinking it concealed a beauty parlor. In good weather, however, you can't miss the place: a gray-haired lady draped with sandwich boards telling her side of a dispute with the state's welfare agencies walks up and down, chanting: "I know you're in there, Governor Rockefeller. I'm hungry, Governor Rockefeller. I know you're in there. . . ."

Not long ago, curious at Nelson Rockefeller's strategic retreat from the national stage after the 1960 elections and wishing I knew as much about the man as the gray-haired lady knew about his whereabouts, I called up his press secretary, Robert McManus, and asked to be included for a while among the reporters who regularly shag after him. From an earlier experience, I expected Rockefeller to remain at arm's length. Historically, he has defended himself at all times in the presence of journalists. He has fraternized with them from time to time, but he hasn't chanced an intimate relationship with any. *Who needs it?* he might ask. (It's interesting to note that no "inside" books about Rockefeller have been published. The literature contains no suggestion of the kind of chummy co-operation Earl Mazo must have received while preparing his biography of Nixon.) But in spite of his aloofness, I hoped to learn something by watching him operate. It would be useful to know, I thought, how his strategy was working. After all, like his choice of offices, his choice of strategies is a revelation of himself.

I remember covering Rockefeller in the Spring of 1959. Suffering from the presidential fever that is endemic in New York governors in any season, he was touring western New York on official and political business. As he went from meeting to meeting and crowd to crowd, his mood was exuberant. He was an amateur doing well in the role of a professional. He was full of fresh-minted charm. He made crowds quiver. Under the guidance of his patronage man, Carl Spad, the local Republican organizations got the people out at the right time in the right places. The people had such a good time looking at him that you refrained from cynical comment on political crowdsmanship. They laughed at his jokes. "Young fellow called on my grandfather and found him down on his hands and knees looking for a dime. 'Leave it—it's only a dime,' the young fellow says. And my grandfather said: 'Young man, do you realize that a dime is the interest on two dollars for a whole year?' " And: "Sometimes you make a slip of a tongue that's embarrassing, like the time I was talking to some doctors and said: 'The two biggest killers of our time are heart disease and candor.' " And: "Well, the judge asked the condemned man if he had anything to say before they hanged him and he said, no, he didn't believe he did. So, a politician stepped up and said, 'Say, judge, as long as he isn't going to use his time, do you mind if I say a few words?' And the judge said it was all right with him, but he'd have to ask the condemned man. And the condemned man said, 'It's okay with me, just so you hang me first.' " Best of all, people liked to shake his hand. He did have the "air of unreality" about himself that J.P. Marquand once identified as the special ozone of the very rich, but this only added to his magnetism: "They look at him as though he was a prince or something," Leonard Hall said when explaining how Rockefeller had won the 1958 gubernatorial nomination from Leonard Hall. "Everybody ought to get into public life at one point," Rockefeller exulted, "just for the experience—it's tremendous! I love it!"

He was then, in 1959, already planning for the 1960 Republican presidential nomination. His disagreement with the way President Eisenhower was running things was a poorly kept secret. We were, he said, in a mortal struggle: we needed to resume nuclear testing, increase our defense appropriations, and provide fall-out shelters for the citizenry. At the same time, he said, we had to tend to our schools, the aged, civil rights, and the growth of the economy, lest our domestic problems overwhelm us and give the victory to the Communists by default. Rockefeller was a crisis-man for a crisis-time. He had momentum that spring and, should the White House door be slammed in his face, he would nevertheless be recalled—when the history of that period was written—as one of the most attractive, forceful and perceptive statesmen-on-the-make in U.S. life.

Now, two years later, the momentum has been dissipated. He lost the Republican nomination to Vice-President Richard Nixon and, in spite of four hundred Rockefeller campaign speeches in New York, the state's electoral votes went to John F. Kennedy. Senator Barry Goldwater's early bird campaign for a place on the 1964 G.O.P. ticket fills miles of space in newspapers and magazines. Nixon exercises his prerogatives as titular head of the party and writes newspaper articles. President Eisenhower speaks out on domestic affairs from a position hardly distinguishable from Goldwater's. And Rockefeller, like St. Francis before Doomsday, is tending his garden. While Democrats fear he may win re-election in 1962 by a million votes because (a) they haven't got a candidate and (b) the Republican ticket includes Senator Jacob Javits (an extraordinary vote-getter up for re-election), Rockefeller professes some anxiety about the outcome. His apparent strategy is to tend strictly to state affairs, campaign hard on state issues, and come through the election with more than his 1958 majority of 573,000 votes. While Republican Senators, Henry Luce, and influential parts of the British press criticize the Kennedy administration, Rockefeller declines to comment. Presumably, when he delivers the Godkin Lectures at Harvard in November, he will present a critique of national policy, but out of many such opportunities available to him, this is the only one he has accepted for this year. He is, it seems, lying low, outside the glare of the limelight. Finally, while Republicans debate the nature and content of the New Conservatism, Rockefeller ignores all factions. The theory seems to be that a dispute with, say, Goldwater, would enable Nixon to emerge as the party's peacemaker; that as the leader of the liberal wing of the G.O.P. he cannot afford to irritate the Party

Regulars too much or too soon; and that there will be time to take up ideological questions after he has won going away in 1962. Rockefeller has, in short, adopted a restrained, cautious, logical strategy. It makes sense, but it doesn't seem to work very well.

One day, Press Secretary McManus (seven children, ex-excellent reporter, ex-Harriman speech writer) invited me to go on a junket with Rockefeller to Camden, New Jersey, and Syracuse, New York. When I arrived at LaGuardia Airport that afternoon, the Governor and his entourage (secretaries, department heads, stenotypist, photographer) were already on board his personal twin-engine Convair. The plane is as comfortable as your living room, with single seats on either side of the aisle, a divan in the rear lounge, a TV set and kitchen in the back. For the sake of privacy and because he suffers an occasional bout of airsickness, Rockefeller sits forward. The press sits in the rear. As I passed on my way to my seat, he was standing in the aisle. "Hi, fella!" he said and we shook hands.

The Governor was two years older, but still youthful. And familiar: ginger hair, small blue eyes, big nose, wide mouth, strong jaw; the nasal twang in the voice that sounds like Will Rogers out of Dartmouth by Standard Oil; still the rumpled, square clothes, apparently snatched off the pipes at Robert Hall's; the athletic framework persisting in spite of his age (now fifty-three) and a graceless tendency to hunch like a halfback (Rockefeller's posture is affected by a chronic back ailment which is treated regularly by a doctor of osteopathy); still the emanations from his personality—optimism, great expectations, warm-heartedness, and generosity. "I saw him greet friends at the amphitheater in Chicago," Congressman William Cahill of New Jersey has said. "Now I've *met* some personalities—but there was in me a spark generated by the personality, the smile, the charm of this man that came to me from two hundred yards away." To this refrain, Rockefeller has replied: "I sometimes think that this personality talk is a result of lack of penetration. I've always felt that the record would take care of it. Why should I argue about it? It isn't really personality. It's a genuine liking of people. People respond. It's not a calculated act. I haven't changed since I was little." He has, it seemed, everything going for him: power, money, ideas, and potential—a do-good billionaire, a governor, a man who would be President. Above all, he has the vaunted, celebrated, feared Rockefeller Personality which, like beauty in women, is both given and self-created.

After take-off, Rockefeller consulted the Camden schedule, which called for a joint press conference with former Secretary of Labor James Mitchell. Rockefeller was making the trip, his first out of the state since election day, to help Mitchell launch his campaign for governor of New Jersey.

"What are we going to talk about at this press conference?" Rockefeller asked.

"They'll want to ask you about New York City," McManus said, referring to the Republican slate for the mayoralty campaign.

"I'm not going to talk about New York," Rockefeller said. "Or my personal future. My purpose on this trip is to make friends."

The stenotypist and the steward served coffee and hors d'oeuvres. Rockefeller passed. McManus asked him about a certain New York politician anxious for a judgeship.

"Never met a more sensitive man," Rockefeller said, sympathetically. "He bleeds to make you understand him. Then when the blood is all over the floor and you're slipping in it, he gets through talking and you still don't know what he wants."

Getting off the plane at Philadelphia, a Rockefeller man commented that Camden was the town where, last year, Nixon had offered to "answer" Rockefeller's "questions" about the G.O.P. platform, but declined to debate him—which is how politicians identify cities. Then, behind a police escort, the Rockefeller party wheeled up to a roadside restaurant outside Camden which had been taken over for the press conference. The main dining room was jammed with local Republicans, Mitchell's people, reporters, television-types, and free-loaders. While the TV lights were being set up, most of the action was at the long bar table. Rockefeller grabbed Mitchell, shook his hand, pounded his back, and cried: "Hello, Governor! Can't call you Mr. Secretary any longer." Mitchell put his arm around Rockefeller and they posed for pictures. The conference produced the questions Rockefeller had anticipated.

How about '64, Governor Rockefeller?

"Absurd to speculate now about 1964. If I can just get back in '62, I'll be happy." (Laughter.) "I'm going to leave no stone unturned."

"You're going to win, Nelson," Mitchell said.

"If I get the nomination, Jim," Nelson said.

"Overwhelming majority," Mitchell said.

"I don't like to take anything for granted, Jim."

What about Senator Goldwater, Governor Rockefeller?

"Well, Senator Goldwater has done a lot to arouse a certain faction of our party. He gets them out and gives us all a chance to talk to them." (Laughter.)

Is Vice-President Nixon going to campaign for you next year, Governor Rockefeller?

"Well, now, I'm always glad to sit down with Dick whenever he comes to New York. But I'm telling you, frankly, I want to run for office next year on my own."

The press conference ended before anyone got around to asking candidate Mitchell a question. Then thirty-odd members of the Camden County Republican Club filed past Rockefeller and had themselves photographed shaking his hand. As the line thinned down, someone announced over the loud speaker: "Last call to shake hands with the governor," and two women rushed to the end of the line.

Later, in the foyer, these same women were talking about the next item on the schedule, a Republican dinner at a local night club; Rockefeller would speak, followed by a full-hour revue starring the McGuire Sisters.

"Let's go over and maybe we can shake hands with the Mc-Guire Sisters," said the first woman.

"What I want to shake hands with them for when this hand just shook hands with a Rockefeller!" cried the second woman.

"That's right," said the first, who hadn't looked at it that way. "What've the McGuire Sisters got?"

After the press conference, until dinner, Rockefeller and Mitchell were, as they say, closeted, talking politics. They attended the dinner, made their speeches, and returned to Rockefeller's room at a motel to continue their talk. Getting into the bathtub later that night, Mitchell slipped and broke his left leg.

Next morning, somebody said, "How 'bout that, Governor?" and Rockefeller replied: "Say, you do have to be careful."

Over the next two days, Rockefeller helped "bring the government closer to the people" of Syracuse, New York. Accompanied by as many as nine heads of state departments, eight reporters, and uncounted local politicians, he made fifteen appearances, delivered eight speeches, and talked with every major interest group in town, including the general public which was invited to a town meeting at a downtown auditorium. Typical of a Rockefeller operation, the schedule had been studied for months, organized down to the minute, and held together by expert communications. Traveling in a police-escorted, twelve-car motorcade (autos loaned by local dealers), the group was never more than five minutes late for an appointment. On the way, Rockefeller told businessmen he was putting New York State in "a better position to compete with other states," told community planners he wanted to "maximize intelligent planning which will inure [sic] to the people of the state," told educators that he had "deep faith in the values that have made this country great," and told a meeting of the Onondaga County Republican Committee that he had once been asked why he wanted to get into such a dirty business as politics, to which he said he had replied: "If you think it's dirty, you damn well better get in and clean it up." He spiced each talk with a joke or two. The punch lines were familiar: " 'Young man, do you realize that a dime is the interest on two dollars for a whole year?' " " 'The two biggest killers of our time are heart disease and candor.' " " 'It's okay with me, just so you hang me first.' " One of Rockefeller's aides explained about the jokes: "We had some new ones that he used for a while, but he's reverted."

Late on the second night in Syracuse, the motorcade delivered its cargo to Rockefeller's plane. Airborne and headed southeast toward New York City, Rockefeller dropped back to kibitz the reporters' gin-rummy game.

"How'd it go?" he asked.

"Fine, Governor," a reporter said, collecting quarters.

"*Great*, wasn't it?" Rockefeller said. "We're going to do this all over the state!"

After two years, Rockefeller appeared to be the same consummate organizer, the same master of the heartfelt cliché, the
same vigorous proponent—yet he was not getting the same results. Neither in Camden nor in Syracuse was there the kind
of quivering excitement among people that had once made his
appearances such triumphs of personality. It was not that his
strategy had failed. It just hadn't been very successful. The
crowds were turned out. The meetings were well-attended. The
newspapers went for the story. But, at last, one felt that something was missing. And the same feeling returned again and
again.

At the Concourse Plaza Hotel in New York City's Borough
of the Bronx, a thousand of the faithful paid 50 dollars a plate
to come to the Annual Dinner of the Bronx County Republican
Committee. The Governor would speak. They sat twelve to a
table, each table with its own number marked on a pink paper
elephant. For dinner, they had roast beef and ice cream and
strawberries. The waiter at table 67 scraped crumbs, humming
and chanting, "Vote for Kennedy." Before Rockefeller arrived,
the orchestra had time for *Tea for Two* cha cha and *Makin'
Whoopee* cha cha. Then the word was passed and the band
broke into *Hail, Hail the Gang's All Here*. The applause was
sharp, but brief, when Rockefeller entered. "No explosion, no
confetti, no nothing," said a reporter. "Whatever magic he had,
these politicos know now that he's less than God. He lost to
Nixon, and Kennedy won the state. Good-by, magic." Rockefeller read an eight-hundred-word speech attacking Robert F.
Wagner, the mayor of New York. The Republican faithful in
the rear of the banquet hall whispered throughout, pausing
only to whoop at the mention of a local politician and to applaud
lightly at the end.

On Cornelia Street in Plattsburgh, New York, Rockefeller
helped dedicate a new state housing project for the aged: forty-
eight apartments in four barracks-shaped buildings, with window boxes. The crowd numbered less than a hundred and
most of them were school children. "People up here don't trust
him yet," said a native. "He tried to be President too soon."
A light rain began to fall. "I'm glad to see that these homes have

window boxes," Rockefeller said. "When I was in Dartmouth, I grew English daisies and lilies of the valley in a window box. My roommate warned me not to, but pretty soon other boys had window boxes, too. I guess the moral is, do what you think is right in this world. Others will follow." By the time he had finished speaking, less than half the audience remained.

And so on. The spark was missing.

In these moments at least, the name Rockefeller could not have been used as a synonym for charisma. Having decided on restraint and caution, he succeeded in diminishing one of his most priceless political assets—the Rockefeller Personality whose charisma depends upon crisis. It needs a context to match its content. Unlike beauty, it is not its own justification. The crisis about which he had raised the alarm in 1959 and 1960 was still on. "Time is running out," he had said again and again. Yet, the crisis-man deprived himself in 1961 of the sense of urgency that made his Personality viable. For urgency, he has substituted irony.

Thus (at arm's length), Nelson Rockefeller reveals himself. His strategic record has been ambiguous (reflecting, it has been said, the presence in his life of different advisers) but, by now, one can see that he has at least four traits which limit his effectiveness—excessive cautiousness, followed by a willingness to shoot the works and stubbornness matched with a zeal for conciliation. Let us look at the record.

After quitting his job as Special Assistant to President Eisenhower in 1955, Rockefeller went back to New York to go into state politics. He wanted to be, he says, *un auténtico representante del pueblo*—one of those authentic representatives of the people who had the power to make policy. Obviously aware that the distance from Albany to Washington needn't be measured in miles, he had determined to run for Governor. As an adviser, Rockefeller selected a former lieutenant governor, Frank Moore, who had served with Govenor Thomas E. Dewey. Then he interested himself in the New York State constitution and was appointed by Governor Harriman as chairman of a revision commission in 1957. Apparently, Harriman was unaware of Rockefeller's ambitions: the commission work gave Rockefeller legal access to masses of state data that otherwise would have been unavailable. By 1958, Rockefeller was able to prepare both a case against Harriman and a seemingly constructive program for the state. Despite the negative advice of his long-time public-relations adviser, the late Francis Jamieson, Rockefeller decided that 1958 would be his year. He remained adamant, even though Republican state leaders attempted to sidetrack him into a Senate race. Then, to sew up the nomination, he visited every county in New York, making both the party leaders and their wives happy. At the polls, Rockefeller overwhelmed Harriman against a Democratic tide running in the country that autumn. Such was the Rockefeller charisma that even the liberal New York *Post* in effect endorsed him just before election day. Rockefeller was straightaway cast as a potential antagonist for Nixon. The new Governor himself did not hesitate to speak out on national and international affairs while struggling with the New York State Legislature for a 277 million-dollar tax increase (he got 272 million dollars). He was, it seemed, running.

By mid-1959, Rockefeller's campaign for the 1960 G.O.P. presidential nomination was in full swing. Studies, plans, and communications were developed with painstaking attention to detail. The blue-brownstone on West 55th Street was turned into a central command post. Organizers and fund-raisers fanned out across the country. Citizens-for-Rockefeller clubs bloomed in city after city—each marvelously equipped with literature, supplies, and mimeograph machines. An inside cadre of advisers was assembled, including New York Republican State Committee Chairman L. Judson Morhouse, Rockefeller-family chief legal counsel John Lockwood, brother David Rockefeller, Jamieson, lawyer George Hinman, and Emmet John Hughes, former chief of foreign correspondents for Time, Inc. and ex-speech-writer for Eisenhower. They advised; Rockefeller decided.

From October to December, 1959, he looked and behaved as a man would who would fight all the way, battling Nixon in the primaries and fighting it out at the July convention as long as an uncommitted delegate survived. Such a strategy might have been effective. Rockefeller had everything to gain by entering the primaries (beginning with New Hampshire, March 8,

1960) and little to lose. A struggle with Nixon would force Rockefeller's name into the consciousness of the American people while conceivably nudging Nixon off dead-center toward the G.O.P. right (where many are named, but few have been chosen). Should Rockefeller lose in the primaries, the damage would not be irreparable. After all, he had been in politics little more than a year.

In spite of the flurry of activity on his behalf, Rockefeller was, in fact, moving cautiously. Whatever principle may have been at stake, he wanted to know the odds against him before he would fight Nixon in the primaries. For months, his men had been sounding out potential delegates, party leaders, and financial backers. Rockefeller pollsters sampled voters' attitudes in every major state. When the summary of soundings, polls, and intelligence was presented to him, he learned that Nixon had more than enough delegates to win, plus commitments from virtually all of the major Republican financial backers. Rockefeller was shocked. A senior Republican strategist said: "It's difficult to understand what else Nelson could have expected. He was an unknown compared to Nixon. Besides, the people with money knew they could deal with Nixon. If he didn't win, he'd be nobody. But it's almost impossible to deal with Rockefeller. Even if he loses he's still an important figure. The Rockefellers don't need anyone else that much." Without a primary fight, Rockefeller's chances were nil. And even in the primary states, polls showed Nixon well ahead. Given the gloomy news and the advice of Hughes, Hinman, Lockwood, and Jamieson, Rockefeller made up his mind. He declined the risk of the primaries. Day after Christmas, he announced: "I am not and shall not be a candidate for the nomination for the Presidency. This decision is definite and final." The last sentence did not say absolutely.

Between January and May, while Rockefeller study groups crystallized programs on the major issues before the country, Rockefeller developed better relations with the Republican legislature in Albany. Blessed by an upturn in the national economy, he was able to present a record-breaking 2,035,000,000-dollar state budget, increasing outlays for education, mental health, and highways, without new taxes. Then the U-2 incident in May gave him new hope for the Republican nomination. The new crisis called for a crisis-man. He decided again to shoot the works. Early in June, he fired off a challenge to his party, offering a ten-point emergency program based on the reports of his study groups: "The people, I am convinced, are ready," Rockefeller said. "The question remains: Is the party ready? The path of great leadership does not lie along the top of the fence. It climbs heights. It speaks truths. The people want and need one thing above all others—leadership of clear purpose, candidly proclaimed." A less-cautious man could have been proclaiming his own right to lead during the spring primaries; then, with the U-2 incident, he might have had the necessary thrust for a Willkie-style assault on the Republican convention. Making the best of it in July, Rockefeller pushed mightily, fighting first for a G.O.P. platform reflecting his view of the emergency, and second for a possible upset on the convention floor. In a dramatic New York meeting with Nixon, the adversaries agreed to a fourteen-point treaty that "composed" their viewpoints on the issue. It appeared that Rockefeller had won, at least, a small victory from a man whom he dislikes intensely. He had asserted his right to speak in Republican councils and had placed himself in contention for 1964 should Nixon lose. Moreover, he had introduced the Rockefeller Personality to America in what was for him an ideal context—an emergency. Yet, when he appeared before convention TV cameras wearing a Nixon hat, he dissipated much of the effect of his Paul Revere strategy. It was a loss of dignity not shared by Nixon's other competitor, Barry Goldwater, who appeared hatless to announce his support of the Republican nominee.

Between the Executive Chamber and the private elevator in the alcove of the office of the press secretary, in the corridor on the second floor of the New York state capitol, along the path that Governor Rockefeller follows when arriving or departing, a forlorn painting of Thomas E. Dewey, twice-defeated Republican candidate for the Presidency, looks down with raven eyes: *Nevermore?* The painting is a reminder that, since, 1932, no governor of any state has been elected President of the United States, although three have tried; that Senators and ex-

Senators dominated (finally) the conventions of both parties in 1960; and that, focused on Washington, the public may now believe that the men who are personally and deeply involved in the current crisis day-to-day, in Berlin, Vietnam, and Cuba, are serving the best kind of presidential apprenticeship.

Rockefeller may, as he has done this year, better his record as governor. He balanced the 2,400,000,000-dollar budget (as the law says he must) and still managed a ten-percent tax rebate. He increased state aid to education, established a collegiate scholarship incentive program, brought 390,000 small-firm employees under workmen's compensation, pushed through laws prohibiting discrimination in certain types of housing, and increased wages for state employees. But as long as he pursues a political strategy that removes him from the national arena, in which national issues are resolved, he undermines his own crisis argument. Rockefeller has, after all, taken a position on principle and has sounded an alarm.

"We are faced with the greatest challenge. . . . The Communists are ruthless, purposeful, and have a sense of history—they believe they'll get where they want to go if it takes one year or a hundred. . . . I think it is essential that we offer an alternative system in which free people who believe in the values of freedom can find opportunity and security. . . . Thus my basic interest, my ultimate interest, is the establishment of a political framework, a new form of association of free people in their common interest. . . . The American people have to realize that this is our destiny. . . ."

Rockefeller has been likened by his supporters to a de Gaulle or a Churchill, waiting out a call to emergency service.

But in America, home of the two-party system, we have not produced a President since Washington (nominees, yes) who has not first called himself.

Personal

I almost became a specialist in studies of Nelson Rockefeller. In 1959, I wrote about him for *Cosmopolitan*. Then *Esquire* published the above and, in 1962, *Good Housekeeping* assigned me to try again.

This last time was early November at the end of Rocky's campaign for re-election as Governor of New York. I called Robert McManus, the Governor's press secretary, and was invited to tag along until Election Day. I thought this would be an interesting preliminary, to be followed by the routine of interviews and additional research after his foregone triumph. So, I spent three days in Rockefeller's caravan from morning to midnight as he worked supermarkets, schools, and women's clubs in the five boroughs.

I sat through one cold afternoon on the open top of a gold-painted double-decker bus from which Rockefeller spoke to pedestrians down below, on the sidewalks of New York. My teeth were chattering and my seatmate, columnist Murray Kempton, had a runny nose. Rocky twice asked us how we were bearing up, always with a laugh, but I think he thought we were members of his staff. Later on, at 96th Street and Broadway, Murray and I got off for a cup of coffee and let the bus go on uptown without us.

However, next day, which was the day before election, I rejoined the campaign somewhere in the Bronx. Despite rain and cold, Rocky splashed from hand to hand among crowds at a shopping center, a bus terminal, and, at last, a restaurant, the name of which I have forgotten. It was one of those places that serve free cottage cheese and little roasted red applies on a lazy Susan while you are studying the menu. Every seat had been filled by Republican women who were to have lunch and hear a few kind words from the Governor. Thus, the gentlemen of the press could retire to the bar until the campaign moved on. I bought myself a martini and stood drinking alone until Bob McManus, the press secretary, tapped me on the arm and suggested we sit in a corner booth.

Not without regret, McManus told me that the Governor refused to co-operate with me. The story in *Esquire*, he said, had been "unfriendly," so there would be no interview for *Good Housekeeping*. When I asked him to explain, McManus said that I knew very well that Nelson Rockefeller had never said what I said he said about the politician anxious for a judgeship: "*Never met a more sensitive man,*" *Rockefeller said, sympa-*

thetically. "He bleeds to make you understand him, then when the blood is all over the floor and you're slipping in it, he gets through talking and you still don't know what he wants."

I offered to show McManus my verbatim notes, but McManus said Rockefeller wouldn't believe my notes. He said he *knew* Rockefeller didn't talk that way. I protested that no one could make up a quote like that and, besides, why do it? Weren't Rockefeller's reactions to James Mitchell's broken leg, "Say, you do have to be careful," and dozens of other remarks in the same half-serious, half-joking spirit? This, indeed, *is* Rockefeller's spirit, a combination of arrogance, courage, fatalism, Dartmouth, and gregariousness that one billion dollars had welded into a potential Presidential candidate. McManus and I exchanged some angry words and then I left the restaurant.

I went to an outdoor telephone booth and called Ray Robinson, the editor with whom I had been working at *Good Housekeeping*. I told him what what happened, calling his attention to the fact that Rockefeller and McManus had waited until the day before the election to announce their decision. They could be sure that any objection I might raise would not affect the Governor's charisma.

Robinson told me then that he had been calling me all morning to cancel the assignment. He had been so instructed by the editor-in-chief, Wade Nichols, who said he was acting on orders from Richard Berlin, chairman of the board of the Hearst Corporation. Berlin, Robinson said, had told Nichols that Rockefeller did not want me around him. I asked where Berlin got such an idea, but Robinson could not answer that. A few days later, *Good Housekeeping* sent me 200 dollars for my trouble and that was the end of it. I had lost my chance to become a Rockefeller specialist.

I won't speculate on who told Berlin that Rockefeller did not want me around him, although I doubt that it was McManus, who is a good soul. One of my hobbies is collecting newspaper clippings of speeches that Nelson Rockefeller has made since November, 1962, to various publishers and journalists, about freedom of the press.

Blaze Starr
Blaze
Starr
in
Nighttown

Blaze Starr is a quixotic barroom-burlesque house stripper, age twenty-nine or so, who has very large, very round breasts. She is not tall, but she has a head of bushy red hair that somehow makes her seem statuesque. Her face, sandwiched between the hair and the bosom, is sometimes missing. But she has fine, heart-of-gold dark eyes and angry cheekbones, which are inherited, she says, from long-ago Indians who mixed with her mountain kin in southern West Virginia. "I'm part Indian," Blaze drawls, "so I tell myself that's why I'm dangerous on a few drinks. I want to go cut up my ex-husbands." Her other feature is a well-made, good-humored mouth. When neither puckered nor pouted for effect, it is full of love and obscenities. She has some scars: the left breast has a pale white crescent above and a darker slash just below it and the left upper arm has a long, ugly gash on the underside. Blaze earned these in Baltimore two years ago after she discovered a thief with steely blue eyes and a long knife lurking in her bedroom at three in the morning. She tried to reason with him, but he refused to leave without a bagful of jewels that Governor Earl Kemp Long of Louisiana had given her before he died.

"Well, let's fight for them!" Blaze said to the thief, and grabbed the pistol under her pillow. The thief lunged as Blaze pulled the trigger. Nothing happened for a moment. The pistol had long since rusted and would not fire. "So I fought him," Blaze says. "I kicked him between the legs. I grabbed him by the throat. I almost had him, but he cut me up, knocked me out, and stole the jewels."

When she performs, Blaze covers her scars with make-up. She is right proud of them, but she has concluded that they do not enhance her self-appointed rank as "Undisputed Queen of Burlesque" and "Nation's No. 1 Exotic Star." Unless you know how she got them.

"I'm not gorgeous," Blaze says, "but I got a little of everything." Thus endowed, she may be working tonight east of the Mississippi in any one of a dozen strip cities. "I play all the best clubs wherever I go," she says, "like the Champagne Club in Washington. But no matter how much I make or where I go, I'll never get too big to play Baltimore."

Baltimore!

She must be seen in Baltimore, the place she calls home, her special and essential city. Eleven years ago, she began there at the Two O'Clock Club on East Baltimore Street. She not only went on to the nation's capital, but also to the Midwest burlesque circuit, to Bourbon Street, and off-Broadway. She even made a movie called *Blaze Starr Goes Nudist*, in which she appears stark naked, and which recently played off-Delancey Street in New York until a neighborhood vigilance committee compelled the theater owner to change his nudie policy and return to Western flicks and monster shows.

In Baltimore, Blaze lives after the fashion that has inspired her work. She owns the holy grail—a new house in a swell suburb. A while ago, she even canceled a long-delayed holiday in order to play a lucrative date in Tampa because, as she explains, "It hurts to go on vacation when there's money you can grab. . . . I like that loot. . . . You can't pay for that house if you don't work, my dear."

Since 1953, Blaze has often played Baltimore, but not for the bread alone. She enjoys real status in her adopted home town. She is a civic asset, like Johns Hopkins University and the memory of H.L. Mencken. "When I was involved with Governor Long," she says, "I had my picture in *Life* magazine. I don't care what I had to do to get into *Life*, I just got there." The photo showed Blaze dressed in a sheath of white gauze, gamboling at Earl Long's "little ole pea patch," a farm in Winnfield, Louisi-

ana. Baltimoreans still tell strangers about that picture. And
they love it when she rides in their parades and snips blue rib-
bons. During Preakness Week, they like to see her swaying on
a swing in a Baltimore hotel ballroom wearing a cape, two
daisies, a *cache-sexe* and that's all. "I don't get paid for it, but
I get lots of space," says Blaze, who belongs to the just-spell-
my-name-right school of publicity seekers. Best of all for Baltimore, local paranoia can be soothed by her. The city is bigger
than Houston and only slightly smaller than Detroit. Its port is
second only to New York in handling foreign tonnage. It has a
number of decent restaurants. But it has no image. It is that
congested area through which New Yorkers used to drive to get
to Washington and can now avoid by staying on the Maryland
expressway. "What the hell else we got in this town," asks any
philosophical Baltimore cab driver, "besides Blaze Starr?"

Not long ago, Blaze spent a month of days enjoying her house
and appearing three times a night at her old stand, the Two
O'Clock Club, amid the strip joints, pizza parlors, and pornog-
raphy shops of East Baltimore Street. The Street, as the local
hipsters call it, has an evil reputation, apparently encouraged
if not actually cultivated by Baltimore's convention and tourism
promoters. It is not very much—one block long, eight peeling
places. Policemen patrol it not in pairs, but alone. Pasties and
G-strings, almost no flashing, and nothing fancy are the rule.
It is probably better than sitting alone in a hotel room watching
Donna Reed on TV.

During her recent run, Blaze had only minor-league competition on the Street. The Villanova Show Bar featured Kim Chee,
Bubbles Darnell, and Pat Craze. Someone called Toni Varges
topped the bill at the Clover Burlesque Theater. Lloyd's Bookstore had nothing sexier than *Fanny Hill* for sale. If there was
any action, it had to be at the Two O'Clock Club.

The club is one flight down, and consists of two narrow rooms.
The first is small, with a cloakroom run by a gray-haired lady
plus an "overflow" bar tended by a wiry young man in shirt-
sleeves. The TV over the bar is on all night, and the music of
its commercials sours *Night Train* and *Love for Sale,* played in
the second room by a four-piece combo. The second room, where
the show goes on from nine-thirty P.M. to two A.M. nightly, is

a long chamber with a horseshoe bar seating and standing about a hundred fifty customers. Perhaps another sixty or seventy can sit up on the banquette that runs along the side walls. Within the bar area, a runway shaped like a flat propeller reaches out from a tiny, curtained stage. Four plain-looking lady bartenders work the bar with their backs to the strippers. The musicians—piano, drum, trumpet, and saxophone, all Negroes—are hidden behind a curtain in the rear beside the door to the dressing room. The smell of the sweat of a generation of strippers pervades the atmosphere.

One wintry night, before any of the customers had arrived, Sol Goodman, owner and manager of the club, a balding, pudgy man with fast eyes and beefy hands, was in the first room trying to fix a broken spring in the cash register. He had founded the Club twenty-eight years ago and knew the secret—brighter lights: Blue spots and other impediments to clear vision may hide dirt on walls and improve the mood, but people pay all that money ($1.55 for mixed drinks) to see what they have come to see. Sol probably knows many other secrets, but he is not an informative man.

"Before I started in the strips," he said, "I used to have the finest acts in the country. Jackie Miles, see, and Jan Murray. Roberta Jonay, she was a dancer, Eleanor Roosevelt's protégée, she was here. I remember she wore a peacock gown and Mrs. Roosevelt came for opening night. Sat right in there."

Sol walked into the big room. The musicians were setting up, an hour before show time.

"I never have to go looking for girls," Sol said. "They come in off the street, like Blaze in '53. She introduced herself to me. She had all the physical assets. I had a girl fix her up with a wardrobe, see, and she was a hit right off the bat. I'm her personal manager. I manage all these girls—we got seven on tonight with Blaze. I sent Blaze to Philly, see, played her in the burlesque theaters. Pretty soon, some of the boys in New Orleans wanted her. She stood in New Orleans a long time. Everyone wanted to see what Earl Long saw, see?"

The colored wardrobe mistress, gray-haired and long-suffering, came out of the dressing room going somewhere and Sol sent her back for Blaze. Then he bought me a drink and returned to work on the cash register. The bar lady leaned over the bar just like a man and poured herself a shot of whiskey.

"Well, yes," she said, "business is good when Blaze is in town. She gets in about eight o'clock with her hair up and a wig on. Takes her hair down, gets in her costume and goes on after all the other girls, the walk-around strippers, you know, about ten-twenty. Her act lasts fifteen or twenty minutes, depending, you know, on the crowd. Then she goes back, gets dressed into something low-cut—but modest, understand?—and mills around with the customers. She doesn't *mix* exactly, she doesn't need that kind of money. She just goes around shaking hands and taking a drink once in a while. Then she goes back, gets undressed, gets dressed, and does her act again about eleven-thirty, maybe eleven-forty-five. Then she goes out, gets re-dressed, and mills around again until it's time to undress and get dressed for the one-forty show. She closes the place at two and gets dressed again and that's it. . . . Here's to life!"

The bar lady slugged the whiskey and growled. "Ha, ha," she said.

On the far side of the bar, two girls who turned out to be strippers belted one straight drink apiece and moved on to the dressing room.

Blaze Starr, the Queen, under a red bouffant wig, no make-up, and street clothes, joined me at the bar. Without make-up, she looks younger than she seems onstage. She was not drinking. She said she had not been feeling too well and was laying off. Besides, she said, three drinks knocked her out. A fellow she knew had infectious hepatitis and she wondered if she was coming down with it. "I'm so tired," she said. On second thought, she decided maybe one drink would make her feel better. Hoping to cheer her up, I said I had seen her movie, *Blaze Starr Goes Nudist*. "I'm glad I made that movie," she said. "It was just awful. Made me look old. I'm really only twenty-nine and I've got a police card to prove it. But I am glad I made that movie. I got five thousand dollars for it. A theater in Kansas City paid me a thousand dollars to stand in the lobby and advertise it. And bad, sick as it was, the boobie men all come to see it and it plays and plays. Now I'm going to sell my house and make one of those art movies and I'm going to own that can of film. That's where the money is—when you own a piece of the action. I'm going to sell my house even though I just got it built. I started it three years ago and put in a twenty-by-forty-foot swimming pool. It's got a flat roof—my own design—one story on one acre in the best section of Baltimore. It looks like a bank. Now I'm going to sell it and make the movie. I'll get older, but I'll still look good in the movie. And it will have some real entertainment in it besides me just bouncing the boobs all the time. It's like anything a person does—you accomplish something and then you want to go on to something else."

Blaze slid off the stool and we walked back toward the dressing room. She had recently opened and closed in an off-Broadway production called *Burlesque on Parade*. The reviews were not terrible, but the timing was—the show arrived in New York during the mourning period for President Kennedy. Blaze was hoping to get the show rewritten and refinanced in time for the World's Fair. She was certain that more than the timing had been wrong with it. "Our show was too slow," she said. "The girls didn't strip fast enough. In burlesque today, people don't want to see the slow tease anymore. It doesn't mean a thing. They want to see bodies and lots of them."

At the dressing-room door, Blaze met Leon Owens, the saxophone man. He was tall and trim and wore a thick black moustache. He carried a tattered musical score. His trumpet player had turned up with sore lips and Blaze's number needed an adjustment. Blaze nodded at the music. On one margin, someone had penciled instructions for the drummer—*Finale: Hit everything in sight.* Just then, two more strippers came by in street clothes. One was Debbie Starr and the other, Faye Harlow. Debbie was thin and shy, Faye was husky and all brass. They were Blaze's younger sisters. Sol Goodman had started both of them in the business. Debbie hurried into the dressing room, but Faye paused, looked at the musical score, and cracked: "I don't know what you're showing her them sheets for. She can't read music anyhow." Blaze smiled patiently. Faye blinked and went on through the door.

"Survive, survive," Leon said and returned to his horn.

Blaze informed me that Leon had studied in Paris and wanted to be a dress designer. "Colored people don't have a chance in

this world," she said. She started talking about money again.
She said she preferred splitting profits to collecting fees. At the
Two O'Clock Club, she said, she had earned as much 2,300 dollars in a week. And once, in Toronto, she got 2,500 dollars. Another time, at a night club in D.C., she agreed to take one dollar
per customer and employed a friend with a hand counter to
click off the dollars as they walked through the door. It is a
cutthroat business, Blaze assured me. Recently, she had participated in a TV panel discussion of burlesque and the subject
of money came up there, too. "We were sitting around this
table," Blaze said. "Sherry Britton and four or five other girls
who were much *older* than me. One of them said she was good
for two thousand dollars a week and another said twenty-five
hundred dollars. So, I said my salary was three thousand dollars a week. . . . Well, in a week's time, the income-tax boys
descended. I always pay my taxes, see. I was lying on TV and
that's what I told them. I was shooting off my mouth to save
my face. That's half the battle, making people think you earn,
like, a lot more than you earn." Blaze said she earned 60,000
dollars last year.

There was a sudden rush of customers into the showroom.
Blaze watched them from behind the curtain. They came alone,
in pairs, and in groups. The ones who looked like barbers were in
Baltimore for a barbers' convention. They were neatly dressed.
Most of the non-barbers were neat, too, wearing suits and ties,
or light jackets over clean work shirts, but some of them could
have used a shave. The barbers were noisy, but the loners and
lonely pairs seemed to have serious thoughts. Most men who
sit alone in strip joints apparently suffer from melancholia, aggravated by the prices. This separates them from the boys in
authentic burlesque theaters who go because they find it cheaper
and, as a rule, hotter. Two young men entered with their hysterical wives. Blaze said lots of women love to see her perform;
they come on weekends and "don't miss nothing." But the reactions of men have always been her measure of artistic success.
She will watch their faces for signs of enjoyment and work
harder when they really like her. "Not that I want any of them,"
she explained. "I'm around so many many men that finally, when
I'm doing my act, I'm like emotionless."

Leon Owens tapped his foot four times and the music started. *Boom-boom-pow!* went the drummer. Blaze said she'd see me later and slipped into the dressing room. A gaunt woman named Laura Shane jumped up in front of the curtain and started talking into a hand microphone. "It's show time at the Two O'Clock Club, friends . . ." she cried. Miss Shane turned out to be the mistress of ceremonies and in the next hour introduced seven walk-around strippers. Roxanne Lynn, also known as Miss Perpetual Motion, worked with tassels. Miss Personality Plus, Pat Michel, walked, stripped, and made knowing faces. Shirley Anne, the Queen of the Strobelight and an elderly woman as strippers go, worked in darkness wearing luminescent pasties. Just Plain Carla danced part of the time on her knees. Cheyenne, the Lovely But Not So Shy Cheyenne, did deep knee bends. Debbie Starr walked and stripped nervously; her awkwardness, almost childlike, made her seem more naked than the others. And Faye Harlow took a sponge bath in a swan-shaped fake bathtub. When each girl had finished her act, she dressed and circulated among the customers. Life went on as though nothing was happening. A barmaid discussed her diet with a fat man. She was on vegetables and boiled meat and had lost seven pounds in two weeks. A short, kind-looking man wearing rimless glasses sipped a drink and clutched a heart-shaped box of Fanny Farmer candies for Blaze Starr. He was a deaf-mute. He wrote on a pad that he thought she was wonderful. And a Marilyn Monroe-type professional blonde in a white woolly sweater methodically worked her way around the bar gulling the gullible for an occasional split of watery champagne. She moved in on a wide-eyed nonbarber from Oregon.

"Hello," she said. "I'm Marilyn. What's your name?"

"Roy," he said.

"Where you from, Roy?"

"Portland. I just got here."

Marilyn ordered champagne, Roy ordered whiskey, and the tab was $4.65. Somehow, this destroyed Roy's illusion. He *knew* and Marilyn knew he knew, so she drank up, excused herself and went to the ladies' room. Then she smoked a mentholated cigarette, sitting next to me on the banquette. "I go up to these guys and I could puke," she confided, "but I have to say hello."

She saw herself as an actress, believing that her real self was
not involved in the way she lived. She agreed that she could be
a stripper, but wouldn't try. It was a question of personal pride.
She waved her hand as Faye Harlow's bathing scene ended.
She said *she* knew what she had, and therefore did not have
to show it. Besides, she could make as much in her line as your
average 125 dollar-a-week stripper. She had always hated Baltimore; but her own Philadelphia was gripped by a wave of
law and order. Under the circumstances, the only place she had
to go was the Two O'Clock Club. "If I could choose one man
in this work for a father," she said, "it'd be Sol Goodman."

After Faye Harlow, Laura Shane sang *I Wish I Was in Love
Again,* told three blue jokes, and then introduced Blaze Starr.
The curtain parted revealing a long red couch, three electric
candles on a small table, and a lamppost marked PASSION
STREET. The band played *Pomp and Circumstance,* a customer
shouted, "Go, girl, go!" and Blaze entered. She wore a wrap
and gown that she had made for herself out of real Somali
leopard skins. On her gown, the leopard in front reached around
in back so that his paws grabbed at her buttocks. In one hand,
Blaze held a long cigarette holder trimmed in leopard. She
smiled insouciantly until the applause died down. Then to a
stripper's version of *Night Train,* she dragged her cape once
around the runway. She switched on the electric candles and
again minced up the runway, sans cape and holder, but now
with a rose between her teeth. She bit off a mouthful of petals
and tossed the stem and pistil to the deaf-mute. Then she bared
one bulging breast and used it for a launching pad, flicking rose
petals to a middle-aged barber with glazed eyeballs.

Blaze tripped to the microphone. Looking down at her exposed breast, she said, "What are you doing out there, you
gorgeous thing?" Then she covered herself. "You got to tell them
they're pretty," she said; "it makes them grow." The drummer
whacked a cymbal and the boys laughed. "Strip, already," a
youth shouted. He wore a red and white shirt with a black collar and an arm patch identifying him as a winner of the National
Duck Pin Bowling Congress Triplicate Award. "You l'il evil ole
tomcat," Blaze said and threw her pelvis at him. Then she flung
herself on the couch and quickly stripped down to a transparent

bra and black garter pants. She produced a powder puff and asked, rhetorically, "Who's going to powder my butt?"

To the tune of *That's My Desire*, a volunteer leaned over the bar and did it. Another was allowed to dust her breasts. And a third received permission to peel off her pants. "You're fogging my glasses," he said. Blaze replied, "Oh, suf-fer." She returned to the microphone and shook out her pants. Powder flew; "That's not dust," she said, "it's r-r-r-rust." On the couch again, Blaze removed her bra, caressed herself, leaned over pendulously, and shouted *"Lunchtime!"* Then she lay flat, undulating, and pushed a secret button so that chemical smoke began to rise between her legs and shreds of red cloth stood on end rippling like fire. After this climax, she dressed in a frilly peignoir. Her line, "We must keep covered and be a lady almost all the time," cued the music for her exit tease. She stooped, gnawed at the electric candles, and simulated the act of blowing them out. The drummer hit everything in sight. The audience howled for more, but Blaze let them suffer.

Blaze did not return to the showroom until Miss Perpetual Motion was on the runway twirling her tassels. Dressed in black lace, Blaze greeted the deaf-mute and thanked him for the candy. He read her lips and nodded excitedly. Then Blaze circulated. She shook hands with the bowling champion, but refused a free drink. "How you doing, Blaze?" he asked. "Survivin'," she said. The champion stared at Miss Perpetual Motion whose left and right tassels were spinning clockwise and counterclockwise, respectively. "I can do tassels real good," Blaze said, "even throw them over my shoulder." The two drinking strippers were drinking, surrounded by barbers. Blaze's sister, Debbie Starr, sat at the bar alone between two loners. She nursed a light whiskey. Blaze had encouraged her to quit her job at a White Tower restaurant in Baltimore and try working on The Street. She lacked Blaze's commitment. "I'm a little nervous at the start of the evening," she said. "Sometimes, I really feel faint up there—and if my boyfriend ever came in, I think I'd walk off the stage."

Stretching on until two A.M., it was an average evening for everyone. The two hard-drinking strippers survived, although smashed. Sol Goodman survived—he had fixed the spring on the

cash register; and there were no fights and no complaints. Even
Marilyn-the-Blonde survived, more or less. About one-thirty,
she had moved in on a heavyset, white-on-white businessman.
For the first time all night, she switched to straight whiskey.
The businessman meant well. He squeezed her hand and she
seemed apprehensive.

"You're a good-looking girl," he said.

"So?"

"So, I've been on the bottom myself, honey—I know how it is."

Marilyn pulled her hand away as though he had burned it.

"This isn't the bottom!" she said.

"It's close, honey."

Marilyn snatched up her purse and her cigarettes and slid
off the stool. "Why don't you shut up!" she said.

Above all, Blaze Starr survived. In the overflow bar, she refused a nightcap with Don Somebody, a bespectacled enthu-
siast who would be driving her home. Blaze's former husband,
who ran a competing strip joint on The Street and sold used
cars on the side, had been her customary escort, but they were
divorced in 1962 after eight stormy years of marriage. So she
needed someone like good old Don. She told him about her
suspected hepatitis and that now her stomach was upset.

"Aw, nuts," she said, "I work too hard. Let's have one for the
road."

The next afternoon, I called Blaze and she invited me to her
house. She was right: From the outside, especially in the snow,
the place looked like a bank. It was a buff-colored brick cube
set back on a narrow lot on Queen Anne Road in the sub-
urban section called Villa Nova. Blaze came to the door in a
red sweater, black lounging slacks, and gold shoes. Two loud
white toy poodles accompanied her. Blaze said that she sometimes dyed their hair—one pink and one blue. There were no
servants. Blaze lived alone. Right off, she said that everything
in the house was her idea. "I love beautiful things," she said and
showed me around. Her living room was a vast expanse of green-
figured carpet. She had three enormous round chairs and a long
L-shaped sofa, but they were mere islands in the sea. She also
had a small round fountain with a statue in the middle surrounded by tufts of artificial grass. This dominated the center

of the room. She had followed the Oriental fashion in selecting her phonograph cabinet and prints. An exotic tree with artificial pink flowers grew up one wall. A cross-legged Buddha, smiling enigmatically but with love, sat on an oval cocktail table. And a gold chandelier in modern design dangled from the ceiling. Blaze's bedrooms were more modest. In one, she kept her collection of dolls, not the fluffy, sophisticated kind, but the real children's dolls that cry and wet and close their eyes when you put them to bed. Her TV room had a color receiver, some books (*The Prophet*, by Kahlil Gibran, *Tallulah*, and *Word Power Made Easy—The Complete Three-Way Vocabulary Builder*), and a collage that combined a Gordon's gin bottle, artificial roses, and a WANTED poster for Blaze Starr who was "carrying two 38's . . . approach with caution." In the bathroom, Blaze's pride, there was a huge sunken tub shaped like a coffin enclosed in an arbor of real grapevines and artificial grapes. "Don't get me wrong," Blaze said here. "I love stripping. It's been good to me. I know my limits, eighth-grade education and all. But I'd be an interior decorator if I could make the same money."

We returned to the living room. Blaze stretched out on the sofa and took the rest of the afternoon to tell what had happened to her.

She was born and christened Belle Fleming once upon a time in the blue-green, puritan Appalachians, the same year Dr. Carl Weiss, Jr., assassinated Huey Long. "Wilsondale, West Virginia, is my home town," she said, "but it was really Dogpatch. The closest neighbor was three miles away and everybody was poor. My greatest fear was going to the poorhouse." She was one of eleven brothers and sisters, ten of whom are living. Her father was a brakeman on the Norfolk and Western. "Even on the railroad," Blaze said, "man don't make enough to feed ten kids. We lived in two rooms. Mother and father slept in the kitchen and the kids in four or five big double beds in the other room. You can say I went to the eighth grade. There was no high school we could get to. Christ, it was two miles on foot to the highway. It was forty miles to Logan. We never saw a movie. No regular newspaper. All we had was a radio. I used to wonder what was over them hills." Blaze was full grown at fourteen. Her mother told her how babies were born, loaned her a few dollars, and let her leave home. She worked about three years as a carhop in Logan. Then she rode a bus to Washington and got a job at the Mayflower doughnut shop.

One day, the country girl was working at the doughnut shop and this man came in and said you're gorgeous and why don't you let me put you in show business. "I fell for his con," Blaze said. "This guy owned a trick horse and cowboy act. It was booked into a joint called the Quonset Hut in Washington. I was willing to go along because I'd always played the guitar and sang hillbilly. The guy took me shopping and got me a cowboy suit and all the time he was trying to get my pants. Well, the cowboy didn't want me in the act. So, says this guy, why don't you strip? And I said, what's strip? He took me to see a stripper. I got more than she's got, I said to myself. Then he started showing me pictures of Gypsy Rose Lee and some of the others and I had to admit I looked better than they did. He said, long as I had the cowboy suit, I'd be the first girl to strip out of a cowboy suit. He changed my name to Blaze Starr. I was scared! The idea of taking off my clothes and letting people look at my body was awful, but it paid good. I could get fifty dollars stripping on weekends and I only got thirty dollars working all week at the doughnut shop. Just before the first time I went on, I vomited. Then I stripped. And when I came off I vomited again.

"Well, one day, I went to this guy's house. I'd never had a guy, you know. Sex was to me like filth. So, this guy said he was going to turn me every way but loose. I told him he'd have to kill me and he said he'd do that and bury me under the house. I said, pardon me, I have to go to the bathroom. I turned the water on, climbed out the window, and ran for dear life."

Once exposed, Blaze wanted to strip. She found her way to the Two O'Clock Club and introduced herself to Sol Goodman. "He asked me do I have any scars? Is that all you? Them club owners would practically fight over a young new face." At seventeen, Blaze was underage for the club, so Sol put her into the chorus line at a burlesque house on The Street. The first day, she stripped out of her street clothes. Despite the law, she soon moved downstairs and onto the runway at the club. "I wasn't eighteen yet and I'd made up my mind I was going to be a star,"

Blaze said, "and I didn't care who I hurt to get there. I knocked my brains out. I invested all my money in costumes so I'd look good. Some of the jealous old broads took scissors and cut them up. They were all mad at me. But the break came when this stripper, a star, told Sol Goodman, 'I'll tell you frankly, with her boobies and red hair, I don't want to follow her.' That made *me* the star. I just did a walk-around strip, but you never saw anything like it." She signed a three-year personal-management contract with Sol Goodman. When it expired, they continued on good faith. "Sol's been good to me," Blaze said. "I'd never do anything bad to him." She developed an animal act, first with a leopard and then with a black panther. She trained both to strip her. But one day in New York, the panther bit her face, hand, and leg and she had to give up the act. Her success remained limited. She traveled back and forth in a world bounded by 52nd Street in the North and Bourbon Street in the South.

On a night in February, 1959, she met Earl Long, who was serving his third and most hectic term as Governor of Louisiana. Along with members of his entourage, Long had seen her performance at the Sho-Bar in New Orleans. He was in an amiable mood between wild scuffles that threatened the Long dynasty and all its work. "Earl said, 'Bring us over some of them girls,'" Blaze recalled. "He picked me. He tried to give me a tip and I wouldn't take it. I said it was an honor to sit at the Governor's table. I knew I was after him as soon as I met him, but if you want to win a Governor, you have to be ladylike. He was a good ole man. Mentally ill, he was not. He gave me diamonds and furs. In the spring, his wife got members of the family to say he was a mental case. She put him in the nut house. But soon as they got him in, he talked his way out. He filed for a legal separation from his wife and, for a year, we had an apartment on Esplanade right off Bourbon Street. It sure was nice for me. I got all kinds of publicity and offers of three thousand dollars and three thousand five hundred dollars a week I couldn't take because he wouldn't let me leave."

Blaze's eyes lit up as she reminisced. She had loved Earl Long. She used to go on trips with him, handing out smoked hams and food baskets to back-bayou poor folks. Long's enemies were scandalized, but Blaze blunted their needles with such public declarations as "I think that he is one of the finest men alive." As a rule, Uncle Earl kept her out of sight at political rallies because she stole the show. But when Senator John F. Kennedy came to town with his wife, both were Long's guests at the Sho-Bar. "I was meeting Senators all the time," Blaze said, "and Jack Kennedy was just another Senator. Little did I know what he had upstairs, in his mind." The Governor assured Blaze that Kennedy would be the next President. He himself had decided to run for Congress. Therefore, Blaze discreetly disappeared from New Orleans in the summer of 1960, a month before Uncle Earl swept to victory over Representative Herbert B. McSween in the Democratic primary runoff. He died ten days later: Back in Baltimore, Blaze knew something was wrong. Uncle Earl had always called her at midnight.

"Those were my golden days," Blaze said. She went to the funeral with Debbie Star, José Martinez, manager of the Sho-Bar, and Polly Kavanaugh, another stripper. (In its reportage on the Governor's last rites, the New Orleans *Times-Picayune* said, "An unexpected visitor was Blaze Starr, showgirl friend of Long." In *The Earl of Louisiana*, A. J. Liebling corrected the impression created by this report: "I expect Long would have expected her . . . she had been on his side when a lot of the political mourners weren't.") Blaze returned to the Two O'Clock Club four nights after the funeral. She was a celebrity now and Baltimoreans jammed the place. During the first show, just at the point where she shakes the rust out of her black pants, a woman shouted from the banquette: "Hey, Blaze! How did old Earl look laid out in his casket?" The music stopped. "Shame on you," Blaze said and finished her act. She returned to the dressing room, but Debbie Starr and Faye Harlow found the woman, dragged her from the banquette, and gave her a beating. "Down here in Baltimore," Blaze said, "I'm not lying, they call us the Dalton Sisters. You know, we thought this woman would sue—and two weeks later, she did come in demanding to see me. I was waiting for her. I was going to, like, bust her in the mouth. But do you know, she apologized and honestly cried. She was really touching."

The afternoon was gone. Blaze said it was time for work and

she had to stop at a florist's for fresh roses. She called a cab and we waited for it at the end of her long driveway. We might have driven one of her cars, she said, but her Jaguar was in a repair shop and she had loaned her white Cadillac to a friend. She wondered where the hell the friend was—he had promised to return the car days ago. Then she heaved a terrible sigh. She said she had fallen in love again, this time with a man closer to her own age. "Hard as I've worked," she swore, "I'd quit stripping for him." The romance had faltered. Blaze was sure his friends were talking against her because she was a stripper. "They think there's something wrong with it, I guess," she said. "But that's the way it is in my business. You get used, abused, reused, and de-used. You hate to get used, but it always winds up that way. Sometimes I wonder if I'm a born loser."

Personal

A few years ago, I met a stripper in St. Louis who called herself Tinker Bell. She, too, was a philosopher, a social critic, and a walking advertisement for Norman O. Brown or Georg Groddeck. Indeed, Tinker Bell had read *The Book of the It* and agreed with its message. "I love myself," she said. Like Blaze, Tinker Bell enjoyed her work most of all. It gave her a logic for living. "Clothes should only be worn for warmth," she said. "The reason for all the trouble in the world is that people are so inhibited by clothing."

I suggested that perhaps she should become a nudist.

"I've tried that," she said, "at a nudist colony in New Jersey. I was nervous at first, but it was fun. I had a wonderful time."

"You weren't embarrassed?" I asked.

"What's there to be embarrassed about? I feel absolutely no shame. Aren't we God's most wonderful creations?"

"We are."

"So?"

"So, why be a stripper?"

"I love money," she said.

Like Tinker Bell, like Blaze Starr, every stripper I know is an unsinkable idealist. It is as though undressing in public cleans the mind, sharpens the tongue, and stiffens the spine. Strippers are exposed, but protected by the spirit. They look upon the problem of morality as the moralist's problem. When they speak, their lingo is somehow free of cant. They are, I think, more to be contemplated than censored.

As you might have guessed, Blaze Starr did not get her show rewritten and refinanced in time for the World's Fair. She has not sold her house. She has not (as I write) made the movie. And younger, she is not; she must be thirty by now. But, just the other day, I heard that she was back in Baltimore on The Street making the boys suffer, and survivin'—I hope forever.

David Susskind
The
Latest
Tycoon

After spending an appreciable time with David Susskind, the mainspring and half-owner of Talent Associates, Ltd., the independent TV-program packaging and production company which has put together eighteen million dollars-worth of shows in a single season (more than a hundred this year, including the Art Carney show, the DuPont Show of the Month, The Play of the Week, two Sid Caesars, and an Eleanor Roosevelt), it is almost inevitable that one should go back and have another look at F. Scott Fitzgerald's *The Last Tycoon*, which Susskind himself once produced on television. One feels as Susskind goes through his paces that this kind of thing has happened many times.

There are important differences between Fitzgerald's character, Monroe Stahr, and Susskind. Susskind is a TV producer-packager, Stahr a movie maker, which means that the rules of the jungle for each are as different as East Coast and West Coast. Susskind wants to have his *name* mean something in TV production, whereas Stahr never put his name on his movies because he believed a man with the power to give himself a credit line did not need it. And Susskind, though successful at an early age, was not a boy wonder as Stahr was, which accounts for a kind of maturity in Stahr at age thirty-five that Susskind hasn't attained as he approaches forty. Given these differences, the similarities are both more striking and more poignant. Susskind and Stahr are in essentially the same business: producing entertainments. That means they earn their living by organizing writers, actors, directors, sets, lights, cameramen, and various craftsmen, modifying the talents and temperaments of all in the interest of satisfying a large public, and making a profit for the people who put up the money. As a packager of the shows he produces, Susskind also sells basic ideas to sponsors and manages the business side "above the line" after they are sold. Because Susskind-Stahr is very, very good at production, both the creative people and the money people come to respect his judgment, whatever they may think of him as a person. This respect is Susskind-Stahr's power and the accretion of it gradually isolates our hero from almost all of life except business life. Its satisfactions are not material, because the hero has no time to enjoy much of anything in the usual sense of enjoyment. He is forever in meetings, on the phone, or at rehearsals, cajoling, arguing, freezing, charming. He is being cantankerous, gay, brilliant, cruel, aggressive, opportunistic, calculating—until, to the outsider, at least, the self is lost. He seems determined to be alone and unreachable. In *The Last Tycoon,* Fitzgerald gives an opinion on what the final pleasure of such a way of life may be. He suggests that Stahr had a "definite urge toward total exhaustion. . . . Fatigue was a drug as well as a poison and Stahr apparently derived some rare almost physical pleasure from working lightheaded with weariness."

Susskind, at age thirty-nine, is a well-built, average-sized man with no fat on him. His hair is gray-brown, short and curly. The eyes are squeezed between heavy lids which tend toward puffiness. He has a bulldog upper lip and a wide mouth. His voice is deep and brisk. He uses it a great deal more than most people because his job is not to listen, but to tell. He's not flashy: the suits are modest; the only ring he wears is his Harvard ruby (Class of '42); and except for the expected Lefcourt shoes, his money is not seen on his person. He pays himself 150,000 dollars plus expenses a year, owns a Brougham Cadillac, and may net personally more than a million dollars this year through a capital gains sale of a major share of Talent Associates, Ltd. stock to Paramount. His working control over his own organization will be undisturbed, at least for now. Susskind's office is a corner room on a middle floor of the Newsweek Building on Madison Avenue; the view is pleasant—St. Patrick's Cathedral, other skyscrapers, etcetera—but he only looks out to check the weather. He has furnished the place without much concern for taste: antique French table for a desk, modern couch and chairs, second-rate paintings of Paris on the walls. This is not important, however, for he is not hired by DuPont, General Motors, Esso, Westclox, and the others for his taste in furnishings. Besides, in his eighteen-hour day, he spends most of his time elsewhere.

There is no such thing as a typical day or week in the life of David Susskind. Yet all days are more or less the same. He comes to work at ten, rarely goes home until well after midnight, and stays up until the small hours reading scripts. He tries to save Sunday for his three children, but often he can't because Sunday night he has *Open End,* a panel show for which he is the moderator. From time to time, his wife, Phyllis, joins him on his visits to rehearsal studios. Not long ago, Susskind was seen in the process of getting five shows on the air in one week (after months of planning), including two on the same night: a ninety-minute version of *Oliver Twist* for DuPont, a sixty-minute Art Carney revue for General Motors, a ninety-minute re-make of M-G-M's *The Philadelphia Story* for Westclox and General Mills, a two-hour Play of the Week—Langston Hughes's *Simply Heavenly* (with several sponsors, but running at a loss) —and *Open End* for a local New York sponsor. *Oliver Twist* and Art Carney would overlap on a Friday night on two different networks. To help him accomplish this feat, Susskind had help from his partner, Alfred Levy, and a staff of seventy-eight people, but, as one of them said, "David does everything."

That week for David Susskind was an endless series of incidents out of Fitzgerald. A straight narration of it would be six chapters in a novel. I propose only to dip in here and there to show the tycoon in action.

TIME: *Afternoon.* Susskind, in his office, was just saying, "Look, when you're dealing with sponsors and advertising agencies, you've got to come on—pow! They're like women. They keep shifting ground. After you explain that you got lipstick on your collar kissing your mother, they accuse you of being late for dinner. So you have to handle them. I hate it, but you have to." The phone rang. Susskind took a call from an executive of the advertising agency representing the sponsor of the Art Carney show. The sponsor does not like one of Carney's sketches that satirizes television commercials. Susskind to the barricades: "But goddam it," he said, "that kind of shivering and trembling can't go on. Good God, man! The sketch is funny!" The agency man said it was offensive to the agency as well as the sponsor. Susskind, outraged, said, "Offensive! My God, Sid Caesar has already done it. Steve Allen's done it. Now you say we shouldn't do it. For God's sake, we're creating so many sacred cows you can't satirize anything but Red Riding Hood." The agency man protested. Susskind hurt, said: "You're being arbitrary and capricious. What are we—aboriginals [sic]? I think for grown men to be debating on that final script is ridiculous. We've got to stand up in the interest of humor, satire, and *truth!*" The agency man said the sponsor was worried about libel. Susskind, *à la* Bogart, said, "I don't care—you might get one letter from Charlie Revson and I say to hell with him." The agency man, weakening, said maybe the sketch was in bad taste. Ominously, Susskind said, "Friend, is this the climate of opinion? If you're called before a Congressional Committee, will you be able to say you never laid the cold, clammy hand of censorship on me? I think any industry that can't afford to exercise a sense of humor about itself is sick. Sick. Sick." The agency man asked if Susskind thought there was any maliciousness in the script. Susskind in the home stretch said, "None. None. None. What's more, this Carney show is better than the first Carney show and you know what great reviews that got!" The agency man attacked again, reminding Susskind that the Arbitron rating service reported that Carney's last show, *Our Town,* did not get a high rating. Susskind, outraged again, said, "What do I care about ratings! Besides, we're building. I've fiercely concentrated on making this a great show. I think you're going to be applauded in *Variety* and the New York *Times.* I'm inclined to think that you fellows would be happier sponsoring the Shirley Temple Show." The agency man capitulated, finally approving the sketch. Susskind, soothingly, said, "My whole instinct is for peace. Let me congratulate you in advance. I know it's going to be a great show!"

Susskind hung up the phone. He buzzed his secretary to call

a man in Hollywood. From a pile of scripts on his desk, he selected a movie treatment of *Raisin in the Sun* which he would be producing this summer for Columbia Pictures. "I haven't got any hobbies," he said. "Almost never take a vacation. When I've got nothing else to do, I read scripts. I'm a scan reader. The sheer number of things to read is overwhelming. I have just one talent. Can't remember names, but I have a photographic memory. When I read, even scanning, I can remember lines and page numbers exactly. It frightens writers when I tell them to change a line on a certain page—" The Hollywood call came through. "Hello, Paul," Susskind said. "We have the script of *Raisin in the Sun. A Raisin in the Sun. Sun*, Paul. Paul—you spent three hundred thousand dollars for it, you should at least remember the name of it. Yes, I'm sending it to you." Susskind sent for his secretary and for his assistant, Mike Abbott. He handed the script to Abbott. "Send this to Paul," he said. "You got to let them know what to think out in Hollywood before they start reading. So put a note on the cover and say Susskind thinks this is a pretty good first draft." Abbott departed and Susskind turned to the secretary. He began dictating a letter to an agent in Cuba who was to get Castro to agree to a taped interview with Susskind for *Open End*. "I am not," he said, dictating, "in the vanguard of those who look upon what has happened in Cuba as a foul plot poised at the throat of America. . . ."

TIME: *Later the same afternoon*. Susskind put on his camel's hair coat and ran down the hall, heading for the *Oliver Twist* rehearsal hall on Second Avenue. In the elevator, he stood next to the operator. "How did you like the show?" Susskind asked. "What show?" said the operator. "*Miracle on 34th Street*." "That was last week." "Well, how'd you like it?" "The kids like it fine."

Susskind flagged a cab. "Ain't you David Susskind?" asked the driver. "Yeah." "I thought I recognized you. I never miss *Open End*. I mean, some of it's way over my head, but I never miss it."

At the rehearsal hall, Susskind found a run-through underway. The floor was marked with white tape to indicate the location of sets, and chairs were strategically placed to represent scenery. Using his body and hands to simulate the position of the camera, the director, Dan Petrie, was working a scene with

Robert Morley. Susskind took up a position just behind Petrie and followed the action from scene to scene. Now and again, he scratched a note on the back of an envelope. Until the show went on the air, Susskind would attend each rehearsal, functioning as drama critic, technical adviser, and morale booster. In contrast to his relations with most advertising people, he assumed a deferential air when dealing with directors and actors. After the run-through, he went to a private office on the floor below the rehearsal hall with Petrie and a script editor. "What did you think, father?" asked Petrie. Susskind smiled. "They don't make them like Dickens any more. Jack O'Brian won't like it, but it's great." O'Brian is a Hearst TV critic who has, on occasion, referred to Susskind as a "cultural carbon copy" and a "congenital pest," but who gives him a fair share of favorable reviews. "Well, I know we have some changes to make," Petrie said. At this point, Susskind pulled the envelope from his pocket. He looked at it doubtfully. He had half-a-dozen major suggestions to make; each one would impose a small mark of his personality on the final form of the play. In general, the values he would stress were simplicity and suspense, a heightening of the drama, and clarification of the plot—sometimes at the expense of meaning. When, for example, the script was being prepared, Susskind saw to it that the character of Fagin was sufficiently softened so that a charge of anti-Semitism could not be leveled at the program, but the effect was to make Fagin's violent end seem unjust. Now, with Petrie, he began: "I kinda thought there was something wrong in the plot—the business about Oliver's mother's locket. It doesn't come off." Petrie agreed that the business was confusing. "So, let's get the writer in," Susskind said. "Maybe we can drop the whole incident. This is a classic, but it ain't the Bible."

After an hour, Susskind left the director and script editor to work out his changes. He was late as it was for the run-through of the Art Carney show at another hall uptown. In the cab, Susskind was thinking about the phone conversation with the agency man in Detroit. "You'll see that the sketch is funny," he said. "You know, once a dairy sponsor complained that one of my shows wasn't selling any of their ice cream. I told them, maybe your ice cream is lousy. God, sponsors! Our watchmaker demanded that every actor in *Miracle on 34th Street* wear a watch, even Santa Claus. So they passed out watches—without works, mind you—and the actors had to wear them."

Susskind walked through the Carney-show rehearsal beside the director, Burt Shevelove. With Betty Garrett and Gloria Vanderbilt, Carney struggled in and out of the sketches. The supporting cast repeatedly fluffed lines. When it was over, no one was laughing.

Susskind saw that there was no sense trying to be cheerful. He put a hand on Shevelove's shoulder and drew him aside. "What's the matter with everybody—the supporting cast. Jesus!"

Shevelove threw his hands up: "You got to remember, David, that these are scale actors and when the guy comes in who can give them work maybe thirty weeks a year, it's only natural they tense up a little."

Susskind walked over to Carney.

"Do I make you nervous, Art?"

"Naw, you don't make me nervous. I'm always nervous."

Later, Susskind settled down with Shevelove for a critique. They got around to discussing the sketch that the sponsor had criticized.

"The thing that troubles me," Susskind began, "is Gloria Vanderbilt's satire of the commercials is sans laughs and it really has to be funny."

"I think it's funny," said Shevelove.

"How can we make sure it's funny?"

"You've just heard all the yacks, David."

"It's too subtle. Not simple enough."

"Okay, David, I'll change it. Of course, we've got one thing I can't change—Gloria's talent."

"But she could be very funny."

"I'll try to fix it, David."

"I know it's tough, Burt."

"You're the boss, David."

TIME: *Noon, another day.* Susskind was joined at Sardi's East by a representative of his watch sponsor and an account man from the sponsor's agency. Susskind had one drink, a Bloody Mary, while the others braced themselves with Martinis. The discussion centered on watches. To illustrate his faith in the client's product, the agency man had unstrapped his wrist watch, dropped it in a glass of water, and let it soak until the waiter began to get nervous. When he retrieved it, it was still ticking. Without bothering to reassure the waiter, he returned it to his wrist and asked how Susskind was getting on with *The Philadelphia Story*, which was scheduled to go on the air in forty-eight hours. "It'll be fine," Susskind said. "It's pre-sold."

According to Susskind, the contract to produce old M-G-M movies depended upon getting *The Philadelphia Story*. "First it was a movie, then it was a musical, and then it was on TV in the mid-Fifties, but the sponsor had a fetish on *Philadelphia*," Susskind said. He had made a special trip to Hollywood to get the rights to the movie from M-G-M. "Then we got it," he recalled, "and we also got a co-sponsor, who thought it was *too* sexy. We had a big session and cut fifteen lines. I thought we had already seen everything when we put on *Moon and Sixpence*. Sponsor didn't want Gauguin to leave his wife and children—'Couldn't he take them with him to Tahiti? And does he have to die of leprosy? Couldn't he recover?' Well, this sponsor didn't like the phrase 'virgin goddess' in *Philadelphia Story*, and they weren't going to let it go on. Finally, we traded them two hells and a damn and the phrase stayed in the script."

At Sardi's East, the wrist-watch man said he expected big things from *The Philadelphia Story*.

Susskind did not enthuse.

The watch man wanted to know what was the matter.

"Goddam it," said Susskind. "I'd like to do some originals."

The watch man said: "I'm up to my ass in watches. What do you want us to do—*Macbeth*?"

Susskind returned to his office after lunch for a three-hour meeting with a group from an automobile sponsor and their agency to talk further about the Carney show. During the meeting, Susskind and his partner, Alfred Levy, who has a stomach disorder, were reminded that *Our Town* had received only ten per cent of the audience and not thirty-three-and-a-third per cent, as expected. The suggestion was also made, indirectly, that the show could be canceled. At one point, Levy excused himself and, in the men's room, vomited. Later, in Susskind's office after their guests had gone, Levy was feeling better. He is ten years older than Susskind, short and sallow, a former lawyer from Arizona. Susskind's assistant, Mike Abbott, joined them.

"What happened?" Abbott asked.

"What happened—it was rough, that's what happened," said Susskind, bowing his head.

"Now, David," Levy said in his usual quiet voice, "they didn't say they didn't like the Carney show. They just said they didn't like the size of the audience."

"Al, they laid it on the line. If they knew they were only going to get ten per cent, they would have killed *Our Town!* I have a vision of the whole rating system consisting of two men in the basement of a poolroom."

"Oh, *David*," said Abbott, "you won out in the end. You must have charmed them."

"And how about that guy accusing me of being 'show-biz people,' out of touch with real people?" Susskind cried. The phone rang; the secretary announced that a friend was calling. Susskind picked up the receiver and said: "Hello, out there! Are you show-biz people or are you just plain people! I think I'm people. I really think I'm people. . . ."

TIME: *One evening around midnight.* As is his custom after a long day, Susskind arrived at Sardi's on the West Side and ordered a steak. He had been through four rehearsals—*Oliver Twist, The Philadelphia Story,* the Carney show, and *Simply Heavenly.* Besides, he was working ahead on shows scheduled for the next week, next month, and so on. "You know how I feel today?" he asked me. "There's no time to savor the victories. When a show's done, it's done. The only thing that excites me is what comes next." Susskind stayed at Sardi's until after one. Chester Morris stopped by his table, saying: "Why don't you do *Detective Story* on Play of the Week?" Cliff Norton came on then: "David, I just did the Four Star Theater on tape. I did it for money. I have a wife and kids. It's a pity there's no more live television." Susskind accepted the confession, not sure what it meant. Then Frank Loesser and Jo Sullivan took the table next to him. Susskind: "Frank, why don't you let me do *Most Happy*

Fella?" Loesser: "Let's talk. Let's talk." Finally a tall, black-haired girl, smartly dressed, walked by, stopped, and pretended to look at the caricatures on Sardi's wall. Susskind obliged her by staring. "Nice bones," he said, sighing from fatigue. "Nice bones." The girl walked on.

Then, having pushed himself to the limit for this day, Susskind went home to read scripts.

Until Susskind came along, it could be said that the New York television world had not produced a Fitzgeraldian tycoon. No doubt, the nature of television's birth and growth made it difficult to produce one. TV was brought forth out of radio at a cost of millions and immediately became a member of broadcasting's corporate family. It grew at a cost of billions under the pragmatic eyes of account executives and comptrollers who saw TV for what it was likely to become: first and foremost a medium for selling merchandise. Finally, it was governed and run by committees, which, as everyone knows, may produce action but rarely passion. For years, on the business side, there was no deep foothold for a freebooter and the quality of TV industrial life was all the poorer for the lack of a single, sweaty, full-time dynamo who consciously wanted to grow up to be, say, Cecil B. DeMille. Then, in the past few years, the industry changed: the filming of bread-and-butter half-hour Westerns and mysteries was taken over by Hollywood and a demand was created for independent New York producers who could make *live* sixty- and ninety-minute "specials." And there, ready, was Susskind whose personal, burning ambition was to "achieve acceptance of my work so that people will watch my TV show because I produced it—like Cecil B. DeMille could do it."

Susskind was born December 19, 1920, in New York. If he wasn't born with colossal ambitions, perhaps he saw enough going on around him as he grew up which, mixed into a bright mind, fostered such ambitions. His father was an insurance salesman, fairly successful in the Twenties, who covered the New England territory. From the time Susskind was six months old until he left home for college, he lived in Brookline, Massachusetts, "the richest suburb in America." His brother, Murray, who is twenty months younger (and has worked for Talent Associates), and his sister, who is eight years younger, were both born there. The Depression hit Susskind's father hard; he had to start making his calls at 7:30 in the morning and rarely came home before nine at night. Susskind's mother, about whom he has little to tell, was pinned down to the house. They were rather poor, but being middle-class in a wealthy town made Susskind want to excel. He played lightweight football and won a name for himself as a "vicious" tackler. He worked on the school paper, belonged to the debating team, and wrote a weekly column for the Brookline paper. He wanted to be a writer and thought he would surely be one after he copped the William H. Lincoln Gold Medal for Excellence in English. His marks were very nearly straight-A. He wasn't a bookworm because schoolwork came easily. His father, however, saw to it that his horizons were expanded. "My father had a voracious desire for learning," Susskind says. "He used to go to three intellectual nonsectarian discussions every Sunday—morning, afternoon, and evening. From age eleven to seventeen, absolutely every Sunday, he used to take me to hear lectures. At the Ford Hall Forum in Boston, we listened to Harold Laski, Felix Frankfurter, Bertrand Russell, John Maynard Keynes—everybody." Once Susskind's father predicted that David would be invited to speak someday at the Ford Hall Forum. The invitation was extended last year. Today, by any definition, Susskind is no intellectual, but his speech is filled with the language of intellectuals, which perhaps he learned on Sundays in Brookline and Boston. In 1946, when he applied for a job in New York in the Warner Brothers publicity department, the head publicist tried to dissuade him. "You can't do this kind of work unless you're born to it," he said. "I can do anything," said Susskind. The publicist replied: "Can you change the way you talk, with the big words?"

On advice from his father, Susskind spent his first two college years in the Midwest at the University of Wisconsin. When he arrived in Madison, a landlady offered him a room with the assurance that he would be happy because she allowed no Jews in her house. He had grown up without ever experiencing prejudice and, in fact, had little awareness of himself as a Jew. Thereafter, he developed some Jewish sensibilities, but his interest is limited even today. Susskind went steady during his freshman year with Phyllis Briskin, the daughter of a well-to-do New York family, which owned concessions in movie theaters. They were married in August, 1939 (he was eighteen, she was seventeen), lived in a one-room flat in Madison, and were in great demand as chaperons for fraternity parties during their sophomore year. "God knows what erotica took place under my chaperonage," Susskind recalls. Both the Susskind family and the Briskin family helped finance the newlyweds; each father contributed 50 dollars a month.

Having earned a straight-A average at Wisconsin, Susskind was able to transfer in 1940 to Harvard. (After the war when Susskind was a talent agent representing Jerry Lewis, he had to submit to being called "my Harvard agent," by Lewis.) He won a scholarship midway through his junior year and finished well up in the class of '42 even though Harvard had reduced his Wisconsin marks to C's. At this time, Susskind changed his mind about a writing career. He had majored in Government (graduating with honors), planned to get a Master's degree, and wanted to teach. Instead, he went into the Navy for four years. Late in the war, he saw action as a communications officer on an attack transport. His ship carried two thousand Marines and twenty-six landing barges into the invasions of Okinawa and Iwo Jima.

"Everything was so boring in the Navy except for a few brief periods," Susskind says, "that I couldn't see going back to school. Besides we had a new baby and another on the way, so Phyllis and I decided to go to New York." He looked for a writing job, but the best offer was eight dollars a week from *PM*. So he took 60 dollars as a junior press agent for Warner Brothers, writing captions for pictures of Yvonne DeCarlo.

Six months later, he moved over to Universal for twice the salary as a senior press agent. Part of his job entailed escorting movie actresses around the right places in New York so that they would be seen by columnists.

"I hated it," Susskind says. "I was always the *least important* member of an actress' entourage. Her manager was *important,*

her agent was *important*, her lover was *important*. I wasn't. So
I started looking for a job as an agent because what you had
to say then *was* important."

At the reduced salary of 85 dollars a week, Susskind went to
work for an agency representing Judy Holliday, Burl Ives, and
the Andrews Sisters. One of the partners was Al Levy. Susskind
distinguished himself by dreaming up a road-show tour for
Lucille Ball. Then the agency split up and Levy and Susskind
went into business for themselves. From the beginning, they
decided to concentrate on television. They agreed to handle
"creative" people—writers and directors—and to ignore stars
who, as Levy says, "were always ungrateful." For his half share
of the company, Susskind put in 2,000 dollars borrowed from
his father-in-law. They named the company Talent Associates
—to which Susskind added the "Ltd." because he thought it
suggested roots in England. They shared an office and switchboard with Feuer and Martin, who had yet to produce their
first successful Broadway play. They rode buses and ate cheap
lunches while looking for their first client. In 1948, Susskind and
Levy "divined" that the Philco Television Playhouse which had
been on the air for thirty-nine weeks, directed by Fred Coe,
packaged by Music Corporation of America, was in trouble. By
rescuing it, with an idea for dramatizing new books instead of
familiar plays, Susskind and Levy were appointed packagers
by Philco's advertising agency. Suddenly, Talent Associates had
a piece of a 25,000 dollar weekly program and a batch of clients,
including Fred Coe, who had become producer of the Philco
Playhouse, plus many of the directors and writers who contributed to it. Not to be outdone, Music Corporation of America
offered Susskind 20,000 dollars a year, expenses, and a bonus,
and hired him away from Talent Associates the following year.

Susskind lasted three years at MCA as agent (for Martin and
Lewis, Dinah Shore, Kay Kyser, et cetera) and emissary to sponsors. Then he was fired. "I was fired for insubordination," Susskind says. The man who fired him, Sonny Werblen, says, "I have
nothing to say about Mr. Susskind." Bitter as it was, Susskind's
experience at MCA convinced him that "the real burden of a
show is on the producer." He rejoined Al Levy at Talent Associates, Ltd., and began looking around for something to pro-

duce. His opportunity came when Fred Coe decided to take a vacation in the summer of 1953. "The agency said *do* something," Susskind says. "I said I would like to produce the Philco Playhouse. They were desperate, so they gave it to me for five weeks. N. Richard Nash came in with an idea for a play and so did Tad Mosel, who was selling tickets for American Airlines and writing at night. I told them both to go ahead. Mosel wound up doing two of the five plays, and Nash wrote *The Rainmaker,* which went on to be a stage play and a movie. It was a wonderful summer. Today, no sponsor would let you do Mosel's plays about old people. They'd tell you that a play like that wouldn't get a rating. In those days, the sponsor let you alone. You could say to a writer, 'Let's go,' and he'd go."

In the summer of 1954, Susskind produced four more Philco dramas, and the following year the program went off the air, having been defeated in the rating competition by Alfred Hitchcock and General Electric.

Meanwhile, Talent Asociates (having removed itself from the talent-agent business) was packaging, and Susskind was producing the Kaiser Aluminum Hour and two half-hour shows, *Jamie* and *Justice,* all live. Susskind added the Armstrong Circle Theater in 1955; produced a movie for M-G-M (*Edge of the City*) and a Broadway play (*A Very Special Baby*), both of which died at the box office in 1956; and took over the last twenty weeks of the Kraft Theater in early 1957, while keeping all the other shows going at the same time. For Kraft, Susskind produced the memorable two-part version of *All the King's Men* and three one-act plays by Tennessee Williams. With the coming of the 1957-58 season, Talent Associates converted to "specials" and Susskind graduated to tycoon. He became over the next three years one of the few successful producers of live TV drama.

Besides his major network shows, Susskind also developed The Play of the Week on New York's local channel, WNTA-TV —a two-hour taped play repeated daily throughout the week. Working without salary, but with a promise of twenty-five per cent of the profits (if any) in the event that the show was syndicated, Susskind was able to get fine plays (*Waltz of the Toreadors, Tiger at the Gates,* et cetera) and performers for minimum prices. He was able, for example, to hire Judith Anderson for a re-creation of her role in *Medea* for 675 dollars. "You mean," she had said, "I get to kill the children and everything?" The Play of the Week almost failed for lack of sponsor-money, but in the nick of time, after an unprecedented outcry in the New York press, the show was saved. Standard Oil of New Jersey agreed to pay for it, offering a strict policy of noninterference in artistic matters.

With his new freedom provided by the growing power of Talent Associates, Susskind's other activity in the past three years has been incessant, purple criticism of the general level of TV entertainment. In 1957, when he first declared publicly that "TV was going down the drain like dirty water," his press agent, Arthur Cantor, called to tell him he had lost his mind. "They'll kill you!" he shouted. For a while, no one in TV answered Susskind back. *Variety* approvingly tagged him "Peck's Bad Boy" when he said, "Television programming this year [1957-58] has been banal and stupefying—an enervating dosage of entertainment Miltown, *et cetera*."

The attitude toward Susskind within the TV industry stiffened when the headaches of the networks and other independent packagers made front-page news. But Susskind has continued his attack because, he says, "I care about TV, so I'm talking —the programming is lousy, stupid, and cowardly." *Variety* reported, approvingly again, that he had "alienated a large segment of the people in TV." Hubbell Robinson, formerly of CBS, said: "David Susskind has turned out a torrent of regimented nonsense, more notable for rant than reason." Sydney Eiges of NBC suggested that he was a Sammy Glick whose "art of self-promotion [has] obscured the number of mediocre programs he has produced over the years." Susskind denied that he was seeking publicity; rather, he wanted to be *believed*, but he made the mistake of being vulnerable. He condemned the networks for failure to present original, live dramas, while producing only one in three years himself. Backing off this somewhat, he attacked the use of film, but by allying himself with Paramount he inevitably will be expected to make use of film. Indeed, when the Paramount deal is final, his partner, Alfred Levy, will be moving to Hollywood to handle that end of things. Susskind belabored mysteries on TV, but was not above submitting three in 1959 to NBC, which turned them down.

Such inconsistencies, instead of influencing television, detracted from his own achievements, which have been considerable, and made many in TV devoutly wish for his downfall. To Susskind, the controversy is all part of his total involvement in the television business. "I love TV," he says. "I don't care what the finks say. I'm in it forever."

Susskind has a different view of his future. He has had one critical success on Broadway (*Rashomon*) and wants more; he has a contract to produce three movies for Columbia after *Raisin in the Sun;* and his television production next year, at least, should exceed the past season in number, and hopefully, in quality. He has the future planned and taped and, given his own ability to ignore his inconsistencies, rationalized. The end he sees is onward and upward.

Susskind's wife, Phyllis, however, has her fears. She knows him better than anyone and is not sure that it will end that way.

Phyllis Susskind is a dark, trimly attractive woman with a tough mind and caustic spirit. (Fitzgerald could have used her, too.) While Susskind has been becoming a tycoon, she has been an intense participant in New York Democratic politics. She has never been less than outspoken about her beliefs. Once, prior to an *Open End* show, Hume Cronyn asked Peter Lind Hayes the meaning of "iconoclastic." Hayes said: "Iconoclastic is Phyllis Susskind spelled backwards."

The day Susskind had lunch with the wrist-watch man and the afternoon meeting with the automobile sponsor Mrs. Susskind met him for the evening dress rehearsal of *The Philadelphia Story.*

In the control booth, sitting to the left of the director, Fielder Cook, the Susskinds watched the dress rehearsal on the color monitor. Diana Lynn, Gig Young, and Mary Astor were performing in the old, familiar roles.

"It's a wonder," said Mrs. Susskind, "that movies weren't ever any better. They only had to sell the pictures and we have to sell watches."

"Phyllis—" Susskind began.

"David, you never learned that TV hasn't got anything to do with anything except selling goods. Wake up!"

An intense close-up of Diana Lynn, half in shadow, faded from the screen as the first act ended. The director leaped from his chair. "That's it!" he cried. "Beautiful!"

Sotto voce, Mrs. Susskind said, "Bull!"

Susskind protested.

"The directing is muddled," she said, still in the quiet voice.

"You're not here to do any criticizing."

"Oh, I know, but I still say it's muddled," retorted Mrs. Susskind. "I haven't seen any faces on the screen."

"We got lots of faces."

"And why did you spend five thousand dollars for the winding staircase?"

"It looks like Main Line, Philadelphia, that's why."

"You use it so *well*."

"Phyllis, you haven't any official capacity here."

"Maybe I should."

"Yeah—at Goodson and Todman."

"Well, who's got more money," she asked, "Goodson and Todman or you? What have you got? No money, bad shows, no guts, no integrity and Diana Lynn in *Philadelphia Story*. That's what you've got."

"They wanted a name, we got them a name. My conscience doesn't bother me. I fight the battles I have a chance of winning."

Later, at Sardi's, the Susskinds ordered dinner. Over the coffee, Mrs. Susskind laughed for no reason at all. Susskind bowed his head.

"Really, David," she said, "it's going to be a terrible show. You knew it. You didn't have to do it."

"What can you do?" Susskind asked. "If you can't lick 'em, join 'em. Next year I'll do some originals."

"Some strategy."

"Look, I want to do something that's never been done before —function simultaneously in theater, movies, and TV. It can be done. You can really have an effective company. All three are different challenges and I like all three."

"I'm going to Happy Valley."

"In five years, I'll have it made."

"If you keep this up," she said, earnestly, "you won't be around in five years. Who else has five shows in one week—and two of them running opposite each other?"

"Don't you think I hate remaking old movies?"

"David, you have 20-20 hindsight."

"No," said the tycoon, "I have an overpowering urge to express myself."

Personal

When I meet a subject, I always carry in my left hand a ballpoint pen and a 3-by-5-inch looseleaf notebook filled with lined paper. These are my tools, which I carry in the open so that my subject will know from the first moment that (a) I am at work and (b) he is on the record unless he asks me to keep a confidence. If his first words are no more than "Nice day, eh?" I open my notebook and jot it down. I hope that he will become so accustomed to note-taking that he will forget about it. Sometimes, when he remains tense, I write my notes at odd moments, putting down an important statement only after he has gone on to something innocuous. I find that I can remember long discourses for several days, but with rare exceptions, my notes are a simultaneous and verbatim record. I know that I will rely on them for almost every fact and quotation used, so I take pains. So far, Nelson Rockefeller's press secretary, mentioned earlier, and David Susskind are the only two people who have denied a quotation that I attributed to them.

Susskind did not wait a year. He registered his denial *before* the piece came out. I was in Los Angeles at the 1960 Democratic Convention acting as press secretary for the Stevenson Committee. Somehow, Susskind had acquired an advance copy of *Esquire*. He read the piece and then called me from New York to tell me I needed a psychiatrist. He resented the description of his scene with Mrs. Susskind and I told him I hadn't been proud of it myself. I only felt it was necessary. (David and Phyllis Susskind have since divorced.) Moreover, Susskind complained that he had never used the word "fink" as in "*I love TV. I don't care what the finks say. I'm in it forever.*" That was not his language, he said, and symbolized my malevolence. He also attacked the "tone," which I had felt was not without sympathy for him and *"his own achievements, which have been considerable."* The fact is that he is a likeable man seemingly dedicated to his own exhaustion.

Susskind went on for half an hour or so. Then, at last, he said, "Why did you do it to me? Don't you see what it means? You've made it possible for the *finks* to get me!"

Under the circumstances, I wrote down that quotation and later filed it with my Susskind notes.

Frankie, Ricky, Kookie, Dick, et al. The Heroes of Teen-agers

Eighteen million American teen-agers growing older in a world they didn't make—a world overpopulated and underfed, over-organized and yet disorganized, impersonal and self-indulgent, machine-tooled, purposeless, yet filled with unrealized possibility and in danger of coming to an apocalyptic end—have settled a new world of their own. They have established a colony Out There in Teen-Land, a kind of pseudo-adult world. It is not a young world, if youth means daring and imagination, idealism and individualism, skepticism and iconoclasm. But it does have such a definite identity and appearance that one can visit it as a tourist, with camera, dictionary, and sick pills. (A nice place to visit, yes; but no place to live.) Because they have to live at home, go to school, belong to clubs, shop for supplies, and appear in court, the teen-agers' colony is attached to the American mainland and carries on foreign relations with it. The hearts and minds of teen-agers, though, are usually in Teen-Land: they are totally aware of themselves as Teen-Agers, something their parents never were when they were younger. They feel and are made to feel (no doubt by articles such as this) that they are a race apart, a minority in an alien land. Thus, they cling with fierce pride to a private set of folkways that seem mysterious and confounding in the extreme to outsiders. These folkways create pressures to conform and inhibit the individual as insistently as those in the adult world, but they give the teen-ager an illusion of choice. Paralleling the adult world, Teen-Land is built on insecurity and its greatest concern is for safety.

The cost of safety is uniqueness of personality and the measure of it is membership in the herd.

To understand this complex, young world, one should get to know the heroes of teen-agers. Here is what prompted this inquiry: the assumption that heroes directly and indirectly reveal much about the hero-worshipers' values and that the heroes of teen-agers would contribute some understanding of those who idolize them in an era in which communication between generations has all but broken down.

This assumption isn't made because all teen-age heroes have special knowledge. Today, a young man is selected to heroship by teen-age girls who buy phonograph records without regard for his insights. The hero, after a short wait, is then accepted by teen-age boys, who buy him uncritically, perhaps to please the girls. The boys don't have feminine heroines of their own. There are girl singers who are popular with teen-agers, but none receive the adulation that the girls lavish on the males. It seems that teen-age girls, maturing faster than boys, have no interest in worshiping a member of their own sex. They are prepared to accept a male symbol long before the boys have extricated themselves from Mother. It has even been suggested that boys do not care for girl singers because the female voice reminds them of Mom and, worse, Discipline. As it works out, then, both sexes accept the choice of heroes made by one sex, and the weaker sex at that.

What makes the heroes themselves, in the flesh, a potential source of information about teen-agers is that they are, of course, more than mere show-business characters. Most of them are teen-agers and only one is out of his twenties. They not only perform; they also reflect those whom they are performing for and are approved by. They are part of Teen-Land as well as symbols of it. Some are virtually overnight sensations and none are so far from a time when they were nobodies that they cannot remember their own experiences as members of the teen world on the far side of the footlights.

Recently, some of these heroes were tarnished by the payola scandals. But in the outcry over payola, the essential nature of the idols themselves was ignored. The superficial crookedness of individuals in the record business was excoriated, leaving untouched something deeper—the irresponsibility of many who profoundly affect teen-age life.

One recent night, a nineteen-year-old boy named Frankie Avalon, a rock-and-roll ballad singer physically reminiscent of Frank Sinatra, was seen doing his turn at the Steel Pier Music Hall on the boardwalk at Atlantic City. When he stepped on the stage, about two hundred well-fed, well-enough-dressed girls in the first six rows and in the side balconies shrieked in the typically violent and mechanical way we have all come to know and love. The sound was a cross between an explosive high-school cheer and the mating call of the red squirrel. A number of the screamers were not looking at their hero, but at each other, to make sure that they were being seen screaming—i.e., belonging. In general, the Frankie Avalon fans were seated screamers, not the old dance-in-the-aisle kind of the naïve Sinatra days, which had merely been a kind of premonition of things to come. A few, however, left their seats to run up the aisle and take flashbulb pictures of Avalon, screaming a little as they went. Back of the forward wall of noise, row upon row of teen-agers applauded conventionally. This may have been because they were less enthusiastic, but more than likely they did not scream because they were outside the bright glow of the footlights. If the management had turned up the house lights, they might have achieved a more perfect pandemonium.

But perfect or not, by enabling post-pubescent girls to express themselves within the damp warmth and safety of the crowd, a modern teen-age hero, such as Avalon, fulfills his function and collects his money. The expression takes many forms. In New Haven, Connecticut, girls in summer frocks pulled the shoes off Avalon's feet in an attempt to drag him from the stage, into the audience. In Buffalo, New York, a wild herd of little women trampled him and sprained his back, while in Milwaukee twenty-one girls fainted during one show. When Avalon sang *Boy Without a Girl* on a television show, the camera panned on girls sobbing in the audience. After that, wherever he appeared in person, girls who had seen him on TV sobbed while he sang this song. Avalon's merchandising business keeps the idolatry percolating at long distance: among his wares for young women are Avalon shirts, sweaters, bracelets, buttons and authentic locks of hair. The latter are collected when Avalon goes to the barbershop—which reminds one of that old boast of the hog business: "We use everything but the squeal."

Now the stimulus for all this is 5 feet 7 inches tall and weighs less than 135 pounds. On stage at the Steel Pier Music Hall, his hair was wavy, his face sweet-to-babyish, eyes sad, skin sallow under make-up, and mouth uncertain. His clothes were a careful combination of show-biz elegance and Pat Boone purity: silk suits and white buck shoes. By nature or design, his manner was gentle, a little frightened, and awesomely humble.

This humility, which is characteristic of many teen-age heroes (Fabian, Ricky Nelson, and the like), was a response to the felt need of the audience to identify with one who was celestial and yet not far out of reach. Since the aspirations of many teen-agers seem to be at the lowest level in the history of America, too much self was taboo and anyone too far away (or out) would be ignored. The cardinal principle of the successful hero would be that humbleness creates an indispensable aura of accessibility.

Avalon first sang *Pretty-eyed Baby*, the words of which were totally unintelligible, followed by *De De Dinah*, his first recorded hit song, which was also unintelligible. He sang with a microphone, but his voice was almost inaudible. He did a little soft shoe, which must have been intended to tell those who couldn't hear that the music was playing. Avalon was drowned out not only by the repeated squealings of the audience down front, but also by the orchestra itself, which played loud and hard, driving the backbeat. The trumpet was loud, in part deliberately and in part due to the fact that the trumpet player had cotton stuffed in his ears against the waves of sound from the teen-agers. The drummer accented every second and fourth beat, which is the standard rock-and-roll accent. He kicked the bass drum like the pit man in a burlesque house. Indeed, Avalon's performance contained echoes of burlesque. His least suggestive movements produced ear-splitting cries for more, such as when he merely kicked the toe of a shoe out toward the audience. While this may not seem erotic in cold type, the girls who saw it sighed mightily.

The sum of his performance was very young, very immature,

and even tender (all said at the risk of sounding old), because Avalon had so little audible singing ability and his audience needed to believe otherwise. Moreover, though they screamed like baby banshees, the girls were making believe they were adults. They struck poses which seemed to represent their idea of *adult* poses: in a moment of sudden restraint, some would sit back, place an index finger along a cheek, tighten their eyes, and listen critically. Like opera-goers, they whispered knowingly between numbers. When Avalon's half hour was over, they wore expressions of adultlike sophistication on their faces: cool, satisfied, almost blasé.

At the stage door, still another crowd of girls gathered to wait for Avalon, held back by a chain. They might have been the same two hundred girls who had had the choice seats in the Music Hall. They milled about the door impatiently. A uniformed guard taunted them ("He ain't never coming out, girls!") while stealing looks through a small window into the hall that led to Avalon's backstage dressing room. When Avalon appeared in the hall, the guard unhooked the chain and demanded that the girls form two lines so that the star and his entourage could pass through to a waiting auto. Instead, the girls surged forward, breathlessly. Nonchalant at first, the guard swung the chain at them, rippling it softly. Then he cracked it hard across the front rank at chest level. The girls, who had been about to crush Avalon, fell back. Avalon walked behind a phalanx made up of his guitar player, the Steel Pier press agent, and three other men. "Touch me, Frankie!" girls shouted. "Over here, man. Just look at me!" Looking neither right nor left, Avalon escaped into the back seat of the waiting car. The entourage piled in after him. Female hands, heads, and torsos surged in at the windows and jammed open the front door. Two well-aimed, shoving blows from the driver cleared the front door, the windows were rolled up, and the car drove off with its precious cargo. The girls waved, disappointed but not angry. They had enjoyed the melee, the mob violence of which was the other side of the group sex rites that had taken place inside.

Ten minutes later, safe in a restaurant, Frankie Avalon said: "I think it's great to be a teen-ager."

Avalon had no more to say, really, than this one line. Yet even

that underlined the modern, crowd-cultured teen-ager's deep
and novel sense of belonging to a special group. Avalon was as
unaware of his function as a hero of that special group as he had
once been of his own potentialities. (He had started in show
business as a trumpet player.) He was their outlet for vicarious
sex and real violence, those primitive means of self-expression
to which one turns when prouder means—ambition, creativity,
ability, the sheer desire to change the world—have been denied,
devalued, or have failed. Avalon did not know it and, not knowing, felt no sense of responsibility for it.

While Avalon was in New Jersey, six teen-age heroes were in
Hollywood pursuing their various commitments to television,
movies, and night clubs. Ricky Nelson was taping "The Adventures of Ozzie and Harriet" with his mother and father. Edd
"Kookie" Byrnes was acting in "77 Sunset Strip," a filmed weekly
TV show. Pat Boone and Dick Clark (the non-singer of the
group) were making movies and, simultaneously, Clark was
producing some of his TV programs for tape. Fabian was working in a movie called *Hound Dog Man* and Bobby Darin had
an adult-world night-club date. One could see them individually
in the surroundings of their trade.

Ricky Nelson was rather well protected by his father and the
family press agent in a barren office across from the "Ozzie and
Harriet" TV-show sound stage. When they let him in edgewise,
it was apparent that he was at least partially conscious of the
nuances of his appeal to teen-agers. His commodity is sincere
sex. He was most aware of the need for sincerity. It seemed
crucial to him that no one should get the idea that he was different—"I'm just another teen-ager," he said—or that he was
anything but sincere. Like most teen-agers, his sentences were
larded with the phrase "you know," partially from habit, but
also, it seemed, to impress one with his complete frankness and
desire to be understood.

In 1957, when he was sixteen, Ricky studied guitar for a while,
then walked on the stage of Hamilton High School in Los Angeles for his first public appearance as a prospective solo performer. He did not swing his hips or otherwise attempt to excite

the audience. Yet, the screaming began before he sang a note, the girls got out of hand, and the members of the football team had to help him escape. Thus the hero was born, as all teen-age heroes are born, in the presence and at the pleasure of screaming young women. Six of his records have since sold over one million copies each, representing a cool net of 40,000 dollars each. His personal appearances have been smashing, thanks in some degree to the careful organization of 10,000 fan clubs all over the country. His income last year was estimated to be 400,000 dollars. To earn it, Ricky selected each hit song by himself from hundreds of demonstration records submitted by publishers and song writers. He knew exactly what he wanted.

"The record should not be too complicated," Ricky said. "If it's not, you know, sincere, it's not too good. In a song, you know, I hate to hear lingo, you know, about hop and bop. I like a song that tells a story without meaningless words, you know, like 'dig that crazy chick.' Now you listen to *Lonesome Town*. It should be a simple song like that, you know? *Lonesome Town* is about this fictitious town called Lonesome Town, you know, where you can forget this girl. I mean lots of times you get jilted and feel like the end of the world's come. So, it's from what I feel sincerely, I decide to do a song. Now, you asked me about teen-age values. I feel my values are pretty good. I mean, I like anything I feel is sincere."

Edd "Kookie" Byrnes touches a different chord out of necessity. He is perhaps the only teen-age hero who achieved his exalted position by playing a role—that of "Kookie," the jive-talking parking-lot attendant of "77 Sunset Strip"—and maintains it by continuing to be what he isn't. In public, his speech sounds like a tape-recording made at the bar in Birdland. The rest of the time he talks like a conventional twenty-six-year-old. Seen at lunch and between scenes at Warner's, there was nothing about him that suggested the character of "Kookie" except the long brown hair and routine good looks. To teen-agers, however, he is "Kookie" whose long suit is a devilish narcissism. His trademark is a comb which he is endlessly passing through his locks. Teen-agers might be expected to frown on such self-conceit, but "Kookie" manages to convey the impression that he is just kidding. If teen-agers were really in revolt against the adult world instead of merely huddled together in their own adultified colony, Byrnes's "Kookie" probably would not be a strong enough character to appeal to them. As it is, he is a symbol of a small rebellion. He says that the "77 Sunset Strip" adventure that won the teen-agers for "Kookie" involved an incident in which he was falsely blamed for an auto accident. "They think I did it," "Kookie" said, "because I'm young." The line could have been the title of a rock-and-roll golden record. Inevitably, as his fame grew, Byrnes turned to the teen-age record market. After a dozen or more attempts to record his first tune on key, the A & R man sent him home and pasted together a master out of pieces from each of the tapes. The result was *Kookie, Lend Me Your Comb,* which sold two million single records, a monument to the taste and perception of our teens.

Fabian, like "Kookie," became a teen-age hero in spite of the fact that he was no bundle of singing talent. "Maybe I would have never made it if I could sing," Fabian has said. His appeal is similar to Ricky Nelson's, but also he elicits motherly sympathy from the girls because he is so obviously awkward and inept. It is now one of the hoary legends of Teen-Land that Fabian was discovered sitting on a doorstep in South Philadelphia by Bob Marcucci, a former waiter who is himself not yet thirty. With his partner, Peter De Angelis, Marcucci had discovered and then promoted Frankie Avalon to stardom. Having developed the magic touch, he searched for and found Fabian two years ago. Fabian was fourteen, had never sung a note in anger, and thought that the six dollars a week he was earning in a drugstore was fair money. When last seen, he was getting 35,000 dollars for acting (not badly, by Hollywood standards) in Fox's *Hound Dog Man.*

Sitting just behind the camera in one of those canvas chairs, Marcucci was watching every move his gold mine made. Marcucci is a short, swarthy man who reminds one of a nervous assistant director at a boy's camp. He has the ability to analyze precisely the demands of the teen-age public and to know what to do about it. He has found a career in exporting talent to Teen-Land. First, he selects promising raw material. Then he molds it. He indoctrinates it for three months. Then he takes it to live TV shows so that it can see what the business is like. Then he lets it make a few test records. Since it cannot sing too well without an orchestra and the electronic facilities (echo chambers, bass and treble modulators, tape splicers and the works) of a recording studio, he teaches it to pantomime while its records play over the loud-speaker during its first public appearance before an audience of two hundred. He dresses it, first in sweaters and white bucks, then in open-Belafonte shirts and big belt buckles. He coifs it by modifying the duck-tail and getting more of the Ricky Nelson bob. He postures it, taking advantage of good shoulders, which should bunch forward, and narrow hips, which should always be off-keel. He takes it on the road, shows it to disc jockeys, and advertises it in trade papers. He decides (brilliantly) to use only its first name instead of its last. He interests Dick Clark in it, and after one shot on TV, it breaks up an audience of 24,000 in Albany, New York. It sells 300,000 copies of a record called *I'm a Man,* then 750,000 of *Turn Me Loose.* It records *Tiger:*

> . . . You kept my heart jumping like a kan-ga-roo
> I'm float-ing like an on-ion in a bowl of stew . . .
> Come right now, 'cause I'm on the prowl
> Like a ti-ger oo-oo-oo, like a ti-ger

After these lyrics (tiger is the word you *hear*), it is known not only as Fabian, but as Tiger, too. It is a hero.

In Fabian, Marcucci consciously or unconsciously produced a caricature that combined the sure-fire qualities of Ricky with those of his own Frankie Avalon. The mood in Teen-Land permits even such an obvious construction to become a hero. What Marcucci could not have planned, however, was the fact that Fabian's inability to sing would really be an asset. Marcucci tried to teach him; he went through four singing teachers trying. Fortunately, all efforts failed. Here was the ultimate in humbleness and teen-audience identification. Nobody in the audience could sing either, so that made the inept sex-pot, Fabian, seem all the more accessible. Mediocrity fell in love with its own image.

Bobby Darin has what Fabian doesn't have and vice versa. Instead of half-closed eyes, a build, and a hairdresser, Darin has the most low-down, mature, masculine voice of all the teen-age heroes. During the past year, his records have sold more than five million copies (*Splish Splash, Mack the Knife,* which got the Grammy award, et cetera). Found at a Sunset Strip night club, Darin (without teen-agers) demonstrated that the humbleness required by them does not become him; he fairly bursts with self-confidence before an adult audience. He is about twenty-four, short, average-looking, and honest with himself. "I know I'm not a pretty boy," he said. "I feel a little out of place in front of teen-agers because even though they buy my records they don't have that fervor for me when they see me. It's a physical thing with them. I don't put them down for it, but I don't think I'm one of them." He said he would sing anything teen-agers wanted to hear—*à la* Avalon, the sense of responsibility was missing. "It's bad the way the papers have screwed them up. The kids have got the idea now that they all have to band together and act like teen-agers. They have phony heroes and no individuality. They don't know who's leading them. I feel for them, but I'm *not* going to lead them, Charlie. You call the roll of commercial guys, put me first."

Pat Boone would save the teen-ager from himself if he could. His book, *'Twixt Twelve and Twenty,* was a tender try in that direction and he has said, "I hope that fellows like me and Ricky and Elvis aren't distracting kids from the real things in life and from becoming people instead of just fans." Boone has been around longer as a teen-age hero than anyone except Elvis Presley. He was a married man with a baby and a second (with two more in the future) on the way before he became a popular idol. He was deeply religious. Thus, he was absolutely safe and pure, too. This combination was immensely appealing to many teen-age girls. His records sold twenty million at last count, second only to Elvis. On the movie set, *Journey to the Center of the Earth,* a wholesome Jules Verne tale, Boone seemed made for Victorian costumery. He does not have conventional good looks, but rather a strong, open boy's face which suggests ball games and picnics. He does not simmer like the members of the

Presley-Nelson-Fabian-Byrnes syndrome. In his time, though, he had had his share of screaming and fainting and clothes-grabbing by teen fans. "I can't believe it's bad or abnormal," he said. "It's fun and a form of recreation and a release of tension."

Dick Clark has defended the teen-agers' *status quo* even more stoutly than Pat Boone. He has become virtually a go-between in the two worlds. To the teen-ager, he is an adult who likes them, a big brother who watches out for them, and an authority who sanctions both their idols and their folkways. For the adult world, he is an emissary from Teen-Land not many years out of the age group himself (he's thirty, looks twenty), a young man whose taste and judgment are respected (after all, indecent lyrics are banned from his programs); and a celebrity who approves of their children. With all this going for him, it's no wonder that Clark is one of the hot properties in show business. He has six TV shows a week on ABC, many magazine-writing assignments, and a fat contract with Columbia Pictures. (Until recently, when he was advised to withdraw, he had a music-publishing and record-pressing business.)

Television is Clark's first love. Both *American Bandstand* and the Saturday *Dick Clark Show* are major outlets for teen-age heroes and their music. The shows are so popular that Clark is probably the most powerful personality-and-song plugger in the teen field. Such power implies responsibility, so Clark is due his share of credit for conditions that prevail in Teen-Land. Last summer, after watching two Saturday shows from the wings (Clark tapes his summer Saturday shows mid-week), one could be sure Clark would never have one of those "There, that'll hold the little bastards!" episodes in his career. He is a careful man and, besides, he believes in teen-agers "the way they are." All of his TV programs devote many minutes to camera views of teen-agers.

Clark's magazine-writing career is based on a column in *This Week Magazine,* but his "talks to teen-agers" have also appeared in *Seventeen, Look,* and others. He is the teen-agers' Norman Vincent Peale. His position is reassuring: the way teens live is pretty much okay. Nothing downs his optimism. Typically, he sums up his advice with, "Keep at it and I know you'll be successful"; or, "I think you will be surprised at how soon there will be nothing to worry about." Once, however, in a conversation, he said:

"I don't think teen-agers are doing anything today that adults don't do also. They have all the same problems that adults have nowadays—money problems, success problems, appearance problems. They are appreciated as a group as never before and they want to be looked on as adults. They're worldly, so much more worldly than we were. They're practically adults. They're sophisticated at a very early age. Take the day Sal Mineo was leaving my studio. He got in his car and a teen-age girl threw herself under the front wheels. 'Run over me, Sal!' she cried. That was dreadful, yes; but a week later in Atlantic City, a forty-year-old woman in a mink coat threw herself in front of Frank Sinatra's car and cried, 'Run over me, Frankie!' That's what I mean. There's no difference between teen-agers and adults."

Clark apparently meant this as a justification for himself as well as the teen-agers who idolize him. In any case, it was an accurate description of juvenile adults and adultified teen-agers.

What Clark and the others suggest in symbol and sentiment is that millions of teen-agers have taken refuge in a pseudoworld that is spoiled and banal and hypererotic and in headlong flight from reality and easily fooled and commercialized and exploited and fatuous. Such a world may be satisfactory for adults, but somehow one has greater expectations for youth.

Every world has means of expressing itself—a culture. Our eighteen million teen-agers (exceptions duly noted) spend ten billion dollars to support theirs. They have publications written in their own language (Teenglish?) which keep them abreast of their times. *Dig, Ingenue, Seventeen, 16, Teen,* et cetera, instruct them in custom, ritual, propriety, sex mores, and properthink; their goal is to inculcate group values. One magazine not long ago defined "What is a Square?" for its readers, who were told, among other things, that a square is one who refuses to go with a group to a movie he has already seen. Then there are motion pictures, television shows, and radio programs, which provide a kind of cultural game of ring-around-the-rosie. The teens influence the adults who provide the entertainments which in turn influence the teens and so on, and on. After sex and violence, the main theme of these entertainments is a kind of dead-pan morality which would be funny if it did not border on madness. Thus, the producer of *I Was a Teenage Franken-stein* defended himself against an attack on his very popular picture by pointing out that none of the young villains and monsters in the movie drank or smoked. And in the basic boy-meets-girl film, scripts are adjusted to make sure that a curious kind of justice, appealing to teen-agers, triumphs. In a teen picture, after the boy gets the girl pregnant, he's got to get stabbed. Watching rock-and-roll programs, citizens of Teen-Land may learn the newest folk dances while they follow the fashions of the times. Hearing disc jockeys on radio, too, teen-agers can absorb their culture. They are infused with mean-ingful backbeat rhythms and simultaneously absorb the philoso-phies of the modern jocks, which are a mixture of Beat, Babbitt and Payola. Beyond these visual and aural items of accultura-tion, there is the automobile. What the frontier was to our pioneers, what Miami is to our modern adult culture, the auto is to the teen—the means of getting away.

Finally, away out on the fringe of Teen-Land, heroin takes some teen-agers where they cannot get by car.

The primary focus of the teen culture, however, is the teen-age hero who, like heroes of all cultures, represents the final expression of those values by which it lives. The seven afore-mentioned heroes are the Apollos and Zeuses of Teen-Land. A few years ago, the movies supplied most of the heroes for adoles-cent Americans. Marlon Brando and James Dean were two, but the former's receding hairline and the latter's death discon-nected them from the young. Chances are they would have faded anyway, because rock-and-roll was bigger than both of them. Now, except for Dick Clark, every first-class teen-age hero is a recording star. No athlete, politician, businessman, or in-tellectual is accorded comparable esteem, nor could he be, given the teen-agers' demand for safety. The ideal athlete is admired for courage, the politician for principles, the businessman for enterprise, and the intellectual for devotion to hard truths—all represent values that tend to separate the individual from the crowd, that expose him, and that lead him into an uncertain and dangerous future. Teen-agers make virtues of conformity, mediocrity and sincerity. It is a simple matter of survival: there's safety in the crowd. They can express themselves through their safe-sex heroes, each one of whom represents his own brand of sex—rebellious sex, sincere sex, clean sex, low-down sex, motherly sex, cool sex—at no risk. It's perfect: it's sex, but it's safe. Without leaving the warmth and security of the crowd, you can say what you want to say to the world.

You can have your cake without being eaten.

It is not easy to know precisely what the teen-agers want to say through their heroes. The means of expression is primordial; the words are often indistinguishable from straight static. In that they are designed (often willfully) to hold a mirror up to the nature of teen life, they offer perhaps our most significant clue.

Two of the most successful people in the teen-age song business are Jerry Leiber and Mike Stoller, a words-and-music team which seems to know precisely what it is that teen-agers want to say. Their rock-and-roll songs have sold over thirty million records: *Hound Dog* sold more than five million records; *Black Denim Trousers,* a supposed spoof of motorcycle bums which was taken seriously by teen-agers, sold more than two million records; *Love Me, Loving You, Searching, Don't,* and *Jailhouse Rock* also sold more than two million; *King Creole, Charley Brown, Yakety Yak, Along Came Jones,* and *Poison Ivy* sold more than one million. After eight years of song-writing (each is now but twenty-six years old) Leiber and Stoller have sold four times as many records as Jerome Kern sold in his lifetime.

It did them no harm that Elvis Presley performed several of their songs. Along Tin Pan Alley, it is still generally assumed that Presley, the king of the teen-age heroes, could sell one million records of himself singing Clementine Paddleford's recipe for boiled beef to the tune of *Juanita*. He is expected to resume the throne upon his discharge from the Army.

Leiber and Stoller had the good fortune to begin writing songs for teen-age heroes in the early Fifties when Negro music known as "rhythm and blues" was being discovered by white teen-agers. About 1953, this music was taken over for the commercial teen market although it had been played for years on Negro radio stations and had been sung down South as a form of the blues since the Civil War. At the same time, "country music" with its strong influence from both the Baptist church and white folk music was discovered. The two themes—one earthy, the other moralistic, both plaintive—came together and were revised downward to the teen-age level; they became "rock-and-roll." The rock-and-roll fad spread like a pox, carried first by independent record companies with singing groups, and then by Elvis Presley, with his country guitar and Gypsy Rose Lee hips. In Presley's larynx, songs that had arisen out of realistic needs for a job, a woman, or a drink were replaced by teen-age needs and expressions that were only dimly related to the sources of the new music. "Cold pouring down rain blues" became "They don't understand us because we're teen-agers rock."

Presley was followed by a horde of imitators. The surprise was that the newcomers were almost as successful as he was. Always before, a segment of youth had zeroed in on a single personality—a Vallee or a Sinatra—and had disdained copies of the real thing. Elvis, however, was more than a personality; he was the leader of a movement which provided a hero for every boy and girl, and finally resulted in the identification of teen-agers as a race apart. Leiber and Stoller wrote on the head of a drum.

"Anger and protest, self-pity and adulation, these are the things the teen-age heroes sing about," Jerry Leiber says.

Repeating the same salty, nasty phrase again and again, such a song as *Hound Dog* is a pure expression of hostility, while *Don't* is equally pure self-pity. What teen-agers seem to want to say is, "I'm mad at the world, at authority, at the way things are," and "I can't do anything about it, so pity poor me." Both would be perfectly legitimate statements, loaded with potentialities, if that was what teen-agers actually meant. "Basically," Leiber says, "these songs are a means of escape from reality. We write the lyrics deliberately vague. The songs aren't addressed to anybody real, but to dream characters. The songs are egocentric and dreamy. Lots of basic blues ideas wouldn't work as rock-and-roll ideas because the blues are too real, too earthy.

You have to make them dreamlike and very moral. That's why you're rarely going to hear even a plain *happy* rock-and-roll song, because happiness is a real emotion."

We have, therefore, not only rebels without causes, we have a generation with nothing to say. All that seems real about teen-age self-expression through the safe-sex heroes is their dedication to unreality, to songs of watered-down, self-pitying blues-that-aren't-blues, and to aimless hostility.

One can hope that in some area of life, teen-agers are giving as much passionate attention to the real business of youth—which is growing up as well as older—as they are giving to their heroes. But if Dick Clark is right, that there is no difference between the generations as he sees them, growing up may be as outmoded as the 78 r.p.m. phonograph record. There may be nothing to grow up to. Yet a comparison must be made. The adult world has an existence apart from its obvious responsibility for what has happened in Teen-Land. There are adults and there are teen-agers. Even on the teen-agers' terms, if a choice had to be made, one would a hell of a lot rather have his woman run over by Frank Sinatra.

Personal

Some stories are more difficult to write than others. For example, before I produced a single useable sentence, John Wayne had me stumped for two weeks. I sat empty-headed before my typewriter, first in earnest, then in despair, and finally in terror until the title, *God and Man in Hollywood,* miraculously came to me.

I seem to need a metaphor to help me begin organizing my material, like "the Adjustable Man" for Roy Cohn. I had given up on Roy after a week or so of concentrated confusion and treated myself to a movie called *Hiroshima Mon Amour.* I was sitting through it a second time when the metaphor popped into my head. I ran out of the theater, hurried to my office, and wrote *The Pleasures of Roy Cohn* in twenty hours, non-stop.

Another troublesome piece was the one about Bennett Cerf. I began shuffling my notes, pencil-tapping my forehead, and shaking my right leg on November 16, 1963. Nothing had happened by the time President Kennedy was assassinated. That afternoon, with friends, I drank a series of double martinis at the Barberry Room on 52nd Street. At eight P.M., they folded me into a cab and sent me home. By mistake, the driver let me off in front of the Sixth Precinct police station, which is next door to my place. Fortunately, a kindly detective pointed me in the right direction. I slept until midnight. Then my wife fed me and for the rest of that terrible weekend, with the TV turned on, I wrote about fun-loving Bennett Cerf. It seems impossible now, but at the time, I thought I was proving to my children that Life Goes On.

The Heroes of Teen-agers was more difficult to write than any other piece. I had collected an enormous amount of material —extensive interviews with seven rock-n-roll stars and a score of songwriters, disc jockeys, and press agents, plus a pile of data on teen-agers that now fills a six-foot shelf in my office. Days and then weeks went by as I sifted each fact and quotation, never quite believing that any single metaphor could apply to eighteen million teen-agers *and* their heroes. In the second week, I began writing the vignette about Leiber and Stoller, the songwriters, but I soon stopped for fear of delaying the Moment of Truth. It happened in the third week when I was taking a stroll with my daughter. The idea that teen-agers, in fact, lived in a world of their own and that Frankie Avalon and the rest were its gods provided a base that could support all of my research. But still it wasn't easy and another two weeks went by before the piece was finished. It was then titled *Teen-Age Heroes: Mirrors of Muddled Youth.*

Not the least of my regrets about the death of President Kennedy has been the loss of one who was a responsible hero of teen-agers. He had managed to get their attention. Had he lived, he even might have annexed Teen-Land for the nation-at-large. As it was, many of the very same kids who were hooked on rock-n-roll idols at the end of the Eisenhower era discovered that there was a world outside during the thousand days of Kennedy.

A while ago, I interviewed over 200 high school seniors on a cross-country assignment for *Look.* They were, to be sure, self-centered denizens of Teen-Land, but they were at least as serious and idealistic as *my* generation imagines it was at the end of the Roosevelt era. This is what was lost under the benevolent eye of Dwight Eisenhower. Youth simply turned their backs on society in the Fifties. And Kennedy turned them around again.

I am not one of those who detects a positive qualitative difference between Beatlemania today and the behavior of teenagers toward their idols six or eight years ago. What Ed Sullivan exploited then, he exploits now. I even have a certain nostalgia for Elvis Presley, whose wiggly hips made more sense than Ringo's flying hairdo. But before the Kennedy era fades, the late President's effect on youth should be underscored. The commercial interest in the continued isolation of teen-agers will be served, it seems, but we know now that the character of a generation needn't be left to the tender mercies of disc jockeys, television networks, and automobile salesmen. Kennedy proved that the formidable barrier between youth and age can be breached by a believable opportunity for service. He was an experience that teaches there is more hope than one might expect.

Bennett Cerf
The
Long Happy
Life of
Bennett Cerf

Bennett Alfred Cerf is perhaps the most fun-loving corporation president in America. In New York, our real fun capital, Cerf presides over Random House, Inc.—publishers of Random House books, Borzoi Books, The Modern Library, Pantheon Books, Vintage Books, Beginner Books, Landmark Books, All-about Books, Easy to Read Books, Legacy Books, and L. W. Singer text and reference books; owners of 9.5 per cent of Grosset & Dunlap, Inc., which owns 70 per cent of Bantam Books; distributors of Bernard Geis books, J. B. Read books, and the Looking Glass Library; and joint-book-publishing venturers with *The Catholic Digest* and *McCall's* magazine. "It's a lot of fun," Cerf says. Even more fun for him is the place he has found in the bosom of the people. Millions of TV viewers know him as the man standing on Arlene Francis' left who archly introduces John Daly, the arch *What's My Line?* moderator, and then, sitting down, earnestly plays the game in the interest of various sponsors' products. Millions read his *Try and Stop Me* joke column, syndicated to 660 newspapers across this fun country, and millions more read the humor anthologies he has spun off at the rate of one every two years for the past two decades—about ten million copies of all editions, hard-cover and soft, are in print. And thousands in the East and Midwest, in auditoriums, gymnasiums, and hotel dining rooms, hear him tell about humor, literature and "Authors I Have Known" when twenty-five or thirty times a year, with a smile and a shoeshine, he rides out on the professional lecture circuit managed by the Lee

Keedick Lecture Bureau. A few years ago, *The New Yorker* magazine *poked* fun at Cerf for his nonpublishing activities which, "culturally speaking, leave practically *everything* to be desired." But Cerf acknowledges only a calculated risk, willingly undertaken. "I might be considered a much more distinguished publisher," he says, "if I hadn't had so much fun on the side. But goddamnit, I honestly don't think the television, the jokebooks, and the lectures have hurt my publishing interests, principles or results one bit. And there's a return: ask the average man how many publishers he knows by name—it'll be Bennett Cerf. . . . Think of the vanity! Think of the pleasure!"

Cerf loves fun and apparently has a congenital aversion to its opposites. Friends say that his sentiments are liberal and warm-hearted, but he avoids like the plague any public inference that he might have a profound or painful thought. Despite two degrees from Columbia University and a lifetime membership in Phi Beta Kappa, he seems to have no taste whatever for intellectual discourse. Even the mention of a Random House author's name doesn't provoke him. He likes to discuss *his* relationships rather than the author's work. Say "Irwin Shaw," and Cerf says, "We've published everything of Shaw's." Ask about Harold Humes and he says, "Humes actually slept on the couch in *my* office when he was writing *Men Die!*" Agree to this level of insight and Cerf can talk about William Faulkner for hours:

"Great guy, Bill. Great, great. I loved him. I remember one time he came to New York, he arrived late for a cocktail party I was giving in his honor. Bill walked in and fell flat on his face in front of half the town. Dashiell Hammett and I put him to bed. But next morning Bill was up and ready to work. He had marvelous recuperative powers. Marvelous. . . . Faulkner would walk into my office, sit down and say, 'Don't let me bother you.' I'd then say, 'What the hell, let's go get a drink.' But he'd go sit in a next-door office and put his feet up and then I'd take young writers in to meet him. Faulkner would say, 'Howdy.' Once he said he liked his editor, Albert Erskine, but he wouldn't tell him. He said, 'When my horse is running good, I don't stop to give him sugar.' Another time . . ."

A Cerf dialogue is about the same as his monologue. His blitheness, like the sea turtle's shell, is virtually impregnable.

He listens well on any subject, but when he talks, he likes to enjoy himself, which he does, and you are to roll along with him, merrily. You say something about, say, the Sino-Indian dispute and Cerf puns, "Did you hear the one about the Indian cook who got fired for favoring [Cerf's laughter begins here] curry?" Ho! Ho! Ho! The laugh is a break-out, an explosive cackle, building to a guffaw, eyes closed, mouth wide, with the habitual pipe removed just in time. Mention Roy Cohn and Cerf puns again, "I've often imagined a photograph of G. David Schine (Roy's friend) astride a horse named Harvest Moon, captioned 'Schine on Harvest Moon.' " Followed by another cataclysmic whoop.

Ironically, with his wholly owned subsidiaries, Alfred A. Knopf, Inc. (acquired in 1960, still run by Alfred and Blanche Knopf) and Pantheon Books, Cerf can muster one of the longest lists in publishing of the better and, almost by definition, more desperate writers of the day. Random House publishes the aforementioned Shaw and Humes, Dwight Macdonald, William Styron, Robert Penn Warren, Ralph Ellison, John O'Hara, Truman Capote, Philip Roth, James Michener, Jerome Weidman and Par Lagerkvist, besides such Knopfmen as John Updike, William Humphrey, William Maxwell, John Hersey, Muriel Spark and Elizabeth Bowen, and not to mention a backlist of departed tragic visionaries, including Faulkner, Eugene O'Neill, Marcel Proust, Gertrude Stein, Sinclair Lewis and Isak Dinesen for Random House, Boris Pasternak for Pantheon, and Thomas Mann, H. L. Mencken, Willa Cather, George Jean Nathan, André Gide, and Albert Camus for Knopf. In contrast to some book publishers, Cerf even reads many of his authors' works, especially the fiction. But they can't calm his breezy disposition. Given their gloomy, mad, or otherwise literary notions, Cerf is most typically Cerfian when he tells you, "My theory is we're always in some crisis or other, it's always something, but this is a hopeful time. I think people should be happier. What the hell, I'm an optimist."

Thus, by choice, Cerf leads a fun life. You see that, once you get to know him. An energetic, effervescent, endearing man, he looks at life through horn-rimmed glasses; stares at it nearsightedly, brown eyes wide and eager; and smiles. It seems that his most persistent facial expression is one of benign and boyish self-satisfaction. He is tall and trim. Frequently, he throws back his shoulders and inhales deeply as though remembering a long-ago command to stand up straight. Since his carriage is normally erect, perhaps he does this, as he does most things, because he likes to. Cerf likes to wear expensively modest, tailor-made suits and he has lots of them. He likes to smoke pipes and collects them. Full of nervous energy, he occasionally puffs a filtered cigarette, but when he's really nervous, he likes to pace the floor and chew on the end of his hankies. Cerf likes money, of course, and he has it. His publisher's salary is 60,000 dollars a year, plus pension benefits, and his other labors, altogether, probably bring in more than this. If he retired tomorrow, the Random House pension would yield him nearly 20,000 dollars a year for life. His 200,000 shares are worth roughly two million dollars at present market prices. Were he to sell these someday, possibly in order to free himself from the more tedious aspects of corporate management (dealing with stockholders, S.E.C., I.R.S., and the like), he would undoubtedly command a fat fee for staying on as a general consultant. Cerf sputters at this last suggestion. "I love my publishing house," Cerf says. "They're going to have to carry me out of here the way they carried Sewell Avery out of Montgomery Ward."

Cerf always seems to be having fun. Strolling on the grounds of his forty-seven-acre estate in Mt. Kisco, he says, "Isn't it just great—*great!*" Or, sitting in his vast office looking across Madison Avenue at the rear of St. Patrick's Cathedral, he says, "Gosh, I'm *happy!*" Or, standing in the luxuriously cluttered sitting room of his five-story home on East Sixty-second Street, he says, "I dunno, I'm just lucky." Or, walking down Park Avenue, where two perfect strangers (TV viewers, probably) inform each other, "Hey, there's Bennett Cerf," and call to him, "Hi-ya, Bennett," he says, "I *really* love it!"

In his private life, Cerf has almost more fun than anybody. He says he is a contented husband, married twenty-five "wonderful" years to the former child movie actress Phyllis Fraser, whose cousin (Cerf often repeats) is Ginger Rogers. She is not only a fun wife and mother, but also she's done "great things" helping to run Beginner Books, the high-profit Dr. Seuss group at Random House. The Cerfs' two boys are also "great." Chris, twenty-two, graduated from Harvard with honors last year, worked on the *Lampoon,* and coauthored a book satirizing James Bond that sold 100,000 copies. Jon, seventeen, graduates in June from Deerfield Academy. Both sons are expected at Random House. "They would never think of working anywhere else," Mrs. Cerf says. "They idolize Bennett." Cerf's friends, most of whom are associated with him in the literary-show business-communications establishment, are generally "dear." He responds to them with generous evenings at home, weekends in the country, and check-grabbing at Lindy's, one of his favorite after-theater hangouts. Some of his friendships go back to college days and before. Howard Dietz, for example, and he have been friends since before the First Great War. As teenagers, they lived in the same apartment building on upper Riverside Drive in New York and later went to Columbia University together. Their friends included Herman Mankiewicz, Richard Rodgers, the late Oscar Hammerstein, and other famous Lions. "I remember one time Howard and I walked all the way to Asbury Park," Cerf recalls. "We had to stop overnight on Staten Island and I remember telling him there that I wanted to be a book publisher. He said he wanted to write songs. We both got what we wanted." Cerf also has happy memories of himself as a son, the only child of Gustave Cerf, a lithographer in New York who designed labels for cigarette packages, cans, and bottles, and Fredericka Wise Cerf, daughter of a wholesale tobacco merchant who willed fun-loving Bennett the 100,000-dollar-ace-in-the-hole that eventually enabled him to start near the top in publishing. Cerf's mother died when he was sixteen, but his father lived to see him become rich and famous. "My father," Cerf says with feeling, "was a wonderful man."

Random House headquarters is a fun place, occupying the north wing of a low, U-shaped, Italian Renaissance building on the Madison Avenue block between Fiftieth and Fifty-first streets. It was built in the 1880's for Henry Villard, the railroad tycoon, and four other families of his choice. The Roman Catholic Archdiocese of New York owns and occupies the central and south wings; Random House owns its wing, which used to be the mansion of Harris C. Fahnestock, of the banking Fahnestocks. Cerf's office, formerly the Fahnestocks' master bedroom, is on the second floor; it is somewhat smaller than Yankee Stadium but larger than a squash court. Cerf chose it for himself in 1946 when the company moved down from offices on Fifty-seventh Street. Two walls are lined with books, a third wall presents an elaborate mantelpiece plus the door to Cerf's telephone-equipped bathroom (a fun idea), and the fourth wall displays a few pictures, including one of Faulkner dressed in a fox-hunting costume. Faulkner inscribed it: "Love and kisses. Tallyho." The office furnishings are contemporary—Cerf's big desk, enough chairs for a small conference, and the couch that Harold Humes slept on. The publishing business masterminded from here, as Standard & Poor's report on Random House says, "involves selecting and editing works for publication, supervising production, and promoting and exploiting these works. . . . The company contracts directly with authors, obtains reprint rights to books previously published, and also publishes works which are in the public domain. . . . The company does not do its own printing and binding." The core is the author's work. The publisher is essentially a middleman. His basic function is service. He runs a business hopefully like a profession. His success depends upon his ability to place the works of other men and women before the public. Aside from the Knopf list, Cerf shares the sensitive selection function with his old friend and partner, Donald S. Klopfer, who is executive vice-president of Random House, and with a cadre of editors. Cerf takes particular interest in the company's advertising budget; he writes many of the ads and supervises the publicity. "I'm a ham," Cerf says. "I like being concerned with publicity." Otherwise, he handles, manages, invigorates, or lets alone several hundred authors and some 650 Random House employees, including Klopfer, who also supervises production (annual salary: 53,000 dollars); Alfred and Blanche Knopf (combined salaries: 94,500 dollars); Albert Erskine, top editor (35,000 dollars a year); and numerous well-to-fairly-well-paid executives, editors, salesmen (more than 130 of them), technicians, editorial assistants, long-suffering first-readers, who annually reject untold scads of over-the-transom manuscripts, and office boys. "You're never through in publishing," Cerf says. "You can't take off the way a writer does. It's a job with no beginning, middle, or end. Days and nights, you have fun."

From time to time over a recent period of weeks, Cerf was seen just for fun carrying on more or less as usual. At the office one day, for example, he said, "Ask me some questions," and gnawed on his pipe.

"How's business?"

Cerf leaped from his leather chair. He snatched up two sales reports and a photocopy of the New York *Times* best-seller list and whipped around to my side of the desk. On the ledge behind the desk, a loose photo of Cerf posing with a couple of beauty-contest winners fell over, but he ignored it.

"We've got number two and number four on the best-seller list," he said. "And we've got three books on the backlist that together sold over two million copies in the last eighteen months —*The Cat in the Hat, The American College Dictionary,* and *The Prophet* by Kahlil Gibran. That's where the money is in the publishing business—in old books. I wouldn't sell the Random House, Knopf, Pantheon backlist with all the rights for ten million dollars—and that's a modest estimate."

Cerf began to pace. He said *The Cat in the Hat* was a so-called Beginner Book by Dr. Seuss. "My wife, Phyllis, that's her baby," he said. Then he grabbed a magazine from a nearby stack and thumbed it until he found the page he wanted. "Picture of my wife," he said, pointing to an attractive, businesslike face. "She's kid cousin of Ginger Rogers."

Cerf sat down again. "Haven't you got any questions?" he asked. I told him I was interested in what makes a publisher. He jumped up and began pacing again.

"What makes a publisher?" he said. "First, being able to spot talent. Second, keep the talent happy. The way you handle him, the way you show that you appreciate him—it's very important and very personal. Every author has vulnerable points. You have to pay attention to them. It always helps to give an author a big ad in the *Times.* They're childish. Sinclair Lewis spent his last night in America at our house. He had dinner and we were all still sitting at the table. Then Bill Faulkner called up and said he was in town. I told Lewis and asked him, could Bill come over? Lewis said, 'Certainly not. This is my night.' Then, at nine-thirty, Lewis went to bed. Phyllis and I stayed up, talking. At ten-thirty, Lewis shouted downstairs, 'Bennett!' I answered him and Lewis said, 'I just wanted to see if you sneaked out to see Faulkner.' "

Cerf laughed till tears came to his eyes. Then he continued: "Anyway, first you have to spot them. Irwin Shaw wrote a play called *Bury the Dead* and we published it. I wrote Shaw a letter and he came in. He was bursting at the seams, so full of vigor. But he seemed down-and-out. I asked him if he needed a job. Turned out he was making five hundred dollars a week writing radio shows—more than Donald [Klopfer] and I put together. . . . Truman Capote came into our lives when he was eighteen. His story, *Miriam*, appeared in *Mademoiselle*. We wrote him a letter and that's how we published *Other Voices, Other Rooms*. Then, right away, there was his picture in *Life*. Truman did that, not us. Some people have a natural flair for publicity and some don't. I don't know what the difference is. . . . Budd Schulberg was editing the college paper at Dartmouth when I went up for the Yale-Dartmouth game. There was a story on a strike in Vermont in the paper and I wrote a letter to Schulberg saying I'd like to meet the editor who had the courage to put a strike on the front page the day of the game. We became friends and the book turned out to be *What Makes Sammy Run?* When you get older, you have to get young editors who can do this for you. My lectures help—following a visit to the universities, a flood of manuscripts come in. We encourage many writers, but only a few pay off. . . . Of course, every publisher in the business has turned down at least ten books that wound up on the best-seller list. We picked up *No Time for Sergeants*, Mac Hyman's book, poor Mac, after four publishers turned it down. We knew just what to do with it. I named it. Cut off the last half. Best seller for twenty weeks. But we turned down *A Lion is in the Streets*, a big best seller. We had the manuscript, we read it, and one of our reader reports said, 'Forty pages of this magnolia-laden crap was all I could stand.' Lots of times editors tear up their reader reports. . . . Eugene O'Neill was published by Boni & Liveright where I started in the business, 1923. Donald Klopfer and I bought The Modern Library from Liveright and that's what we started with. We paid something over two hundred thousand dollars for it, added titles, threw out titles, and made it grow. Then, in the early Thirties, Liveright went bankrupt. An O'Neill play like *Mourning Becomes Electra* had sold seventy thousand copies. Every publisher in New York wanted O'Neill. I went down to Sea Island to see him in person and got a verbal contract while the other publishers were still in town talking to his agent. . . . Sinclair Lewis came to us because of Harry Maule, the editor. Mignon Eberhart, same way. Robert Penn Warren was brought in by Albert [Erskine]. Very personal business. . . . A female author left because Albert got married. Bill Styron came here because of Hiram Haydn. Haydn was our executive editor, but when he moved to Atheneum, Styron stayed here. Haydn helped persuade Jerome Weidman to come here from Doubleday after starting at S[Simon] and S[Schuster]. . . . James Michener was a textbook editor at Macmillan until he wrote *Tales of the South Pacific,* published by Macmillan. Macmillan thought it was a good idea for Michener to publish with us from then on. Ten days later, his book won the Pulitzer Prize. *The Snake Pit* came in to us unsolicited. It hit us like lightning. We knew we had a great book. . . . Harold Humes was negotiating with Knopf to take over his Random House contract while the Knopf-Random House merger deal was going on secretly. . . ."

Cerf drew a long breath. "Say," he said, "have you got a novel?"

One bright morning a few days later, Cerf rode in a chauffeur-driven rented limousine to the Rumson-Fair Haven Regional High School in Red Bank, an exurban community beside the Jersey shore. A highly agitated gaggle of tweedy women, representing the local Junior League subscription lecture-series committee, met him at the door. They escorted him first to the faculty lounge, where *they* all had a smoke. Cerf fished in his coat, found a small packet labeled *Bennet Cerf's Mints* (the printer had misspelled Bennett), and popped one into his mouth. After a while, Cerf's escort led him into a 700-seat auditorium packed with upper-class high-school kids and prematurely middle-aged ladies. A mistress of ceremonies, with a catch in her voice, introduced "that warm and dynamic personality, Mr. Bennett Cerf." Cerf grasped the lectern and began a rambling talk about publishing, authors, plagiarism, censorship, and life behind the scenes on *What's My Line?*

"You aren't going to hear any tales of woe from me," Cerf began. "The world gets smaller and smaller and you've got to get accustomed to it. . . . I say the way to get used to it is with a sense of humor and a sense of optimism . . . let's laugh." They laughed when he told how James Michener, in 1938, had gone to an island to get away from it all, "and that island was called Guadalcanal." Cerf had a joke about Yogi Berra, another about John Daly, and a third about himself. One of his most memorable lines concerned fame—"Anyone who says he doesn't like it, is crazy." This was topped by the peroration—"In the words of Will Rogers, our greatest humorist: 'You can get along in this world if you, *one*, work hard, *two*, think big and, *three*, have a dream.' I hope you've had some beautiful dreams and that a lot of them will come true."

In the question period that followed, a lady wearing a bell-shaped hat asked Cerf if *What's My Line?* was rigged.

"Absolutely not," Cerf replied. "There was one time when Sam Goldwyn, the movie producer, had dinner at my house and said, 'Hey Bennett, what kind of questions are you going to ask me on Sunday night?' And I said, 'I'm not going to see you Sunday night.' And Goldwyn said, 'Yes, on that fool show of yours, I'm the mystery guest.' So, I told him now I had to disqualify myself. Then, a couple of days later, Goldwyn saw Dorothy Kilgallen. He said, 'Boy, did I make a fool out of myself with Bennett Cerf the other night.' She asked him how come and he told her. . . . Since two of us couldn't disqualify ourselves we faked it. I asked him wrong questions like, 'Are you a comedian?' "

The students and the ladies roared. They loved Bennett Cerf.

After he had autographed fifty or sixty copies of his recent books, *Out on a Limerick* and *Riddle-De-Dee*, Cerf ate lunch with the power structure of the Junior League at the home of a patron in nearby Rumson. Among the dozen or so guests was a large-eyed, knit-dress lady who briefly cornered him.

"I'd know you anywhere," she said.

"*I love to be recognized!*" Cerf cried.

"You look younger than you do on TV."

"I am younger."

"Who's your favorite author?"

"My favorite author is Plato—no complaints about book jackets, ads—"

"I've been reading Celine."

"Celine? That reminds me of the fellow who lost his false teeth hunting in Ceylon and ever since he's been looking for his bridge on the River Kwai."

By four that afternoon, sans limousine, Cerf was in Philadelphia to give the first lecture in a series on "The Mass Media in Contemporary America," sponsored by the Annenberg School of Communications, a division of the University of Pennsylvania. He spoke agreeably on the state of the publishing business, dined in the faculty club, met with a class of fifty for an hour of questions ("Can a good writer always get a publisher, Mr. Cerf?") and answers ("He's sure to be discovered. The trouble is too many rotten books are being published"), and boarded the 7:45 P.M. train for New York. He sagged in his parlor-car seat, so tired for the moment that he seemed weighted down by the pile of newspapers in his lap. Slowly, as the train rolled, he hunted through the *Inquirer* until he found the book page. He brightened. The local critic had liked a Random House book. Cerf turned to me:

"Did I ever tell you about the time A. E. Hotchner got mad at a critic?"

"No," I said.

"A.E.'s ire rose," Cerf said. "That's what I call a beautiful pun."

The following Sunday evening, Cerf and his son, Chris, an enthusiastic, promising, and modest young man, arrived by taxi at a west side TV theater thirty minutes before the scheduled air time of *What's My Line?* As they entered, the elder Cerf restudied his list of likely mystery guests for the evening's show. He had prepared the list himself based on thirteen seasons of *What's My Line?* experience: mystery guests were usually show-business people, each with a promotional reason (a new play, a new film) for being in New York. "It's got to be Janis Paige," Cerf said. "Or Tony Bennett, Carol Lawrence, or maybe Albert

Finney—no, no one knows Finney out West." While Chris Cerf sought a seat in the audience, his father trotted upstairs to the dressing rooms. In one room Bennett found Arlene Francis, wearing a creamy gown, and Tony Randall, the evening's guest panelist, tuned to the Judy Garland show on television.

"Hello!" Cerf cheered.

"Bennett!" Arlene cried, presenting her cheek for a kiss.

"Hey, there, Bennett," Randall said, deadpan.

In the doorway behind Cerf, Dorothy Kilgallen, the Hearst columnist, paused, then made an entrance. She wore a sexy black dress and unique hairdo, topped by a bit of hat-like black fluff. Cerf's eyes flicked up, closed, and reopened straightaway. Then he warmly embraced Dorothy and moved past her down the hall to the makeup room. On the way, he met Franklin Heller, the dark, jowly, jolly man who directs *What's My Line?*

"What is she trying to do?" Cerf asked.

"Who?"

"Dorothy, with the hairdo. What's she trying to do to her hair?"

"That's her new hairdresser."

"What's she doing? She should know what people in the Midwest are saying about her hairdo."

"She's got this new hairdresser."

"Well, people think she's lost her—"

"At least, Bennett, it's better than the old days when she used to do it herself."

Cerf and Heller walked, single file, into the makeup room. Cerf sat for a brief touch-up. Heller faced him in the mirror.

"Hey, Bennett," Heller said. "What about Dick Condon's new book?"

(Condon, author of *The Manchurian Candidate*, had recently switched to Random House from McGraw-Hill.)

"Joe Fox [Condon's editor at Random House] was excited about the first part of it," Cerf said.

"I hear he's read all of it and loved it."

"Maybe so."

"It's a great novel."

"That's wonderful—what's your interest, Frank? Do you own a piece of it?"

"Naw, Bennett—I guess you'd say I was the catalyst."

"That's good," Cerf said, "we'll put it on our fall catalyst."

Cerf returned to the room down the hall. The TV had been turned off and Arlene, Tony, and Dorothy were warming up for the game with a friend who had volunteered as an imaginary contestant. So far, the panel was off the mark.

"You're Elizabeth Taylor!" Cerf guessed.

"Right!" the volunteer said, gaping.

Elizabeth Taylor's name reminded Arlene of a pet peeve. She said: "Jack O'Brian [another Hearst columnist] managed to drag *me* into his criticism of *her* [Elizabeth Taylor's] TV show from London. He said *she* sounded like *me* when I interview a visiting Englishman or someone from the upper clawsses."

"He has to pick on you," Dorothy said consolingly, "because he can't pick on me. . . ."

Suddenly, Cerf seized Dorothy's hands, swung them up in the air, rose on tiptoes himself, and, around his pipe, exclaimed: *"Dorothy, your performance is mag-ni-fi-cent!"*

"Oh, Bennett, you—"

Then everybody laughed.

Five minutes remained before air time. John Daly had gone to the set. Frank Heller was on his way to the booth. The four panelists scurried. Last man on the stairs was Cerf. Here, he again gave serious thought to his private list of likely mystery guests, intoning, "Tony Bennett, Carol Lawrence, Janis Paige. . . ."

The mystery guest turned out to be funny Groucho Marx and no one guessed.

In Mt. Kisco on a Saturday, Cerf, dressed in a lumberjack shirt, beat-up slacks, and old shoes, walked me from his roomy, off-white clapboard house down the hill past the swimming pool through the bathhouse along the tennis court between the flower beds up the 190-yard fairway and down, visiting two well-kept putting greens, over to the duck pond, up again to the care-taker's house, into the trees along the singing Kisco River and back to the house for one more panoramic view of his 47-acre estate, "The Columns," as he calls it because the royalties from his newspaper column paid for it. "Isn't it beautiful!" Cerf shouted. Back in the house at dusk, he decided it was too late for a rubdown from the lady masseur who had just finished with Mrs. Cerf. The lady masseur, lugging a suitcase, departed. Cerf changed into a white shirt bearing his monogram, BAC, a dark tie, and light suit. Then, he checked the wall of books in the living room to make sure that *Goodbye, Columbus* and *Letting Go,* both by Philip Roth and the latter published by Random House, were visible and in good company. They were—at eye level and associated with William Styron on the right and Henry Carlisle, Jr., on the left. Roth and four other people had been invited for dinner. After they arrived, there was relaxed, amiable cocktail conversation, and a steak dinner was served. Then, returning to the living room, Roth paused at the bookshelf. "Well," he said, "there are *my* books." Later, after Roth and the other people had departed, and Cerf and his wife and son were together in the living room, I remarked on Cerf's good luck with the placement of Roth's books. "I never said," Cerf said, "I didn't do things to be nice to authors." The next afternoon, Truman Capote came calling in his new, robin's-egg blue, XK-E Jaguar, named "Bluegirl." He was short and blond, but stouter than he had seemed in that *Life* photograph of almost twenty years before.

"How do you like Bluegirl?" he asked, settling down on a couch in the living room next to Mrs. Cerf.

"Beautiful," Bennett Cerf said.

"At one hundred and thirty-five miles per hour," Capote said, "you have the feeling that the road is rising up. It's an optical illusion, I know, but I can't get it out of my head that I'm going to run into a wall. So, I don't go quite as fast as that."

Capote went to Bluegirl and returned with a fat brown envelope. He pulled out three installments of a projected four-part *New Yorker* series, titled *In Cold Blood.* Three years of research, assisted by Harper Lee, and writing had gone into telling the story of a quadruple murder in Garden City, Kansas. After *The New Yorker* published it, Random House would do the book. Capote held up each installment, secured by paper clips, and waved them happily in the air. He said that it was almost over.

"Where are you going now?" Cerf asked.

"Back to Garden City."

"For what?"

"That's installment number four."

"Tell me about it," Mrs. Cerf pleaded.

"I will not. *You* have all kinds of secrets at Random House." Somehow, Capote lost a paper clip. After a search under the couches and tables and between the cushions, he shrugged and stuffed the galleys back into his envelope. He said he had to go. Cerf and his wife went to the door with him. Capote opened Bluegirl's door on the driver's side. Then with one foot inside and one foot on the gravel of Cerf's majestic driveway, he turned and shouted to me, "Become a Random House author and you can own one of these." And then, before he roared off, he blew a kiss to Ginger Rogers' cousin and to fun-loving Bennett Cerf, who is sixty-five years old.

Personal

While researching this place, I came across the autobiography of Donald Friede, published in 1948, in which the editor and publisher recalled his first meeting with Bennett Cerf. Working for Boni and Liveright in the summer of 1925, Friede wrote, Cerf had been "as blandly disarming as he is today, and fully as joke-conscious." From this testimony and my own eye witness, Cerf appeared unchanged in nearly forty years. Presumably, such consistency was fun for him and not really anyone else's business, so he wasn't much help when asked to explain his motives. Some of his friends have since told me that reading "The Long Happy Life of Bennett Cerf" enabled them to understand him better than ever before. I find this amazing, because aside from his need for deference, I still don't know what makes him tick.

John Wayne
God
and Man
in
Hollywood

One of the most significant factors in the art, economics, and politics of Hollywood is a strapping, beak-nosed, 55-year-old citizen with an incomparable cantilevered walk named John Wayne. His friends call him "Duke." He is a movie star in a community where love is not only the energy of life, but also box office. His rewards, influence, power are finally determined by his ability to inspire love, admiration, sympathy, hero worship. He really can do it. His pictures have played before four hundred million dollars' worth of loving audiences at home and abroad. A Paramount press agent who knows that love is what makes the industry go round says, "Everybody loves Duke. A hundred thousand people showed up for the première of *The Alamo* in San Antonio. Fifty thousand people turned out in Toronto when he went there for *Hatari!* He delivered a poem at Independence Hall in Philadelphia last June—thirty thousand people for that one. He even went walking down Bourbon Street in New Orleans after dinner one night and you could hear the murmuring: 'Here comes the Duke!' And all the B-girls and the bartenders and the strippers came out and said, 'Hiya, Duke,' and 'Hello, Duke, baby!' That Duke—he draws crowds like the President." John Wayne is also a superpatriot. He really loves this country. In a Chicago night club not long ago when the orchestra leader asked if he would like him to play Wayne's favorite tune, Wayne replied, "No, if you played my favorite tune, everybody would have to stand up." It follows that he is one with the diverse intellectuals, retired colonels, campus firebrands, professional anti-Communists, industrial tycoons, young women looking for husbands, and everyday folk who are creating such a flap on the Right nowadays. "All I care about," Wayne recently told an interviewer from one of the big magazines, "is liberty of the individual." In that spirit, a while back, he publicly denounced thin, beak-nosed Frank Sinatra for offering a screenwriting job to one of the Hollywood Unfriendly Ten. To Wayne, individuality means about the same tingly thing it means to, say, Douglas MacArthur or John Edgar Hoover, both of whom, incidentally, *he* loves. In short, the Duke, who has appeared in four hundred movies and almost as many rightist meeting places, comes close to being the Hollywood apotheosis of the Right-Wing American—but not quite. Getting to know him, one finds that stardom comes first. This kind of love, it seems, conquers all.

In the movies, Wayne is committed to a characterization that is too broad to qualify as a specific symbol for the Right. In his starring role, he is a rough crossing of Gary Cooper and Victor McLaglen. His appeal is less to the adult than to the adolescent, which group is hardly a monopoly of the Right. Wayne used to play his role closer to Cooper's wistfulness, but now he plays it on the hard-nosed McLaglen's side. The factor here, of course, is aging, not ideology.

Wayne came up in the Thirties through Grade-B and worse Westerns. Early on, he changed his name from Marion Michael Morrison to the more masculine-sounding John Wayne and his "personality" from that of an Iowa-born son of a druggist and U.S.C. football-fraternity chap to slow-talking cowboy. Wayne has said it took him years to learn how to say "ain't." After accomplishing this, he still had to wait until his good friend John Ford, the director, was able to find a producer willing to let him play the Ringo Kid in *Stagecoach.* Producer Walter Wanger finally agreed and Wayne became the Kid (the Duke was already in his thirties, but looked younger)—rangy but trim, romantic, lawless, unmoved by violence, aggressive toward men but gentle with women—the Western hero who is part of the fantasy of the Center and Left Wing of America as well as the Right. In 1939, then, nine years after appearing in his first film, Wayne finally created a character that vast audiences could love. He became a big star. As the years went by, he looked the part of a Kid less and less, but he played in that field until he was a fleshy forty. Luckily, Borden Chase, the screenwriter, came along in the nick of time with *Red River*, in which, Chase predicted, Wayne would find a role that he could play "for the next twenty years." What was *Red River?* Chase says he wrote his scenario with the elements of *Mutiny on the Bounty* in mind. Now Wayne could become a middle-aged heavy, a Texas Captain Bligh on a cattle drive that was essentially a voyage. And of course Montgomery Clift would be the Western Mr. Christian. Wayne's looks were suited to the lubbering, finally sympathetic, ruthlessness of the *Red River-Bounty* protagonist. Forthwith a large, loving public responded to the refurbishment of John Wayne, made him top box-office star in 1950 (he'd been sixteenth in 1948) and again in 1954, and has kept him well near the top to this day.

Wayne understands about love and movies. "The way the business is today," he says, "the producers have got to know they're going to get their money out. They don't want me to play any roles but the one people seem to *like*, and I wouldn't want to do anything different anyway." Wayne accepts the basic requirement of the Hollywood star-loving system which is conformity to a screen image. Even if he didn't, he would have had proof of its inexorable logic by now. The one time he did essay a slight change in character, just a little one, he stumbled. In casting his own production of *The Alamo*, Wayne chose to play Davy Crockett, a straight and uncomplicated frontier hero. He could have played the Alamo commander, Travis (Captain Bligh), but instead gave the role to the English actor, Laurence Harvey, who carried it off using a selection of accents: deep Southern, Western, and finally, as if to say the hell with it, pure British. "Travis might have been better for me," Wayne says with the advantage of hindsight, "but I didn't think I ought to be hogging the whole picture." The result was a film, whatever its merits, that did not attain the dramatic coherence hoped for it. One kept waiting for Wayne to go into his hard-man act, but it did not happen. Instead, Laurence Harvey had all the lines. Unquestionably, box-office returns, which are coming in slower than expected, reflect the fact that Wayne was out of character

—his picture fails to satisfy the need to love the star-image of John Wayne. "I believe in the meaning of *The Alamo*," he says. "But let's face it, I made the picture to make money." Of the twelve million dollars said to have gone into the film, Wayne supplied about one million five hundred thousand dollars of his own money and investors, including the Texas magnate, Clint Murchison, provided the rest. The latter have been paid back. And *The Alamo* ranks high among the top-grossing pictures of all time. But Wayne has yet to earn back his own money. He probably will some day, but he is having financial difficulties at the moment and seems unlikely to stray from Captain Bligh again. As a star, he has little, if any, independence of his own image. He must check free will, like a shooting iron, at the studio gate. He may not want to be other than what he is, but it is no less ironic, given his credo of individualism, that he cannot be.

The Wayne character is essentially a property for the movie business. "Wayne is awfully patriotic and we don't always agree on social issues," says Howard Hawks, who directed three of Wayne's best-loved films, *Red River, Rio Bravo,* and *Hatari!* "But he doesn't ask that that stuff be put in. Wayne says, 'Don't tell me the story, Howard, tell me when you want me.' On *Rio Bravo*, he said okay before he looked at the script. On the other hand, I use him a lot in testing whether he feels right doing a scene. He is a better actor than he is given credit for. Look, he has got the ability to play three or four good scenes and not offend the audience the rest of the time. What you get from Wayne is authority. He looks like he belongs in Western clothes. You also get a personality. I do not believe too much in actors playing parts. I believe in tailoring the part to the personality. In a love scene, Clark Gable always forced the issue with a girl. That was his personality. Now Wayne is better when the girl is forcing the issue. That is his personality in that particular situation. So, if you've got a love story in a Wayne picture, you adjust it to his personality. He just wouldn't be effective if he were aggressive toward a woman. Partly that's because of his size. He is too big to be a Rover Boy like Gable was."

Wayne is also his own capital asset. "Motion pictures, see, are made up of personalities," says James Edward Grant, who wrote *The Alamo* and many other Wayne vehicles. "Great acting has nothing to do with it. You have to have a voice that suits your body. Wayne is not ashamed of being an actor, but he doesn't want to get caught acting by the stunt men and the grips. Wayne isn't acting most of the time, see. If you can just get him to feel he's not making a fool out of himself, he'll go the limit. Now, you take Bogart—he used to say Wayne was a fine actor within his limits. Duke walks well and looks good in action. That's the trick. See, here's how you can really judge who's who in Hollywood today: this is the time in Hollywood when the producing company or the bank tells you that they'll give you so much money for stars. Widmark is worth maybe $400,000. That's all you can get to make a Widmark picture and I don't care if it is bound to be another *Gone With the Wind*. Hank Fonda—well, maybe you could raise $600,000 with Fonda right now. Bob Mitchum—he's good for $750,000 or thereabouts. I'm talking about money for the whole picture. Now, Wayne gets practically unlimited money. His personal guarantee against a percentage of the gross is $750,000. Wayne and Bill Holden and Liz Taylor—they're the ones that can get unlimited money. This is the thing you have to have."

None of this, as one can see, has anything to do with Wayne's politics. He may be the apotheosis of something in his movie career, but it is not Right Wingery. "My business is stardom," he says, the way Popeye says he's a sailor. In meeting the demand for lovableness, he has had to keep his politics mostly off the screen. With but two or three exceptions, Wayne's films have been nonpolitical (except insofar as all things in heaven and earth are, finally, relevant to politics). One might look upon *Big Jim McLain,* the story of a two-fisted congressional investigator, and *The Alamo* as overt expressions of his philosophy. *The Alamo,* indeed, was widely promoted as the Duke's "statement." He was the star, producer, director and script supervisor and no doubt intended people to look for the political significance in it. He had no compunction about wrapping it in the flag in trying to sell it. Some of the ads even implied that anyone who didn't go to see it was un-American. Ostensibly, *The Alamo's* message was better-dead-than-Red with a touch of this-is-a-republic-not-a-democracy. But just sitting in a theater, watching it for what it is—a rousing, occasionally spectacular, and somewhat askew Western—one realizes that Wayne is first of all a Hollywood man, an *ifyouwantamessage callWestern-Unionman*. His message, such as it was, turned out to be better-dead-than-Mexican. And, as indicated above, the audience almost loved it.

Outside the movies, however, Wayne comes into his own as a Right-Wing American. About the time he was assuming his new screen character as a "sympathetic heavy," he entered the lists as an outspoken member of the Motion Picture Alliance for the Preservation of American Ideals. With Borden Chase, Clark Gable, Ronald Reagan, with Adolphe Menjou, Gary Cooper, and forty or fifty others in MPA, Wayne determined to drive Communist individuals and fellow-traveler individuals, such as they were, out of the movie industry. Their determination was shared by the House Un-American Activities Committee Looking into Communist Infiltration of the Motion Picture Industry, known for short, in Hollywood, as The Committee. In the late Forties, there was some tolerance for the differing opinions of civil libertarians, MPA members, Communists, and anyone else who wanted to talk on the issue of the loyalty of free men. This ended, for all practical purposes, when the head moguls of the industry decided not only that no more Communists could work in pictures, but that former Communists were also out unless willing to participate in the name-naming ritual of The Committee. The cause of MPA had scored a victory and the organization became a clearinghouse for "converts" on their way to The Committee. Of all its members, none was more assiduous than John Wayne.

As one might expect, his role in MPA was that of sympathetic heavy. "Duke really went into the work of the organization," says Borden Chase, who was a founder of MPA. "He became president after Clark Gable and Robert Taylor. He was no *front*. Duke had guts. We had a split in the group—the 'once-a-Communist, always-a-Communist' group and the group that thought it was ridiculous to destroy some of those who, say, joined the Party in the Thirties in Nazi Germany. Duke and I were in the latter group. We were converting people and wanted to keep on. (I have a hundred twenty converts today.) Duke was sincere in this and was ready to stick his neck out. He was president during the Larry Parks affair, for example, and almost got his head chopped off. I got a call from Bill Wheeler, investigator for The Committee, just about the time Parks was to go on the stand in New York and tell all. Wheeler said that The Committee wanted someone to get up and say that Parks was a good American. I said okay, but would he please send me a letter covering his request? Then I wrote a speech for Duke in which he commended Parks for testifying and said that any man can make a mistake and he hopes Americans will understand and that Parks can come back into the motion-picture industry now. The next night, at eight o'clock—which was eleven o'clock New York time—Duke read the speech at a big MPA meeting at the American Legion Stadium. In the meantime, the papers were coming out in New York with the story that Parks had not done what he'd said he was going to do. And Hedda Hopper had the information, too. Only she was sitting right there listening to Duke. She grabbed the microphone and ate Duke out in public. Duke looked at me as if to say, 'How could you do this to me?' Well, fortunately, the letter asking for the Parks speech came from Bill Wheeler before too much damage was done and got Duke off the hook with Hedda and some of the others. Later, of course, Parks did testify, but you can see how far out Duke was willing to stick his neck in this anti-Communist work. Don't think it didn't cost him, either. When *The Alamo* was coming out, the word of mouth on it was that it was a dog. This was created by the Communists to get at Wayne. Then there were some bad reviews inspired by the Communists. Of course, I wouldn't say that all criticism of *The Alamo* was Communist-inspired, but some of these movie reviewers, who are only liberals, have some best pals who are Communists—now, the reviewers don't know that the pals are Communists and so they are influenced by them. This is why some of them said it was a dog. It's a typical Communist technique and they were using it against Duke for what he did in MPA."

In the early Fifties, Wayne relinquished the presidency of MPA to his friend, Ward Bond, but maintained his interest in the organization until, with the death of Bond, it became defunct. He also lent his support to other causes—especially the two Eisenhower campaigns and Nixon's try for the presidency in 1960—out of a conviction that the country is being ruined by "democracy." "Obviously," he says, "government is the enemy of an individual. My feeling about life is that you're put here and you have to make your own way. Our country used to be small enough so that a man who'd proven himself and who had some understanding could get himself sent to Congress and the people back home would just go on about their business believing that whatever he'd do would be good enough for them. Those were the days when Congress chose the President. Now, though, we've got this democracy and the politician kowtows to whomever wants the most. Instead of going in and running his office the way he should, the politician appeals to the popular vote, that being the mob vote. Believe me, this can ruin America."

A short time ago, Wayne approved an invitation to me that had been extended by Paramount's New York press agent to visit the Duke while he was working on a new John Ford picture called *Donovan's Reef*. Originally, I had hoped to catch up with Wayne while the Ford company was still on location in Hawaii, but failing that, I arranged to meet him in Hollywood at the Paramount Studios. For any New Yorker intrigued by the Hollywood community, it must be a curious experience today to go from the city to the movie colony. In New York, movies are okay now. Almost everybody is writing movie criticism for one magazine or another and he who isn't is, at least, a movie buff, able to quote obscure casts of characters and ever ready to reminisce over a scene from an early Cagney. Movies are today the proper study of man. Where once there were only Leo Rosten, Hortense Powdermaker, and a few others, now there are scores of intelligent and interesting analysts of cinema culture. In Greenwich Village, along the Upper West Side, and even occasionally on Broadway, theaters are piling up lively grosses replaying grainy classics and serving black coffee in small cups for lower-middle-upper bohemians. One theater recently played fourteen Bogarts in a row and did very well with them. For reading material, some New Yorkers say they are getting pleasure out of James Agee's collected movie reviews and others at least carry around *Film Culture*. It may be said that the era of enchantment with the film has arrived in New York. In contrast to this, the atmosphere of Hollywood is mournful. The place has been a shambles for some time, of course. Nathanael West's people have long since switched to TV, moved into the suburbs to avoid the smog, or for all one knows, finally found something to do—like attending meetings of the Christian Anti-Communism Crusade. So many premièreless nights have gone by that, when a finger of klieg light is seen in the sky, the man in the street knows a new supermarket and not a new movie is beckoning. What makes Hollywood seem more desolate than ever, though, is the fact that there are so few *movie* people around. Taking into account those who are abroad dodging taxes, it is still true that fewer people are now making fewer movies. To be sure, many are working in television in Hollywood, but such people aren't movie people anymore. One feels this absence of the real McCoys in the Hollywood bars, or when driving past Fox where three-hundred employees were let go at one time last year, or merely walking by Schwab's, which is just another drug store now. One feels it, too, when talking to the survivors, all of whom say they are living from picture to picture. They display various tics, mannerisms, and tendencies —like drinking too fast—that are more eloquent than words.

And who, the survivors ask you in half-envious, half-despairing tones, is doing better for himself than almost any Hollywood actor; who is the unscathed phoenix still living on the love of what's left of the great audience? John Wayne, that's who.

Wayne was working hard trying to finish up *Donovan's Reef* so that he would have two or three weeks off before the scheduled start of his next picture, *McLintock!*, yet another Western being produced this time by Batjac, his own company. In the week that I was in Hollywood, he arrived at the studio every morning, Monday through Friday, around eight, spent most of the day on the set and, bushed, drove home to Encino late in the afternoon. He was on camera the better part of each day and between times, just back of the set, carried on a continuing chess game with Pat Wayne, his twenty-three-year-old actor-son (Wayne has four children by his first wife, two very young ones by his third and present wife, Pilar, and six grandchildren). The younger, muscular, almost too-handsome Wayne was appearing in the Ford film with his father while his brother, Michael, twenty-seven, and Duke's brother, Robert Morrison, were elsewhere on the lot working on the Batjac project. The one afternoon Ford excused Wayne from the set he spent in James Grant's nearby office, discussing the latest Western script with Grant and Andrew McLaglen, forty-seven-year-old son of the late Victor, whose experience had included the direction of seventy-five *Gunsmokes* and a hundred twenty-five *Have Gun, Will Travels* for TV. He was getting his first big break as a movie director from Wayne, who had loved his father. Well, I hung around all week watching Wayne being busy and then, Thursday evening, he invited me to spend the weekend with him in Arizona hunting up locations for *McLintock!*.

The Friday shooting schedule specified a continuation of the brawl scenes Wayne had been working on for several days under the good, unpatched right eye of John Ford. The Duke, dressed in yacht cap and khakis, was supposed to be a retired Navy man named Donovan running a bar called Donovan's Reef on a tropical island in the Pacific. He was asked now to defend the place from Dick Foran and numerous other drunken British sailors. When I arrived, midmorning, Wayne was just getting set, rearing back, and throwing a right hand at a jutting jaw for the thousandth or ten-thousandth time in a movie. *Pow!* No one does it any better or looks better doing it. Wayne is at least six-feet-four and weighs about two-twenty-five. He is all bulk, but he moves himself gracefully, like a mean tomcat. His head is large, his beaked nose is large and his beefy hands are large. The skin under his chin is holding up well and makeup obliterates the permanent flush in his cheeks. Just above the belt, he has a paunch, minimized by low-slung trousers. For a man fifty-five accustomed to four packs of cigarettes a day and, on occasion, quantities of whiskey, he looks bullish. His eyes, heavy-lidded above and deeply lined in the corners, look old but not tired. The well-known, thin-lipped, bedroom grin is apparently the natural set of his mouth since he is almost always wearing it, even when throwing horrendous punches. (Women, the star theory goes in Hollywood, want to sleep with Wayne. They want to mother a Gary Cooper. Which means that a Clark Gable, with whom mothers want to sleep, is really a superstar.)

The sailor "hit" by Wayne fell in a heap—to the incredulous distress of John Ford, who had wanted him to fly backward into, it seemed, Ford's canvas chair. Ford had been running the set from underneath his baseball cap and around his green cigar in moods varying from cranky irritability to rage. Now, "Goddam!" he shouted. "Forty-five years in this business and never lost my temper, but you, you sonofabitch!" including everyone on the set in his epithet, except Wayne, whom he gentled. The director and the star had known each other for more than thirty years and understood each other well enough for Ford to do most of his directing *around* Wayne. While Ford burned, Wayne moved off the set for a touch-up from Web Overlander, who has been his personal makeup man for twenty years. They are next-door neighbors in Encino.

"Ford's the most even-tempered sonofabitch in Hollywood," Overlander said. "Always *mad*."

"Mr. Wayne," an assistant director cried.

"I guess I got to go belt somebody again," Wayne said.

"They don't let you rest, do they?" a passing grip said.

"No, but Christ—the money is good," Wayne said.

Next time, the sailor flew correctly when Wayne swung at him and the actors took a break. A few yards behind the camera, Wayne and his son Pat picked up their chess match where they had left it. The younger man played a formal game, moving pawns and then knights in logical order. The father, however, moved erratically, worked the flanks, and apparently did not mind that his king was three squares up from the base line while his queen was immobilized by his own pawns. Yet, suddenly, one could see that the son's caution was costing material. He seemed to play as though he expected to lose to the Duke and he did.

At lunch in the studio commissary, Wayne sat with his sons, Pat and Mike, and me. Mike is slighter and less formidable-looking than his father and kid brother. He is president of Batjac and wants to be a film producer. They were a tight group. Someone had dropped off a copy of *Film Culture* in which a critic had praised Wayne as "one of the finest movie actors we have," while another had said Ford's *The Man Who Shot Liberty Valance* was on a par with Welles' *Citizen Kane*.

"That's a lot of intellectual garbage," Duke said.

"My father has always been belted by the critics," Mike explained.

"When they begin to take you seriously," Duke said, "*Look out.*"

Wayne ordered a small steak and tomatoes. Since he had arranged for me to see a screening of *The Alamo* the day before, we fell to talking about it. He said the picture had had a rough time in the theaters on a two-a-day basis, but had taken off as soon as it was changed over to a continuous-showing policy. "The exhibitors wanted twenty minutes cut out of the picture," Duke said, "so I did it and it made it seem an hour longer. But Christ! We're talking like *The Alamo* wasn't a big success. It's a big success."

He ate quickly, virtually between cigarettes. He said *The Alamo* had cost a lot of money and that he felt he had gotten most of the money on the screen even though it was the first time he had ever directed a picture. He attributed his success in this to the fact that he had, after all, been around a lot of directors for a long time. He emphasized that exhaustive research had been done on every phase of the Alamo story and that J. Frank Dobie and other Texas historians had co-operated.

"See how we treated Santa Anna," he said. "He wasn't all bad, although he's always been made out to look that way. We studied him from every angle. You know, he was quite a boy. He got a charter of freedom for the Mexican people that was a lot like ours. But then, when he took over, he pulled a Kennedy and started grabbing the power."

Late that afternoon, doing the Wayne walk under a twenty-year-old, sweat-stained, broad-brimmed white Stetson, the Duke stepped up to the bar at the Los Angeles International Airport. The Phoenix-bound entourage—Mike Wayne, also wearing a cowboy hat, Andy McLaglen, and brother Bob Morrison, included—fanned out around him and everyone had a drink before boarding time. Someone had steamed up the Duke about a recent kidnapping. "If I caught a kidnapper," he said, "I would shoot the sonofabitch in the eye and turn right around and eat my breakfast." Brother Bob, who was shorter than Brother John, younger but looking older, and quieter, savored his drink. He said that twenty-five years ago, in the Thirties, Duke used to get into a lot of fights. "Once he grabbed a director," Brother Bob said, "and shook him and cussed him out right on the set and the crew applauded. And another time, before he'd become a star, he was at a party and there was this crap game going on and Duke caught a big, famous star cheating. So, Duke grabbed the guy by the hair and dragged him around the party, telling people that the guy was a cheat." The Duke was just saying that he couldn't wait to get going when the flight was called. "Because," he said, leading the way to the boarding gate, "any day now, this new boat of mine is going to be delivered and I don't want to be somewhere else when it comes. It's a hundred and thirty-six-foot converted minesweeper. I know that's big, lots bigger than my seventy-three-footer that I don't have any more, but I need the space for the six kids and the six grandchildren and the wife; that makes fourteen people already. A boat's the only place I can relax and forget about my work. And I like to have my kids around me. You know how kids are. The only way you can have them is if you have something they want that no one else has. It was the same way with me. I love my mother—and my father [Wayne's father died in 1937]—but you make your own life and don't see your parents much unless they have something extra to offer." He took a seat toward the rear of the plane and buckled himself in. "I'm the guy," he said, "who, when I get to the poorhouse, I'll be able to look at the guy next to me and say, 'Did you ever have a hundred and thirty-six-foot yacht?' "

From Phoenix, the group drove in air-conditioned hired cars to a motel in Apache Junction, Arizona. As he registered, Wayne was approached by two small boys, one with an autograph book, the other with a half sheet of paper. Wayne signed the book. Then he fished in his pockets, pulled out a small, presigned white card, and gave it to the second boy. "Saves time signing autographs," Wayne explained, "having them written out in advance." He went to his room and unpacked his toilet kit. After a while, he came out refreshed and hungry. He ate steak for dinner, sitting beside a local man interested in promoting film locations in the neighborhood.

"I admit it's a small town," the promoter said. "Local paper has only eighty-two subscribers," he added, picking a small number from the air.

"Well, eighty-two people could take over the whole goddam country," Wayne said.

"How's that?"

"Well, Kennedy's got Schlesinger . . . Rostow . . . Rusk. . . ."

The promoter laughed, but the Duke didn't.

All through the next morning, as the desert temperature rose past the hundred-degree mark, Wayne and half a dozen followers humped over the countryside, over the hills and through the sage, looking at prospective sites for scenes in *McLintock!* Now and then Andy McLaglen took a photograph, but neither he nor Wayne seemed satisfied. By lunch time, Wayne was ready to move on to Tucson. That trip took most of the afternoon, interrupted by side trips to new sites and followed by visits to an "authentic" rebuilt Western town and two likely ranches. It was long and dull in the cars, not really cool, with twist music on the radio and an occasional news flash. This was the day that a Nationalist Chinese U-2 plane had been reported down in Red China.

Then, at last, it was Saturday night in the dining room of a good motel in Tucson. Somehow, the group had expanded to fifteen, Wayne, Wayne, Morrison, McLaglen, the promoter from Apache Junction (still hanging on), a girl, a Batjac production man who had been doing advance work, a couple of fellows from Tucson, their girls, and a few others who seemed to have business. Wayne sat at the middle of a long table, his son sat opposite. They held their own conversation agreeing that it was a hell of a note about that Nationalist Chinese U-2 plane:

"Listen," The Duke said, "all we've got to do is bring four-hundred Nationalist Chinese over here and train them at SAC and give them the equipment they need and they'll keep Red China . . . busy."

"Well, it's up to Jack Kenne—," Mike began.

"*Rusk,*" the Duke said, fiercely but not too loud. "*Rusk* was with Stilwell when they made that coalition government in China. *Rusk* was with Truman and told him, after he'd had the guts to go to war with the Communists, not to go all the way. *Rusk,* he was the one who wouldn't fight the thing all the way in Cuba. And now Rusk, *Rusk*, he's putting up a coalition government with the Commies in Laos. How many mistakes are we going to let the s.o.b. make? Damn it, they ought to let Chiang Kai-shek attack the mainland! He's a dictator, sure—okay, but he's the best dictator the Chinese ever had."

After his outburst, the Duke ordered his first drink of the day, and a steak. From time to time, as the dinner loped along, he signed menus for guests in the motel and once laughed out loud when a frumpy woman in her late fifties exclaimed: "I'm in love with you, now that Gable's gone." Wayne might have sat there the rest of the night, but about ten-thirty a drunk from the bar (gray-haired, bleary-eyed, about sixty years old) pulled up a chair. The drunk began a passionate discourse on the Cadillac motorcar. "I've got two of 'em, Dukie boy," he said. "How many you got?" Wayne shook hands with the man; then, quite suddenly, he slipped away to his room and went to bed.

"Fine thing," the drunk said to no one in particular. "An' I love that man, that Duke. I really love him."

Personal

I thought I should approach John Wayne with caution. After all, I am and always have been a liberal. This spiritual condition derives from my upbringing in Springfield, Illinois. My mother worshipped Eleanor Roosevelt and my father favored legalized gambling. Together, with love and patience, they taught me their own pre-existential political philosophy. "Always vote Democratic," Mom used to say. "Never vote Republican," Dad would add. Today, I even look like a liberal. I wear black-rimmed glasses, smoke unfiltered cigarettes, and always need a trim. More importantly, I *feel* like a liberal: On meeting a real conservative, I expect to get hit with my glasses on.

Imagine, then, my surprise when I found John Wayne approaching *me* with caution! During the first week we were together at his studio, he was either unavailable or monosyllabic. The work with John Ford went on from morning to late afternoon arousing in me a new respect for Wayne as a performer. But he played the subject-writer war game as though waiting for the FBI to clear me.

Anyway, something changed him, because on the eighth day

he arranged for me to see screenings of *Red River* and *Alamo*. And the next day, he invited me to lunch. I lit some fuses and, obligingly, he exploded. Thus, the narrative part of my piece began.

Later, Wayne wrote to thank me for fair treatment in *God and Man in Hollywood*. In his letter—the tone is amazement— he says I have an unusual trait for a Liberal: I have an open mind. Then, Wayne says he hopes *we* agree on the kind of mammals you find in the State Department. They are egotists, ineffective promoters of the national good, and irresponsibles who make decisions that only an elected official ought to make.

I do not agree, but as in the writing of the piece, I decline to comment on the grounds that Wayne, like Barry Goldwater, to whom he lent vociferous support in 1964, looks best hanging by his own petard.

Huntington Hartford
Peripatetic
Patron

George Huntington Hartford, II, is a dead-pan, high-strung man who was born very rich and who has been spinning off expensive "projects" in recent years like sparks from a well-oiled pinwheel. "I am basically a man of philosophical nature," Hartford says. "I am interested in ethics, why we're here, philosophy—that interests me more than anything else in life." But then there's all that money which, like it or not, is basic, too. It comes from two sources: an inheritance from his grandfather (and namesake) who founded the Great Atlantic & Pacific Tea Company, and another (smaller) inheritance from his maverick father who invented the Hartford shock absorber. Hartford's personal fortune has been estimated in the New York *Times* at five hundred million dollars. A close friend of Hartford's confidently ranks him as "one of the ten or twenty richest men in America." Hartford himself insists that such talk is eyewash. "I do not have half a billion dollars," he says. "I do not have a quarter billion. In 1959, to be exact, I had about seventy million. I've spent a lot of the cash since then and I may have to borrow on my A&P stock to keep things going." Hartford is sensitive about the overestimates. "Let's get it straight, huh?" he says. "Let's get it right about the money. Every time I do something, people say, 'Oh, so what? He's a bottomless well.' I'm not a bottomless well." For our purposes here, let's remember that we're talking about only seventy million dollars.

Huntington Hartford may be said to be project-oriented. He chooses his projects carefully, being under some compulsion

from his philosophical nature, the inevitable threat of a dull
life, the hope of immortality, the example set by other sons and
grandsons of American tycoons, and his own inner doubts. He
pursues projects almost as swiftly as ambitious men of ordinary
background pursue status. He is, in fact, pursuing a special kind
of success: deciding late in life to take himself seriously, Hartford has wanted others to take him seriously, too, and to give
him more respect. If and when this happens, here *is* success.
"Hunt has to have projects," says his second wife, Marjorie, who
recently sued him for divorce. "He has to do things—on his own.
If you've made your own money, you know you can make it
again if you lose it. Those born rich aren't sure emotionally.
Hunt spends his money the way he spends it to show himself
that he can do serious things. After that, he wants to win respect
from people he admires." Thus motivated, he works at achieving
his kind of success as doggedly as a Horatio Alger hero would,
given the style of living that seventy million dollars affords.
Hartford spends late winter in Florida and Nassau, springtime
in New York, summer and fall in London and the south of
France, and Christmas in New York before returning to Palm
Beach. He has homes in all those places, plus a week-end retreat in New Jersey, a canyon home in Hollywood, and a hun-
dred-foot yacht. (Joseph Conrad III, the yacht, is in Florida
most of the time, as are his children, Catherine, ten, and John,
seven, who attend school there.) Wherever he happens to be,
more often than not Hartford has his projects on his mind.

Recently, he gave New York City 862,500 dollars for a sidewalk café on the edge of Central Park next to General Sherman
and his horse. Before that, he committed himself to spend about
seven million dollars for a ten-story art museum on the same
street three blocks west at Columbus Circle. He paid fourteen
million dollars for an island in the Bahamas in 1959 and ear-
marked another six million dollars to make a resort out of it.
He has nine million dollars in a foundation for the support after
his death of the art museum, an art colony, and the scientific
analysis of handwriting. He gives healthy grants for medical
research and has nearly $1,500,000 invested in two futuristic
ventures—an automatic parking garage and a process for extracting crude oil from shale. Another 250,000 dollars is loaned out

to a pal who used it to start a liquor store. He's dropped a tidy bundle on a play which he wrote and produced, which flopped twice, and which he plans to produce yet again in London. He has a task force of magazine people working up layouts for *Show*, a new national monthly in the entertainment field, television folks organizing an international TV festival for his island, and himself hoping to produce more shows, write some books, and maybe make some movies.

Of such are Hartford's projects: some interesting, some dreary, some raising the question of responsibility—couldn't the money be better spent some other way? On all of them, there is the mark of a man in sincere pursuit of his goal. But, as Dr. Riesman has pointed out, sincerity isn't quite the same as seriousness.

At forty-nine, Hartford is a tall man, well-built, but giving the impression of being slight. He has appealing features, graying black hair, aquiline nose, and intense, dark eyes. His manner is casual, sometimes self-consciously so. He knows people in all classes, keeps his servants and employees for years, and lives up to G.B. Shaw's definition of good etiquette: he treats everyone alike. He deprives himself of the chauffeur-driven car in favor of the taxicab. He likes to conduct business meetings at home, wearing a sports shirt and bedroom slippers in a room full of Brooks Brothers. He is at pains to seem egalitarian. Like many men in America who are born rich, he has a tendency to self-depreciation. He still plays first-rate tennis and squash, but hastens to tell you that he prefers squash because his "nervousness" doesn't interfere with his game so much. "I am, I know, emotionally unstable," he volunteers. He is also shy. When the phone rings, he seizes the receiver like a ball-of-fire, smashes down the button and, with almost inaudible softness, speaks hesitantly into the mouthpiece. On the other hand, while his politics are conventional (Nixon-Lodge-conservative today), he seems touched with the fear of the haves for the have-nots. Once he missed a boat for Nassau, and had to take a plane. What distressed him most (besides the fact that he would have to fly, which he hates) was that now he would have to "travel with all the peasants." He once wrote that the ranks of the underprivileged were salted with envious "malcontents," "rotten apples in the barrel," whose "peace of mind ultimately depends on revolution and anarchy." His fear contributes to a certain apprehension toward strangers, too, but he has other, better reasons for that: many who come to him simply want a piece of his money. People he never saw before ask him to play banker and finance such schemes as bottling mint juleps, manufacturing bottle tops that don't need openers and cigarettes that don't need matches, filtering salt water, opening a Bible center, and erecting an Eiffel-type tower in Florida. "He's wary of people," says Sy Alter, the pal to whom he loaned the money for the liquor store, "because people are always trying to take him. That's why it's important to bring a proposition to Hunt through the right channels. If he likes you, he'll trust you." In a sense, Hartford is wary of his friends, too. They get few gifts from him, specifically none for birthdays or holidays. As though trying to discourage sycophancy, he warns them not to give him anything either. "It's certainly not that he's a tightwad," says Alter. "He's just a man who worries all the time about doing the right thing with his money and is frightened that he might do something wrong with it."

Hartford often has a distracted, vague expression on his face. If you notice it when he is greeting you, you hasten to tell him your name again, even though you've met him many times. He has a notoriously bad memory for faces. A while ago, a woman stopped him on the street and asked him how he was. Hartford gave her the look—a mixture of concentration and great distance—until at last she said, "I don't think you know who I am." She was his first wife. Hartford wears the distracted expression now and then during project meetings, too. It may mean only that he is trying to remember a name or worrying about the right way to spend his money. But one also feels that, try as he may, his pursuit bores him a little and when it does, he retreats behind the faraway look.

"I know the look," Marjorie Hartford says. "It doesn't mean anything. Hunt's just vague."

When in New York, Hartford works in the living room of his thirteen-room duplex on a high floor of a Beekman Place apartment building. It has a three-sided East River view. Looking south, one sees the United Nations building without obstruction.

A large painting of this panorama hangs over the fireplace. His wife, Marjorie, painted it. "My wife," says Hartford, "is one of the greatest female painters alive, perhaps who ever lived." Elsewhere in the living room are a huge stereo console, a globe of the world, and a massive bust of Joseph Conrad, Hartford's favorite author. (He has named three boats after Conrad and once produced *The Secret Sharer* in a good episodic movie called *Face to Face*.) The floor and some of the sitting places are littered with books, clippings, contact prints of pretty girls hoping to become models (Hartford's first project, now defunct, was a model agency), tapes, letters, learned journals (predominantly psychological or graphological), maps, renderings and brochures. Some of the litter pertains to on-going Hartford projects, the rest represents future prospects and previous unfulfilled passions. In the discard are some whoppers from his West Coast days: data on bringing a monastery from Spain to California stone by stone, drawings for a country club in Hollywood submitted by the late Frank Lloyd Wright, and some of the plans for a Hollywood art center with two playhouses, two movie theaters, an art gallery, and a garden of statuary to be built on Wilshire Boulevard across from the La Brea Tar Pits. In this confusion of past, present, and future, Hartford sees an essential order: "I'm in a position where I have the opportunity to do a number of things," he says, "and I'm doing them. The one link is that they all have a creative element. Nothing routine and nothing that isn't economically sound." As Hartford moves from place to place, the nerve center of his project operations naturally moves with him, but friends say he works harder and more consistently in the Beekman Place living room than anywhere else. He gets up late, goes to bed late, and holds meetings almost any time, day or night. He begins seeing advisers, assistants, lawyers, and collaborators as soon as he arrives from the south in the spring, and keeps them moving in and out like a good ringmaster should until he sails for Europe early in the summer. Here one can meet the director of his foundation, the manager of his theater, the editor of his proposed magazine, and the psychologist from his handwriting-research institute. Having spent some time recently in that living room, it seems to me that there are five Hartford projects that tell most about the man and to some extent offer a measure of his success.

The Huntington Hartford Foundation: In 1949, Hartford put up 600,000 dollars to save the world from its habit of ignoring the struggling artist, writer, and composer. It was his idea that the money might help artists produce better works by providing them with a six-month sojourn free of economic worry in pleasant surroundings. So he created a retreat in Rustic Canyon in the Pacific Palisades on the edge of Los Angeles: studio apartments designed by Wright's son, Lloyd, built without disturbing the landscape, plus free food, swimming pool, and stables. He set up the Huntington Hartford Foundation to govern the project and presented resident-fellowships, in time, to hundreds of applicants who seemed promising to him. To help him choose, he established advisory committees in the various disciplines made up of scholars and professionals. The colony has survived for more than a decade. The work done there has been, of course, uneven; there have been some prize-winning efforts, and a sprinkling of "names" have attended. Among the writer-Fellows, for example, have been Van Wyck Brooks, Max Eastman, C. Wright Mills, and Wright Morris.

But Huntington Hartford himself cast a pall over the experiment soon after it had begun and this has not been dispelled even today.

In the Fall of 1951, while the painters posed their nudes amid sylvan scenes and the composers wrote in their studios with the windows open, Hartford tore off a 7,000-word essay asking, *Has God Been Insulted Here?*, which he had printed and mailed out to four thousand unsuspecting opinion-makers. The essay began with some quotes from James Jones's *From Here to Eternity* (written in a more frugal colony in Robinson, Illinois) which repeatedly used such words as "goddam" and "crap." Before he identified the name of the book, Hartford wrote, ". . . by this time, the reader must be aflame with curiosity concerning the source of this colorful language. A book about the Army? You guessed it! A little pornographic book sneaked under the cot for the boys to peruse when they have been unable to find a woman for a month or two? Good heavens, no! Believe it or not, you have just been reading from the literary masterpiece of the twentieth century." The essay rolled on this way, alternating exclamatory and rather vulgar satire with angry stabs at "vulgarity," at art that reduces life to its "lowest common denominator" (example: *A Streetcar Named Desire* by Tennessee Williams), at Faulkner and Picasso, and at the "blank face of despair." Since Hartford had fostered the impression that his art colony was going to be ideal as well as idyllic, it took a while for the Fellows in Rustic Canyon to understand the significance of the essay as it applied to them.

A few months later, Hartford showed he wasn't kidding. He announced publicly (a tactical error, public-relationswise) that two painters' applications for Fellowships had been rejected because their work was "too abstract" to be encouraged by the Huntington Hartford Foundation. All seven members of his art-advisory committee resigned in protest. Many of the Fellows were shaken (none quit, however) and for a time the project seemed jeopardized. Undismayed by outsiders' criticism, which often took the form of amused satire, Hartford appointed a new advisory committee and said the project would go on. The incident gradually faded into the traditions of the foundation and controversy has been avoided ever since.

Nowadays, Hartford has only passing interest in what goes on in Rustic Canyon, although there's no question of his veto power if he chooses to exercise it. A UCLA professor, Dr. John Vincent, runs the retreat and has most responsibility for the fellowships. "Hunt hasn't been to California in five years," he says. "His mind is on other things. The foundation is going well. I send him regular reports—he likes everything in a nutshell." There are no apparent restrictions on applicants, but one assumes the "vulgar" need not apply. All that really has been lost is that first flush of idealism.

The Huntington Hartford Theater: Out of his grand—but abortive—plan to build an art center in Hollywood in the early Fifties, Hartford salvaged the somewhat smaller idea of building a theater. This idea missed, too, and he settled for remodeling an existing theater. A legitimate playhouse had not been opened in Hollywood in a generation. "I was determined," Hartford said, "to shove culture down their throats out there, whether they liked it or not." In 1953, he bought and had refurbished the old Lux Radio Theater on Vine Street at a cost of one million dollars and had his name put on it.

The Huntington Hartford Theater has 1,050 seats, a seventy-foot café-bar that sells hard liquor, and plush décor. Although there were some early expectations that the theater would provide a showcase for new talent and set an example for Broadway, Hartford opened it with Helen Hayes starring in *What Every Woman Knows*. Since then he has presented culture of a sort: mostly road-company showings of time-tested Broadway successes (*The Caine Mutiny Court Martial, Toys in the Attic, The World of Suzie Wong*, et cetera). As a project, the theater has been as "creative" in the past six years as has Broadway, which manufactures most of its fare. "Hunt used to be interested in what went on," says Dmitri Vilan, manager of the theater. "Now we tell him what shows we are getting and that's about it. He has so many things to do that when people ask him what's playing at the theater, he doesn't know. Why the road companies? Why not? We're mostly concerned with box office, just like Broadway."

The Handwriting Institute, Inc.: Graphology—the study of handwriting—has been one of Hartford's enduring fascinations. He is its leading patron in America through the Handwriting Institute, which he founded in 1955. With a full-time staff of six psychologists, three of them graphologists, and a doctor ensconced in a Hartford building in New York, the Institute investigates "graphological and graphomotor variables" and collates the research of others in this area. One member of the institute is working on a project to find out whether cancer can be detected through handwriting. Others, working with the psychology department at Columbia University, are researching methods for simplified character analysis seeking a new projective technique for psychology.

"I don't feel that current intelligence tests accurately measure the capacity of a person," Hartford says. "The trouble is they don't test the whole personality. We feel handwriting tells more. We feel the need of tests through handwriting to show drive, sensitivity, maturity, humor, and aggressiveness. The I.Q. tests don't tell us these things and people often wonder why some people do well on an I.Q. test and don't achieve anything. If handwriting tests could be simplified, you could actually predict human behavior. You'd be able to predict that a boy who was doing well in school was going out to kill his mother. Or take the guy who graduates *summa cum laude* and never does anything because of his beginning strokes and his unbalanced *f*'s."

Hartford truly believes that "because handwriting is the closest communication with the brain," graphology reveals an individual's personality. "Among other things," he once said, "my handwriting shows I'm something of a perfectionist." The editors of some psychology journals disagree with his belief in all particulars. "They are naïve," Hartford says. "It stands to reason that the more you write as you were taught in school, the more immature you are. Your personality is imprinted on your school copy."

Dr. Larry Epstein, a handwriting Institute psychologist who has co-authored a scholarly graphology article with Hartford, is less sanguine. "Mr. Hartford has a tendency to look at someone's handwriting," he says, "and indict him or her for being immature if the handwriting reveals primary [school] beginning strokes. His wife has them. Lots of people have them. I have to settle Hunt down on this."

Hartford has ordered numerous studies on a handwriting phenomenon which he calls "the figure-eight *g*." This is a *g* in script that looks like this: 8. Hartford personally discovered the figure-eight *g* and believes that people whose handwriting includes such *g*'s are especially sensitive and creative. Hartford's own script includes the eight-*g*. "That's why I picked it," he says. "I think it takes subtle creativity when you're writing fast to make an eight for a *g*."

Dr. Epstein comments: "I have tried to convince Hunt that because Albert Einstein didn't make a figure-eight *g*, he didn't necessarily lack sensitivity and creativeness."

Among other key handwritten letters for Hartford are the *f*, evenly balanced at top and bottom, which is taken as a sign of character, and the *t*, especially the t-bar. He believes that people who cross a *t* only halfway are procrastinators and those whose t-bars slant down are stubborn.

"I've thought about one thing and only one thing for the past five years," Hartford says, as one expects him to bring up the problem of disarmament, "And that is that *slant* is terribly important. Rhythm, of course, is important, too. I worry about the nervous rhythm of my own handwriting. But slant is *so* important. Take Admiral Nimitz and Admiral Halsey. Nimitz' handwriting was straight up and down, and what was he? A desk man. Bull Halsey's handwriting slanted out. *He* was active in the field. That interests me. I firmly believe that people who have forward-leaning slants are more intelligent than those with up-and-down strokes."

Hartford uses his graphology in day-to-day project work by sizing up people in terms of handwriting variables. "You can sell Hunt an idea," a friend says, "if he knows who recommended you, goes for your proposition, and likes your handwriting." Dr. John Vincent, director of the foundation, once told Hartford jokingly that he might find out something wrong about his personality from his handwriting. "Don't worry," Hartford snapped. "I've had you checked." A few years ago, Hartford employed Jane Benford, now an editor of *Ingenue* Magazine, to work at his model agency. "Before he hired me," Miss Benford recalls, "he asked me to write out a sentence. It was the sentence he always asks people for—'I'm walking down the street to get the horse and buggy out of the old garage.' I wrote it and didn't cross my *t*'s or dot my *i*'s. Hunt said it proved I wasn't aggressive and I guess I wasn't. But I did have the figure-eight *g* and that really sent him."

Gallery of Modern Art: Hartford let loose another cantankerous essay in 1955. Entitled *The Public Be Damned?* this one was shorter and focused on the art of painting. It paused only briefly to lash at Hartford's favorite horrible example of what's wrong with modern theater, Tennessee Williams. This was probably fortunate—before the end of the next drama season, Hartford's wife had succeeded Barbara Bel Geddes on Broadway in Williams' *Cat on a Hot Tin Roof*. To make sure that the public got his message about painting, Hartford bought full-page advertising space in six New York newspapers and published the full text of *The Public Be Damned?* in each. The essay tilted with art critics who "admire artists who paint with their toes," and at artists who throw "pictorial garbage" into the public's face. He called upon us all to stand up to "the high priests of criticism and the museum directors and the teachers of mumbo jumbo," to reject Matisse and Rouault and their ilk, and presumably to support more representational painting that was "easily understood."

A year later, Hartford indicated that he was going to put himself in a position to express his views on art more concretely by building his own art museum in New York. Delayed by one thing and another, his Gallery of Modern Art is still abuilding. It was announced as a three million dollar project and now is costing closer to seven million dollars for the land, the construction job (Edward D. Stone, designer of the U.S. Pavilion at the Brussels' World's Fair, is the architect), and the works of art. The site is a small, triangle-shaped island on Columbus Circle. Standing alone, the museum will be ten-stories high, faced in white marble, and monumental in spirit. Hartford intends to display paintings, sculpture, and photographs, but he hasn't yet said by whom.

The Hartford Pavilion: With one exception, Hartford's projects have provided him with a measure of power. The exception is the café pavilion, money for which he gave to the City of New York. First approached by Commissioner of Parks Robert Moses (since resigned) to donate a marionette theater for Central Park, Hartford declined, saying he didn't want to contribute just anything. "I wanted to give something that was *badly* needed," he recalls. Moses countered with an idea for a children's baseball stadium. Hartford rejected that, too, and came up with the thought that what New York badly needed was a sidewalk café. The city lacked, he said, a certain "leisurely charm, that atmosphere almost of country, so characteristic of the older European capitals." Hartford says the idea "simply grew." His friend Sy Alter agrees. "Hunt's been complaining for years that there wasn't enough charm in New York, so why not have a sidewalk café? He first figured it would cost two hundred and fifty thousand dollars. Then it snowballed. You get your foot in and can't get it out." Leaving his foot in, Hartford ended up giving the city checks for 862,500 dollars, to cover the cost of building the café on the Central Park plaza corner next to General Sherman's statue, plus the fifteen per cent designing and supervision fee for the architect—again Edward D. Stone. As soon as the news about the Hartford Pavilion was announced, a small but articulate minority of New Yorkers wrathfully attacked "encroachments" on the "sacred" turf of Central Park. Mrs. Arthur Hays Sulzberger, wife of the publisher of the New York *Times,* wrote a strong protest to Commissioner Moses which was seconded on the editorial pages of the *Times* itself. Walter Hoving, chairman of Tiffany's, started suit against the city to stop the café before it got to the ground-breaking stage. Henry Morgan, the TV entertainer, threatened a taxpayer's suit. New York's Park Association, the Municipal Arts Society, and the Fifth Avenue Association—all three groups representing some of the city's more solvent citizens—thanked Hartford and suggested he take the gift back forthwith.

By now an old hand at tempests, Hartford ably counterattacked. "Those who worry about encroachment [on Central Park] are like misers hoarding their gold," he said. "The restaurant aspect is secondary—this is not a place to eat, but a place to sit down. From 42nd Street to 59th Street, there is no place to sit down. It's like a living room without furniture." Hartford may "win," both because gift horses usually do and because his opponents missed the real point of argument. Since any commercial restaurateur gladly would have built a café for New York on the invaluable plaza corner of Central Park, shouldn't Hartford use his 862,500 dollars in an area of greater public need? New York probably needs a marionette theater or a children's baseball stadium a lot more, not to mention money to deal with its social problems. Hartford could have logically answered that it was nobody's business what he did with his money, but not without threatening his ultimate claim to serious purpose. In any event, the issue was not joined. Now with the support of the Mayor of New York and the new Park Commissioner, the café project has a chance. "If it draws large crowds," Hartford says, "the only solution will be to build another one."

Hartford's ambition—his need to spend the seventy million dollars and win respect—has produced a mixed-bag. Missed opportunities and expensive irrelevancies limit regard for his accomplishments. In his drive to "do things," the doing often appears to take precedence over the substance of the things. Despite his precautions, All That Money does silence most of the disagreement about his works that he might otherwise expect from his friends and associates. He hasn't had to submit to the discipline of criticism in his own living room. Apparently, Hartford senses after each project is underway that *that* isn't it and he must move on, moving for the sake of moving, as he has been most of his life.

Hartford was born in New York, April 18, 1911. His father, Edward V., had no interest in the family grocery business. He believed that "one Hartford ought to be a gentleman," and went to college while his older brothers, George and John, went to work with their father. The A&P thrived. By the time Uncle George died in 1957 it had become a four and a half billion dollar business with 4,200 stores. Our Hartford was left ten per cent of all this by his grandfather, who died in 1917. The stock was held in trust, however, until after Uncle George's death. Hartford was forced to live on the income (in some years, this has been estimated at more than three million dollars). Added to this was the small fortune Edward Hartford had made as the inventor and manufacturer of the Hartford shock absorber. He was a Christian Scientist and died of blood poisoning when Hartford was eleven years old. Hartford's mother was a refined Charleston, South Carolina, belle who raised her son in the tradition of Southern gentility, which helps account for Hartford's soft manner and cranky conservatism today. She didn't like the fact that he was left-handed, saw to it that he became right-handed, and then had to deal with his stuttering. Hartford has no trace of an impediment today. After prep school, Hartford went to Harvard. Although he was married a year later, he managed to play three years on the tennis team, win the college squash championship, and graduate in the normal number of years with a major in English literature. His first wife (he was divorced in 1939) was Mary Lee Epling, daughter of a Bluefield, West Virginia, dental surgeon.

After graduation, Hartford ignored the Great Depression and developed his skills as a playboy. Besides he tried working for "Grandma" (as A&P is known to some of its employees), but Uncle John fired him for taking half a day off from his 65-dollar-a-week clerical job to attend a Harvard-Yale game. "It just didn't work out," Uncle John once said. "There he was, surrounded by people who really had to work for a living, and he was receiving callers who wanted to sell him a painting." In his defense, Hartford's friends say that he was lonely and wanted his uncles to train him, but that they shunned him. At twenty-five, Hartford said the hell with it and bought himself a square rigger that had once been a training ship for the Danish Navy. He sailed about the West Indies, sometimes with DuBose Hayward, author of *Porgy*, and knocked about until after his wife divorced him. He finally gave the square rigger to the U.S. Navy. In 1940, he became a financial backer of *PM*, the short-lived liberal New York tabloid, and went to work for the paper as a crime reporter. He amused his threadbare co-workers by arriving at the office in a Rolls-Royce, then chasing off on assignments by subway. He felt he was competing with other reporters fairly and still enjoying the luxury to which he was entitled. After resigning from *PM*, he joined the Coast Guard and became an ensign. For a time he was an aide to Admiral "Iceberg" Smith on the Greenland patrol. Later, as a lieutenant, he commanded a cargo ship only slightly larger than the yachts he had owned. He spent a year in the Pacific in the vicinity of New Guinea and the Philippines, ran aground twice in bad weather, and came home with his crew intact.

Back in New York after the war, Hartford reappeared along the playboy circuit. At the time, it was a mark of status among social young men to escort fashion models to the more swank clubs. Hartford escorted his share and wound up in the model-agency business. "Working with him was a problem," recalls one of his old employees. "He doesn't involve himself once he starts a thing. He didn't learn the whys and wherefores of the agency business. He would listen and be very patient and understanding, but he never had enough experience nor took the time to understand what was going on." He became, as Helen Hayes has said, the Abraham Lincoln of the playboys, because his agency emancipated the fashion models. In the late Forties, the models worked long hours and often had to wait weeks before the photographers paid them. The Hartford Agency, perhaps because of its solid financing, became the first to pay models a weekly salary and to collect from photographers on a business-like basis. The agency prospered until a year ago, when it was absorbed by a competitor. Hartford is still beseeched by girls looking for modeling careers and, on occasion, still arranges introductions and tests for them in the business.

Hartford discovered California in the postwar period, too. He liked the climate, the sporting life, and Hollywood. For a time, he thought he would stay there forever. He met his second wife, Marjorie Steele, one night in Ciro's where he was playing and she, at eighteen, was working as a fill-in cigarette girl. A drama student and amateur painter, Marjorie was born in San Francisco and grew up wanting to be an actress. Her father was an electrician and a salesman who supported her ambition and let her go to Hollywood at seventeen to try her luck. A lithe, frenetic, strawberry blonde, her interest in art and theater coincided with Hartford's disposition. His interest in serious projectmanship seems to date from their meeting at Ciro's. "She's the inspiration for much that I've done," Hartford has said. They were married in 1949, the year that he founded the Rustic Canyon art colony. In 1953, he produced his first and only film, *Face to Face*, which starred his wife in the episode adapted from *The Bride Comes to Yellow Sky* (the other half of the movie was the Conrad piece). Hartford and wife were both well received by the film critics. *The New Yorker* writer said that Hartford was a new movie producer who "deserves the congratulations of all of us." Undoubtedly, it is the public's loss that he has never made another film. He has since tried the theater, but he won the congratulations of no one for that. His production was a play originally called *The Master of Thornfield*, which he had written himself, basing it on Charlotte Brontë's *Jane Eyre*. In 1957, he signed Errol Flynn for the male lead. The play opened in Florida, but after two weeks Flynn walked out saying he had to make a movie for Darryl Zanuck. "I'm suing Zanuck," Hartford says, "and I'll get even with him if it takes the rest of my life." He brought his play, now named *Jane Eyre*, to Broadway in 1958 with Eric Portman starring. The critics lambasted it, but Hartford kept the show on the boards for six weeks. "I think the critics who panned it were prejudiced," he says. "I kept it going or it would have closed overnight. It was so humiliating. French wouldn't publish it and the goddam *Theatre Arts* Magazine wouldn't print the manuscript." Determined to show *them,* Hartford plans to produce the play in London, starring Claire Bloom and Rod Steiger, or to make it into an operetta depending upon what day you discuss it with him.

Ironically, perhaps the sweetest successes in Hartford's life have been found in the business world where, given his philosophical nature and all the rest, he might seem least likely to succeed. By repuation, he is a maverick like his father, but it may turn out that he is his grandfather's boy after all. He has invested 700,000 dollars in the Oil Shale Corp., a Denver company for which he serves as chairman of the board. Oil Shale has set up a pilot plant to develop a revolutionary means for efficiently extracting a substance similar to crude oil from low-grade shale. Hartford's Speed-Park, Inc., has recently completed a unique parking garage on 42nd Street in New York. With one attendant, the garage can handle 270 cars at a time. Elevators move each car vertically and laterally. Ramps and maneuvering areas are eliminated. The only human hand needed is the one that collects the money. If profitable, Hartford and the inventor, Mihai Alimanestianu, plan to sell the idea across the country.

Hartford's biggest project, by far, is also essentially a business effort, although it does offer some of those aesthetic values that are dear to him. It has not progressed as far as any of the projects mentioned above, but it promises to overshadow all that has gone before. In 1959, Hartford bought 700 acres or four-fifths of Hog Island, a coral beauty spot two hundred yards across the harbor from Nassau. He paid 13,500,000 dollars for it to Axel Wenner-Gren, the Swedish industrialist, who also holds 100,000 acres on near-by Andros Island. Through the public-relations firm of Peed, Gammon and Company, Hartford announced that he planned to develop Hog Island into "a dignified vacation resort attractive to Europeans and Americans alike." He is in the throes of that development now, following in the footsteps of other U.S. millionaires, such as Clint Murchison and Howard Hughes, who have recently found resort development in the West Indies a satisfying pastime. (Even Axel Wenner-Gren departed his Hog Island acres saying that now he would get to work developing Andros Island.) Hartford estimates that his total investment in Hog Island—renamed Paradise Island—will come to more than twenty million dollars. He brims with plans. He is building a 150-room hotel, tennis courts, seaside cabanas, an 18-hole golf course, a 200-boat marina, and a 2,000-seat amphitheater (designer: Jo Mielziner) with separate auditoriums for dramatic and sporting events. Because it means *culture*, the amphitheater commands much of Hartford's attention. He sees it as a compromise between a Greek open-air theater and a conventional playhouse. "Sort of a ruined abbey," he says, describing it. He aims to hold an annual series of international TV festivals in the amphitheater—"bigger and better than anyone else's festival"—to help publicize the island.

Neither Hartford nor anyone close to him entertains any doubts about the outcome of the Paradise Island project.

"We will expect people of quality from all walks of life," Hartford says. "There will be no automobiles, no roulette wheels, no honky-tonks. In that way, I hope we can create an atmosphere of cultural enjoyment."

His friend Sy Alter says: "At the outset, we thought he'd be lucky to break even, but now it looks like there'll be a little profit."

His wife, who has attended to many early construction problems on the scene, is philosophical: "The more Hunt builds, the more he wants to build."

Dmitri Vilan, Hartford's theater manager, is wry. "You know Governor's Island?" he asks. "Off the tip of Manhattan? Last year the Government offered to sell it. Well, Hunt would have bought it if we could have come up with an idea of what to do with it."

Personal

It was soft working in Huntington Hartford's duplex on Beekman Place overlooking the East River, but it was also boring. He was shy. He was vague. He sucked his teeth. Like his dreams, he was humorless. And his attention wandered. When he cared to, he could talk and talk about Speed-Park, Inc., or Paradise Island. But then he would drift off in the middle of a sentence, pause, and launch a discussion of modern art or The Trouble with the Theater. He spoke in a soft, sometimes querulous monotone, often defensively, as though people never understood what he was trying to do. Sometimes, I dozed. In the end, I felt I had failed and the assignment should be junked. But I tried one draft, all written in one evening, and the above is it. It contains everything I know or feel about the man, every last drop.

In the past five years, Hartford has aged five years. Otherwise, he launched *Show*, dropped seven million dollars trying to make a go of it, and then unloaded it on Gilman Kraft, publisher of *Playbill*. He sold the Huntington Hartford Theater in Los Angeles and, for the time being, shuttered the Handwriting Institute in New York. While he made one million nine hundred thousand dollars in a California real-estate deal, the value of his A&P stock fell off as much as thirty per cent from previous highs. He earned no profit from the Oil Shale Corp. The automated parking system called Speed-Park, Inc., remained a one-shot experiment. And the cost of developing Paradise Island soared to twenty-seven million dollars, seven million dollars above previous estimates with no end in sight. The one hotel on the resort island has only 52 rooms, which aren't always filled. Hartford has said he will build more. All things considered, only the nine and one-half-million-dollar investment in the Gallery of Modern Art seems well spent.

If, as Hartford told me, he started with seventy million dollars, the man today may be down to his last twenty-five million. There must be irony in this, and an idea for a "revisited" story. Anyone who is interested may have it.

Alf Landon

The
Late Spring
of
Alf Landon

Early in 1960 at Madison Square Garden along with such ubiquitous liberals as Eleanor Roosevelt, Norman Thomas, Walter Reuther, and Harry Belafonte, a mass meeting of the National Committee for a Sane Nuclear Policy was addressed by, of all people, Alfred Mossman Landon from Topeka, Kansas. In the demonology of American politics, circa 1936, Landon is "the Kansas Coolidge"; the thin-smiling, respectable businessman-politician peering out from the pistil of a cartoonist's sunflower; the desperate and finally fuddled leader of the Republicans' terrible "Life, Liberty, and Landon" campaign against the New Deal. He is America's only ex-candidate for the presidency ever to carry Maine and Vermont and that's all. Yet, said he to the multitude of SANE bomb-banners: "Now—more than ever—world opinion must be aroused to demand that the attempt to ban atomic tests continue in energetic good faith. . . ." (Alf Landon?)

Then, last December and again in May of this year, Landon turned up in Washington to plug another unlikely cause: the establishment of a partnership between the United States and the Common Market nations of Europe. Had he been four-square for the conservation of American independence and sovereignty, he would have seemed more in keeping with his alleged character. He is, after all, dimly remembered for his attacks on Roosevelt's reciprocal trade program. Nevertheless, Landon told his Washington audience: "The time is past for any nation to travel alone. . . . The United States must take the leadership

. . . to unify the military, economic, and political resources of the free peoples." He even said he might consider leaving the Republican Party if President Kennedy's new trade program, first step on the road to partnership, ever became a clear-cut issue between the two parties. "Landon astonished everyone," Washington columnist Mary McGrory wrote after his December speech. "His high-level defense of the Common Market would have done credit to McGeorge Bundy or Paul-Henri Spaak." Alf Landon?

With this question in mind, I wrote Landon last spring and was invited to pay him a visit. I flew to Kansas City and rode sixty-odd miles on the Santa Fe Railroad west along the Kaw River, through the wheat, to Topeka, arriving at nightfall. I checked in at the Jayhawk Hotel and then stopped at a bookstore on Kansas Avenue. I was waited on by a young salesgirl who could find no books, old or new, about the Big Loser, neither Frederick Palmer's This Man Landon nor What It's All About by William Allen White, late editor of the Emporia Gazette.

"You know Mr. Landon?" I asked.

"Who's he?" she asked.

So, I bought a copy of Arthur Schlesinger, Jr.'s The Politics of Upheaval, which covers the 1936 elections, and read parts of it at dinner. Schlesinger says that Landon was essentially a moderate Republican. "He simply did not see the New Deal, as Hoover did, as a conspiracy to subvert American institutions. He was, after all, a man who had offered to enlist with Roosevelt in 1933, who supported the administration's agricultural and conservation programs, endorsed the principle of social security, had never criticized the securities or banking or holding company or labor legislation, and seemed to hold against the New Deal chiefly its administrative inefficiency and its fiscal deficits." As the campaign wore on, however, Landon was impelled to express the true sentiments of his party, "the hysterical certitude that the republic was on the verge of collapse." In the final weeks, Schlesinger says, "The man of modesty and moderation and charm had turned into a tired, groping, stumbling figure, moving somnambulistically from railroad train to limousine to auditorium, reading strident speeches in a flat, earnest voice before crowds which came to cheer him and, after ten minutes, sank into fretful apathy." While FDR went on to his rendezvous with history, Landon failed himself and passed into our folklore.

After dinner, I found Alf M. Landon listed in the telephone directory just that way (as I learned later, only his wife and the New York *Times* call him "Alfred") and he answered the phone when I called. He said I'd picked a good, average week to come to town. He would be running WREN, his Topeka radio station, and keeping tabs on his two other Kansas stations; visiting his oil leases down by Madison, Kansas; and enjoying his hobby, which was politics. He told me to hop a taxi and come on out.

On the way, the hackie circled around the state capitol, a green-domed granite pile lit by spotlights. "Best governor we ever had in there," he volunteered, "was old Alf Landon—um, um, 1932 to 19 and 36."

"You know Governor Landon?"

"And like him, the old buzzard."

We passed the Menninger Foundation, the Topeka zoo, and the city line. Quarter of a mile off the highway on Westchester Road, we turned sharply and drove up to Landon's white house. In the glare of the headlights, we could see that it was only a little smaller than Monticello. Old Alf Landon had been making the best of it.

Upheld by stately columns, the roof extended high over the long, wide porch. When I rang the doorbell, I half-expected Big Daddy or Tennessee Williams himself to appear, but there was Alf himself, wearing a checked shirt, baggy gray suit and un-laced brogans. At age seventy-four soon to be seventy-five, he appeared hale. He was sunburned and weathered, almost bald, with hair like white mist, and his eyes were pursed behind rimless glasses. Around the mouth, he was Will Rogers. He had square jowls and a square frame. He said he was glad to see me and gave me a solid handshake.

Walking heavily, Landon led me from the foyer through a vast living room containing six or seven groupings of splendid furniture and into the study. This room was less grand, just about the size of a four-wall handball court. At one end it had a fireplace and at the other the massive desk he had used as governor. According to a brass marker on it, the desk had been built by the Student Cabinet-Making Department of the Kansas School for the Deaf. It had been given to Landon by his "Democrat successor," Walter Huxman. Two walls of the study were lined with books and the floor space easily accommodated two couches and several easy chairs. Landon sat in his favorite chair under a reading lamp, holding the *Christian Science Monitor* in his lap. He lit a cigarette and turned on the radio so that it would be warmed up, he exclaimed, when the St. Louis Cardinals' night game with the Houston Colts came on WREN. He was in good spirits. He asked me about my trip and about the weather back in New York. He said spring had been very late in Kansas this year. Farmers were complaining. Then he seemed amused by some inner joke, slapped himself on the knee with the newspaper, and said, "I'm enjoying the role in life that I play. After the campaign of 1936, Mrs. Landon and I came back here with the three children and we built this house because I wasn't going to run for office again. We would never have built a house this big if I had decided the other way—I could have been elected to the Senate in 1938 if I'd wanted it. We would have kept the old homestead in Independence, Kansas. It had just a yard and not thirty acres like we have here. It would have been small and crowded, but we would have lived there until we went to Washington. Fellers running for office shouldn't have big homes. Nixon made that mistake. First thing he did when he went back to California was to build himself a two hundred thousand dollar house. Only Kennedys and Rockefellers can get away with something like that. Well . . . I've been playing my role in business and in politics. I think about the issues as they come up and I say something about them when I want to. Don't like to say too much, but I speak up when I've got something to say. I've had a rule for ten years now that I won't make a speech if it keeps me away from home at bedtime. I've made two or three exceptions that you know about, but mostly I don't even go drill an oil well if it keeps me away from this house overnight. A while ago, we brought one in and I stayed up thirty-six hours in the field south of here, but when I slept, I came back and slept in my own bed."

Mrs. Landon joined us. Back in 1936, she had tried to help her husband by emphasizing the differences between herself and the peripatetic Mrs. Roosevelt. She had promised the American people that she would not be seen outside of the White House. As it had turned out, of course, even this prospect had failed to cut any ice with the voters. She was a pretty, matronly woman now, with gray hair tinted blue and an expression of great firmness.

"Just look at Alfred's desk!" she said. It was piled high with newspapers, books, reports, letters and other clutter. "It's always a mess, but if you cleaned it up, he'd never find anything."

"Nobody wants to hear about that, Theo," he said.

Landon turned up the radio and listened for a moment. Mel Tormé was singing. "Game's not started yet," he said to himself, turning it down again. He saw that I had the Schlesinger book with me. He advised me to give the section on the 1936 campaign a careful reading. Schlesinger, he said, had spent a week with him in Topeka while gathering research for the section. He had lunched every day at Landon's and had studied his campaign correspondence on file at the local historical society. "What he's got in there is the most balanced thing that anybody's written on what happened in '36," Landon said. He was openly fond of Schlesinger and pleased that once in a while the younger man called him on the phone from the White House. "The President made a speech a while ago saying that Hoover *and Landon* had been against Roosevelt on social security," Landon said, "and Arthur Schlesinger told me he was going to inform the Kennedy camp that I had not been against social security." Landon laughed as he said this to show that it did not make any difference to *him* whether or not people still thought of him as a reactionary, but it was not really an easy laugh.

Landon was interrupted by a phone call from Dale Gates, manager of his oil leases—thirty-six active wells producing about 110 barrels of three dollar oil per day. Landon was trained as a lawyer, but he had become wealthy in the Twenties on the profits from his oil interests, although not tycoon-wealthy. Now he was getting only enough output to meet his overhead and show a relatively small profit. He listened to Gates' nightly report, gave a few terse instructions and hung up. Then he tried the radio again. The Cardinals were at bat. As soon as the

announcer reported the score, he seemed satisfied and turned
down the volume once more. He said he'd had a very good reaction to his Common Market speech. The coverage in Eastern
papers had been extensive and lots of Kansans had heard about
what he had said in Washington. "That's because news travels
east to west in the United States. You have something to say to
the American people, you go east to say it and then nature takes
its course. You say it here and they might not get wind of it in
Wichita. But you say it in New York or Washington and everybody in the country hears it. By the time I got home from
Washington last December, I was scheduled right away to make
a speech before the Chamber of Commerce. I gave them the
Common Market and they gave me a standing ovation."

Landon stared at me for a moment and said I looked like I
could use a drink before going back to my hotel. He went to
the kitchen, brought out ice and glasses, and suggested I pour
the Scotch. ". . . Now a little branch water," he said, filling our
glasses at the tap.

Back in the study, he sipped his drink and sighed. He said he
could not understand why everyone was so surprised to hear
him support lower tariffs and freer trade. He recalled that his
father had been a Bull Moose progressive in 1912 and that he
himself had been a Bull Moose precinct worker in 1914. He
talked as though it had been only yesterday and nothing had
happened in between. "I didn't have to change. I've always been
a progressive. Didn't I get up on the platform in 1924 and speak
out against the Ku Klux Klan? And who was it, in 1934, that
agreed to introduce Norman Thomas when he was making a
speech here? Nobody else would do it, so I did it. I quoted Vol-
taire—about dying for his right to speak though I disagreed with
what he was speakin' about." Landon piled up further proofs
of his changelessness. In 1929, when one lone Kansan in Congress voted against the infamous Smoot-Hawley tariff bill,
Landon as Republican state chairman sent him a wire of congratulations. In 1944, he was chairman of the Republican platform sub-committee on tariff reform and got through a plank
that somehow satisfied GOP protectionists and still gave the
Presidential candidate, Thomas E. Dewey, something he could
interpret the other way. "Well, sure, I know I took a weasel-

worded position on reciprocal trade in 1936," Landon said, "but I was a candidate. If you're a candidate, you've got to stand on the record of your party. Mr. Stevenson learned that, didn't he? Funny thing about him, Stevenson—I never could understand what he was saying."

After we had finished our nightcap, Landon said he would drive me to the Jayhawk Hotel. He backed the Cadillac out of the garage, turned around in the drive, and we headed for town. On the car radio, he picked out a news station which was just then summing up developments in the fight between President Kennedy and U.S. Steel. "There's one group in this country that don't know anything about politics," Landon said, disgustedly, "and that's the businessmen. They know nothing at all about it. Oh, you find a few country bankers who have a feel for it, but they're few and far between. Businessmen—that's what's wrong with the Republican Party. They ought to quit fightin' labor and start fightin' Democrats." Landon drove in silence for a while. Then, as we approached the hotel, he apparently decided that not only the Republican Party but also the U.S. economy was in a peck of trouble because of poor judgment among business leaders. He said there was a conflict of interest going on right now in every big corporation that gave stock options to its management. "Ever since the war, these business fellers have been payin' dividends instead of putting money into new plants and equipment. And now, they're crying to the government for tax relief so they can get enough money to modernize their plants. They're so far behind! I ask you—why did management in steel, oil, and railroads choose dividends and stock splits over modernization? I'll tell you—it was because those fellers have more interest in their own pocketbooks than they have in running a prudent operation. Stock options are supposed to be an incentive, but they've brought us to the point where now big business has to have more profits and more tax breaks and more depreciation allowances just to compete with old Europe. It's funny, isn't it?"

Next morning about ten, I returned to Landon's house. As usual, Alf Landon had awakened with the sun. Before breakfast, he had thoroughly read the Topeka and Kansas City morning newspapers, some research materials pertaining to the

Common Market, and *Newsweek*, a magazine that he preferred
to *Time* because "those *Time* fellers are too willing to sacrifice
accuracy for a wisecrack." He had dressed in breeches, boots,
and a lumberjack shirt with a gaping hole in each elbow. About
nine A.M. he had eaten a light breakfast, going easy, as he would
say, on the hydrocrabates. Soon after I had arrived, he saddled
up two of his horses (he had three, including a twenty-eight-
year-old mare). We rode across the turnpike that sets the rear
limit of his property, through the backyards of several neighbors, and up to the cliff edge looking over the Kaw River. Landon quietly sized up the river's depth and current and said
spring sure was late this year. Back at the house, he changed
into his city clothes: a white shirt badly frayed around the
collar, a bright blue tie, a shiny gray-green suit, brown shoes
with the well-worn heels, and a brown fedora so old that it was
turning black. Then, as he waited outside for Mrs. Landon to
drive him into Topeka, he was approached by an elderly Negro
driving a polished, well-kept 1937 Ford coupe. The man wanted
a job as caretaker and Landon told him he would think it over.
"You should have seen his Ford car, Theo," Landon said to his
wife moments later. "It was twenty-five years old if it was a day
and it looked like new. Any man who's that conservative about
property might be a good man for us to hire."

Mrs. Landon dropped us on Kansas Street at The Chocolate
Shop, a modest café one flight below street level. It was patron-
ized by politicians, officeholders, and office seekers and Alf had
been eating lunch there for years. He was, of course, different
than the other customers: *they* wore white-on-white shirts and,
once in his life, *he* had played for all the marbles. The difference
was pointed up during the meal as fellers paused at Landon's
table to whisper in his ear or talk aloud in an abstruse lingo
that only a State House denizen could really understand. Ultimately, the difference was that Landon alone wanted nothing
for himself from anybody.

"Did the candidate call you, Alf?" a certain judge asked.

"What candidate?" asked Landon.

"You know who."

"Oh, *him*."

"Did he call?"

"When?"

"You know what I mean, Alf."

"Well, Judge, he did and he didn't."

"Primary's coming—you'll have to make a statement for the voters."

"I don't have to."

"You've got to."

"No—I don't have to go out on the limb anymore."

"But *he* may be the candidate, Alf."

"Well, maybe I'll have to say something."

"You ought to, Alf."

"I might—and then again, Judge, I might not."

"That's good enough for me, Alf. Funny weather we're having, ain't it?"

"Spring is really late this year."

"Sure is. I never saw the like to beat it."

"Me neither."

By two P.M., The Chocolate Shop was all but deserted. The politicians had gone back to work. A busboy was mopping the floor. Landon, however, dawdled over his coffee. He said he was just now, this late in life, having the best time he had ever had in politics. "I was the first Republican to come out and support President Kennedy's trade program. Then the newspaper boys asked me if I was speaking as a Republican or a Democrat. I said I was speaking as neither but as an American. But then I thought I'd just jar 'em a little so I said, near as I can remember, I said I might become a Democrat depending on what happened to this Common Market legislation. But I went on to say that I thought both parties would be split over it. . . . Anyway, I won't make that statement anymore. No, I won't say I'll become a Democrat." Landon finished his coffee and lit a cigarette. As he sat there, at that very moment, many of the leaders of his party were in Abilene, Kansas, not more than two hours' drive from Topeka. They had assembled there for the dedication of former President Eisenhower's library. Landon said he had not gone because I had come to visit him. When I replied that we could have driven over to Abilene together, he said, "Well, I'm just being pragmatic. Not that I know what it means. . . . Everyone is using the word pragmatic these days. I looked it up several times, but I don't see how they can use it the way they do if it means what the dictionary says it means. People use that word almost as much as 'image.' I'll tell you, you won't find many speeches except mine that don't have *image*, *dedication*, or *challenge* in them. I hate those words." And we were off the subject of Eisenhower.

By phone, Landon ordered a car from station WREN. Then we went up to the street to wait for it. The sun was bright and Alf's eyes seemed tight shut behind his glasses. "Yes sir," he said, "once I called publicly for Dulles' resignation—of course, before anyone knew he had cancer. He made the 'liberation' speech and got all those people on the other side all steamed up. We've got to take our share of the blame for the Hungarian Revolution on account of that. And for what happened in East Germany, too. You see, the difference between Eisenhower and me is this: his policies were to the left of what mine would have been, but his appointments were way to the right. Now, that's all I'm going to say about it. I'm still in the Republican Party. . . . I was head of the Kansas delegation to the Republican convention in 1940. We went for Willkie on the fifth ballot and then I returned to my hotel pale and white fearing for my party and my country for the way we voted. . . . In 1944, I was head of the delegation again. We were for Dewey on the first ballot and that's when he got it. I like Tom Dewey, but I wasn't for him in 1948. I'd already seen what kind of a campaign he would run, so I was for Taft. You know, Bob Taft might have got it. You remember the Ohio primary of 1948, he had some difficulties with Harold Stassen? Being the way he was, Taft did nothing to repair the damage and asked me to see what I could do. I called up Fred Seaton and Fred Seaton talked to Stassen and Stassen flew in to Topeka—let's see, it was May 30, 1948—to see me. I told Stassen he didn't have a chance to get the nomination himself but if he acted quickly, he could nominate Bob Taft or Dewey and have a hand in working out the ticket. Now it seemed as though Stassen would agree to that. Meanwhile Taft called and said he'd been thinking of Alf Landon for Secretary of Defense. I replied that I found it difficult to make people believe that neither Mrs. Landon nor I was interested in living in Washington. As it turned out, Stassen seemed to think that

Taft did not want him and besides, he began thinking he really did have a chance for the nomination. So, the upshot was Stassen finally wound up trying to deadlock the convention and Taft didn't get the nomination. . . . That reminds me. I was telling you last night what was the trouble with the Republican Party. Well, there was a good example in 1948. We were all at the convention in Philadelphia and there was a party given by the president of the Pennsylvania Railroad. Wouldn't you know that the leading candidates *went to it!* Sure enough, next morning in the papers, here's this railroad president weighing two hundred and twenty pounds with his arms around you know who—*Dewey and Taft.* That is what's wrong with the Republican Party!"

Landon suddenly realized that the driver of his bright-red radio car (with WREN painted on both sides and the trunk) had been waiting at the curb for some minutes. Alf said he had some appointments to keep and would again go riding with me in the morning. Then he climbed in beside the driver and, lacking only the blare of far-off trumpets, drove off in the brilliant afternoon light.

The following morning, I overslept. I skipped breakfast and read the Topeka paper in the taxi going out to Landon's house. I read all about the dedication of Eisenhower's library and looked over the special picture page. Of all the pictures, the one that was most arresting showed a little girl down on all fours watching the ceremonies between the boots of a soldier standing at parade rest. By the time I arrived at Landon's house, he was waiting for me on the porch and, with Mrs. Landon at the wheel, we headed right back to town. Mrs. Landon drove carefully and never took her eyes from the road—not even when Alf chatted with her at a stoplight.

"Well, I had a call from M——," he said, "and he asked me if I'd been to Abilene for the dedication. I told him no, because I had this feller from New York here to see me."

"You wouldn't have gone anyway, Alfred," Mrs. Landon said.

"Well, I didn't want to say anything like that. It was Ike's day and he'd earned it."

"If you'd have gone, you probably would have had your picture taken."

"Theo, I've had my picture took."

"You'd have been in the paper like that little girl they showed watching the parade on all fours."

"They'd probably've given me a seat like hers," Alf said, happily.

This seemed an opportune moment to remind Landon that he had not said anything to me about the Republican conventions of 1952, 1956 and 1960. "I didn't go to any of those conventions," he said, "I was for Taft in 1952 and knew he wasn't going to be nominated, so what was the use of me going? The convention in 1956 was way out in San Francisco and there wasn't any reason for me to go to that either. The 1960 convention was up in Chicago, but I still didn't see any reason to go. . . . About 1964, it's futile to ask. Who've we got? Nixon, Rockefeller, Romney maybe, and Goldwater. Besides them, I think Fred Seaton is a possibility if he gets himself elected governor of Nebraska. He was a good Secretary of the Interior. . . . Nixon's already said he thought Kennedy would win in 1964. Rockefeller's divorce makes him a dubious prospect. Romney's not tested yet. Now, I must say I've been amazed at the reception Goldwater's been getting. There are more crusaders for Goldwater than any other candidate. He drew twenty-five hundred people to an auditorium in a little town in Wyoming when there weren't but two thousand people in the town. I don't know that he's got much to say, but you can't rule him out. He campaigned against labor in Arizona—he was *for* right-to-work laws as much as I was *against* them—and the Republicans can't carry the big cities by kicking labor in the pants. Yet, I think the 1964 convention might nominate Goldwater. Never can tell."

It turned out that our destination was the WREN studio and offices on Fillmore Street. The station had been founded in 1926 and acquired by the Landon family in 1952. Of the four AM stations in Topeka, it was the only one with a union and an employee profit-sharing program. Moreover, it had given the employees something to share since Landon had managed to double the station's annual net profit in less than a decade. Architecturally, the station was unique; it combined an old Midwestern gothic house with a modern, glass-front extension—but otherwise, it was just another station devoted to music, news and sports. At the door, Landon was met by his station manager.

"How's things?" Landon asked.

"Okay," the manager said, smiling.

"Anything new?"

"Nothing."

"Any new business?"

"Nope."

"So, what are you smiling about?"

"Well, sir, we didn't lose any."

Landon's offices were in the gothic section of the building. Over the mantel in what had once been someone's parlor, he had hung a large painting of sunflowers. On the walls were old cartoons by Berryman, Ding Darling and McCutcheon, photos of Teddy Roosevelt, Abe Lincoln, Landon's father, Tom Dewey, and the first stone hauled to build the Kansas State Capitol, but no pictures of Eisenhower or Nixon. The furniture was old and most of it was uncomfortable. Apparently, Landon did not feel the need to impress anyone with his business surroundings. Instead, he seemed to be running a tight, economical ship. This morning, he read his mail, signed some checks, and talked on the phone. Then two Negroes arrived for a conversation. Landon talked with them for over an hour. When they had left, he told me that they had proposed a partnership with him in a business deal that might be worth a lot of money. He said he had pretty well made up his mind to go into it with them. "I've never had the money that the newspapers have attributed to me," he said. "I'm an oil man who never made his million. A lawyer who never had a case. And a politician who only carried Maine and Vermont. I never was worth a million dollars or even half that much. But I like a good proposition as much as the next man and this seems to be one."

With his son, Jack, an advertising man in Manhattan, Kansas, and his son's friend who was the accountant for Landon enterprises, Alf had spent much of the following day in Greenwood County near Madison looking over his oil leases. There was nothing romantic about the "Landon Pool," just small pumps scattered over the countryside sucking up small quantities of oil and pushing the stuff through pipes into small storage tanks. After a late lunch at Dale Gates', Landon had said it was time to head back to Topeka. In the front seat while his son drove, Alf had been smoking quietly, looking out at the placid, bluestem grass country. Now and then, he had commented on the terrain or on the price of Texas cattle sent north to Kansas for the rich grass.

"Late spring," he had also said.

"Sure is," said his son.

"Latest I ever saw," said the accountant.

An hour had gone by on the highway and there was another hour to go, when the car shot past a farmer pounding metal fence posts into the ground. Instead of a sledgehammer, the farmer was using a more efficient device, a metal hood that he held in both hands and brought down over the posts with a short, hard, driving motion. The scene set off a chain of spoken thoughts about work done with sledgehammers, post-driving and steel-driving and stake-pounding for circus tents. Then Alf touched his son's arm and said:

"Down in Oklahoma, there was Jake Hamon, an ambitious feller with big ideas who was a little short of cash. He had the idea that what Oklahoma needed was another railroad, so he sat down and tried to figure out where he could get the kind of money you need for that sort of thing. He thought a while and then he remembered the days when he'd been a sledgehammer man driving stakes to put up the tents of the Ringling Brothers circus. It just came to him that Mr. Ringling might have some spare cash to spend on a railroad. It didn't bother Jake that Ringling was in New York at the time. This being nearly fifty years ago, people thought no more about spending days getting where they wanted to go than we think about spending hours. Jake just scraped together ticket money and rode the day coach all the way to New York. When he got there, he unwrapped the package he was carrying with his clean shirt and socks, spiffed up in the washroom, and went over to the Waldorf-Astoria

Hotel where, as everybody knew, Mr. Ringling came in for a cocktail every afternoon. Jake got there a little ahead of time and, with his last five-dollar bill, he tipped the bartender to point out Mr. Ringling when he came in.

"So, Ringling came in and the bartender pointed him out to Jake and Jake waited until Mr. Ringling had his cocktail in his hand and was just about to drink it. Then Jake sidled up to him at the bar and bumped his arm, on purpose. The drink spilled on Mr. Ringling and made him a little peevish, but then Jake started talking about how he'd driven stakes for Ringling's circus tents in Oklahoma. And one thing led to another until pretty soon they'd formed a partnership to build Jake's railroad—the Oklahoma, New Mexico & Pacific Railroad Co. They bought up the necessary land and got the railroad about half-finished when, all of a sudden, they struck oil all along the right-of-way. Of course, Jake Hamon and the Ringlings cleaned up—made millions, in fact.

"Well, after that, Jake went on and became an important feller in Oklahoma politics and in 1920, he headed the Oklahoma delegation to the Republican nominating convention. From the first, Jake decided he was going to vote for Warren G. Harding and keep on voting for him until Harding won it. Days later, when Harding finally got the nomination, Jake was right next to him and stayed with him, helping him get elected.

"Now, President Harding was a grateful man and he decided to show his gratitude by making Jake Hamon Secretary of the Interior in his first Cabinet. He told Jake about it and Jake said he'd like it fine. But Harding said there was just one thing keeping him from making the announcement. Everybody knew that Jake had a girl friend back in Tulsa and Harding said he'd have to get quit of her before he came to Washington. All right, Jake said, and got on a train and went back to Oklahoma to tell the girl friend, who, as it turned out, shot him dead.

"Well, if Jake'd been Secretary of the Interior, it might have been him all mixed up in the Teapot Dome scandal, so perhaps it's just as well that Albert Fall got the job instead."

Alf's son, Jack, laughed. "Is that a true story, Dad?" he asked.

"True story? Well, sure it's a true story. The oil's still being produced, son. If it wasn't for that, in this day and age, how do you think the Ringling Brothers could keep their circus going?"

Personal

This piece about Alf Landon feels more like life to me than any other I have written. It is hardly more than a transcript of my notes. The lead is based on my first response to a friend who told me that Landon was in favor of the Kennedy Trade Program. "*Alf Landon?*" I asked. I wrote all of it in about three long days. Yet, I am happiest about its effect. It might have been longer, except that on my fourth day in Topeka, I received word of a death in my family and had to return immediately to New York. Later, I might have gone back to Topeka—I had especially wanted to hear Governor Landon as he talked about the Common Market and his own brand of internationalism to an audience of Kansans. But neither *Esquire* nor I could afford another round trip.

Since I saw him last, Landon has gone on raising the eyebrows of those who remember him only as their favorite symbol of political defeat. Last fall, when Barry Goldwater brought his campaign to Topeka, Landon sent his regrets—an oil drilling in southern Kansas prevented him from greeting the 1964 Republican candidate. And a few weeks later, he became the first American to propose a 1965 conference of the world's nuclear powers, including Red China. He is, I hear, in good health and had no trouble getting to sleep last election night.